International
Conflict Resolution

International Conflict Resolution

EDITED BY

Ramesh Thakur

Westview Press
BOULDER & LONDON

University of Otago Press
DUNEDIN, NEW ZEALAND

Westview Special Studies in Peace, Conflict, and Conflict Resolution

Published in 1988 in the United States of America by Westview Press, Inc.; Frederick A. Praeger, Publisher; 5500 Central Avenue, Boulder, Colorado 80301

Published in 1988 in New Zealand by the University of Otago Press, P.O. Box 56, Dunedin, New Zealand

Library of Congress Cataloging-in-Publication Data
International conflict resolution/edited by Ramesh Thakur.
    p. cm.—(Westview special studies in peace, conflict, and
conflict resolution)
  Proceedings of the Symposium on International Conflict Resolution,
held Oct.–Nov. 1987 at the University of Otago, New Zealand.
  ISBN 0-8133-7567-3
  1. Pacific settlement of international disputes—Congresses.
2. Nuclear arms control—Congresses. 3. Nuclear disarmament—
Congresses. I. Thakur, Ramesh Chandra, 1948– . II. Symposium
on International Conflict Resolution (1987: University of Otago)
III. Series
JX4473.I56 1988
327.1'7—dc 19   87-36868
                                                                          CIP

ISBN 0-908569-45-9 (New Zealand)

Printed and bound in the United States of America

(∞) The paper used in this publication meets the requirements of the American National Standard for
     Permanence of Paper for Printed Library Materials Z39.48-1984.

6   5   4   3   2   1

Contents

Tables, Figures and Appendixes

Foreword

There can be no more vital subject for study and deliberation than conflict resolution. I commend the organisers and participants of this symposium for the valuable contributions they have made. It is pleasing to know that New Zealand provided both the initiative and setting for the discussion of the papers which make up this important book.

While it is easy to agree on the importance of the general subject of conflict resolution, it is more difficult to define just what is meant by the term. Part of the stimulation of this book comes from the diversity of background and national origin of the authors and, resulting from this, some very different perspectives. Through this variety of viewpoints three common elements emerge. The first is the determination to find ways to avoid or end the conflict by means other than military conflict or, to borrow the phrase of one of the participants, "systematic appeasement." The second is a common recognition that the origins of conflict relate less to national boundaries than to the wider and more fundamental issues of equity and justice which underly conflict both within and between nations. Finally, and most importantly, the authors agree that the nuclear threat provides the most urgent manifestation of the inadequacy of war as a means of resolving differences between nations.

On the international stage New Zealand has gained most attention for its determination to exclude nuclear weapons from our territory. The Government took this action because it did not consider nuclear weapons were relevant to the defence of the region. Indeed nuclear weapons add to the threat they purport to meet. This was a decision appropriate to our particular circumstances. It is up to other countries to make their own decisions on how to respond to the nuclear menace.

At the same time the Government has taken decisions to increase the role New Zealand can play in fostering the peaceful development of the South Pacific and promoting the global issues of disarmament and economic development. As a small, isolated island state dependent on international trade, we have a vital interest in supporting international efforts aimed at the peaceful resolution of conflict. As a multi-cultural society, and as a Government committed to promoting equity and justice, we are actively engaged in tackling the economic, racial and other injustices which generate conflict. This book is an important contribution to meeting these challenges at home and abroad.

David Lange
Prime Minister, New Zealand

Preface

From 26 October to 5 November 1987, Dunedin and the University of Otago were host to an unusual and distinguished gathering engaged in a collective reflection upon the causes of conflict and the paths to peace. Planning for the Symposium on International Conflict Resolution began many years ago, the idea having first taken root in the fertile mind of Dr Peter Toma. An ex-Hungarian and expatriate American, Dr Toma was so taken with the tranquil beauty and pure environment of New Zealand and Dunedin during a visit several years ago that he decided to live here. As a citizen of the world concerned to preserve it, he approached the University of Otago with a proposal to bring a distinguished collection of minds from around the world in a common endeavour to halt a seemingly inexorable drift towards war.

After a period of gestation, the University of Otago, under the leadership of its Vice Chancellor Dr Robin Irvine, finally committed itself to the idea of a symposium on international conflict resolution. A planning committee was formed with Peter McMechan, Peter Matheson, Paul Mullen, Peter Toma, Ann Trotter and myself as its members. The chairman of the planning committee was Acting Vice Chancellor Richard Mulgan. The committee was assisted by an executive staff consisting of Anya Besley, Brian O'Rourke, Dorothy Piper and Bill Webb. Even the high-powered planning committee was unable to cope with such unexpected difficulties as Moscow airport being closed by fog on the day that the two Soviet participants were scheduled to fly out; fortunately, one of them was able to rearrange his itinerary and come to Dunedin later. Gordon Parry did a wonderful job as Publicity Officer in keeping the public and the media informed of the planning and running of the symposium. Proceedings of the symposium were recorded under the care and direction of Robert van der Vyver of the Audiovisual unit of the University of Otago, with the Queenstown part of the programme being recorded under Peter Toma's supervision himself. The typing has been in the hands of a capable quartet: Jeanette Bonar, Liz Grant, Shirley Kelly and Betty Larkins.

The most important contribution to the symposium materialising was the generous and substantial sponsorship from Peter Toma. We are grateful for the emotionally moving formal ceremony of Maori welcome performed by Te Kapa Haka o Te Whare Wananga o Otakou, and to Godfrey Pohatu of the Maori Studies Centre for having provided the translation of the speeches. Another innovation for the symposium was the first audio link-up of all seven branches of the New Zealand Institute of International Affairs for a nation-wide teleconference programme on 4 November 1987, made possible by the equipment and expertise of the Department of University Extension of the University of Otago.

Most important to the success of the symposium were, of course, the participants themselves. Most took a fair period of time out of their busy calendars for an exceptionally extended conference. Some travelled long distances to get here, for which we are grateful. Some of those who travelled lesser distances came at short notice: for that too we are grateful. It is a measure of the success of the symposium that discussions initiated in Dunedin are to be continued on an expanding basis through the establishment of the Otago Dialogues.

Ramesh Thakur, Symposium Director

Maori Welcome

Mr John Broughton (Chairman, Araiteuru Marae[1] Council)

I sneeze and it is life![2]
Friends of the University of Otago, greetings! To the distinguished visitors—great is our respect for you. You have come to speak to the theme of man's respect for man. Our wish is that this theme is heard throughout the world. Therefore wisdom and love alight over you.... To the many canoes that have been paddled to this place, your canoe of peace has also brought you here.[3] Thus greetings, greetings, greetings to you all!

Dr Peter Matheson (Representative of the University Organising Committee)

Greetings, greetings, greetings to you all!
We welcome you as guests to this place at the very end of the world. We welcome you as guests to this place of Aotearoa,[4] to this place sacred to peace, sacred to justice, sacred to the integrity of creation.
We welcome you here with your knowledge to this *whare wananga,*[5] to this house of knowledge. We welcome you on behalf of the peoples you represent, on behalf of the aspirations you represent. You who will speak on behalf of those who cannot speak—we welcome you. We hope that the spirit of the great God will be with you in your deliberations; in your discussions; in your conflicts and in your resolutions. We welcome you from the bottom of our hearts for making this long journey, for being who you are, and for bringing what you bring. And we stand here on behalf of this university, of these people of Aotearoa and thank you for your presence with us today.

Mr Karaka Roberts (Maori Elder)

I sneeze and it is life!

Climb up, come up to this place—and may I be given the waters of life so I may watch over the sleep of the great lady of the night—until the great dawning which is signified by the crashing of the waves at Te Reinga [the very tip of the North Island of New Zealand]: welcome, welcome! Welcome to you as for me who must welcome you who come from all over the world who bring your expertise. Welcome here upon the theme of this gathering in this university of the great greenstone island [South Island].

Let us not make small the significance of our departed ones—even those who have left behind—therefore to you departed ones who are beyond the veil of Paerau [the final veil]: this is the greeting to them.

Therefore bring them with you to within this house. Let them gather with those departed ones of this house—of New Zealand itself, let them gather and meet in this house. We will then greet them who are also relatives of each and every one of us, and send them on to arrive at the veil of Paerau. And so I greet them. I greet them because it is customary to do so—as they have left this custom for us. The significance of this is that we have been given the glory to sustain them for whom the glory of their deeds is maintained, therefore we greet them and farewell them. Farewell O departed ones—farwell, farewell, farewell to you all. Farewell to beyond the great void, to the place where the great Creator awaits us all as He has done since time began. And thus when it is our turn to go (and there can be little doubt that we will) we farewell them in order to prepare the way for us and thus is the reason for us sending our greetings and our farewells. Let us complete the farewells to them, completed and ended. The words have been given therefore farewell, farewell, farewell to you all. Rest within the bounds of the Lord.

Let me turn my greetings to you—welcome O experts of the world, welcome! Welcome to you and your expertise. It is excellent that such experts as you will help the people of the world, to assist and to counsel. But the expertise that you possess is different. I know how important knowledge is, but it is not the most important. Much of the knowledge about the world is held by you, for what? Let us turn the talk as we as people do turn to kill each other. Let us take hold of some sayings from the scriptures. It is indeed good to see the younger brother and the older brother live in peace, in the one thought—that is in the scriptures and in the teachings of Christ.

We look at each other—what are we doing in this world? What are we doing? We see that on that side of the world younger brothers are killing older ones; families are fighting; husbands and wives. This is what we are thinking about on this side of the world, especially by us Maori, in our Maori thinking. We observe those circumstances but behind them we wonder what causes those wars? What is it? It is greed. Perhaps you will understand this opinion—it is greed for power, for world power.

So therefore your gathering here is to seek solutions within those ideas that will help resolve conflict that we inherit—resolutions that help us as people. Let us not pursue ideas of arming ourselves with great rockets which are present on that other side of the earth—for when they are released they cannot be seen. They send these bombs from way over the other side of the world—they send them off to land over this side. Go nuclear or no nuclear, anti-nuclear that's how we stand here—nuclear free!

These are the thoughts of the Maori people that are here in New Zealand. Let us look to ourselves; maybe we have reached the stage where we do not know where to turn. Maybe we've got to the crossroads that we're looking for peace. Maybe we've got to the crossroads we don't know which way to turn. But there should only be one policy, one thought if we truly wish to seek world peace—and live in peace. There are the thoughts and ideas (that I have alluded to) to answer those important questions.

Therefore my talk is not going to be dragged out. To you the special visitors, you who have come here to this side of the world from the other side of the earth, to begin this symposium, and to organise this symposium within this university—welcome, welcome, welcome to you all.

NOTES

1. A *marae* is a sacred courtyard upon which ceremonial welcomes are performed.

2. *Tihei mauriora*—sneeze of life: this is a poetic allusion to the sneeze of life of a new-born child. Thus when applied to speech it signifies the birth of a speech.

3. Visitors from afar are called "canoes," especially with regard to the fact that they come from overseas.

4. Aotearoa—"land of the long white cloud'— is the ancient Maori name for New Zealand.

5. The Maori words for university or house of higher learning.

1

The Last Child–Seventh Generation Ethic

Ramesh Thakur

The incidence of war in human society is as pervasive as the wish for peace seems universal. Contemporary references to international conflict resolution appear to regard war solely as pathological. Yet war has been an important means of conflict resolution throughout human history, and it used to be viewed as cathartic or therapeutic.

The use of force and the possibility of controlling it and so controlling others has preoccupied the minds of rulers and scholars alike since time immemorial, from Thucydides, Kautilya and Machiavelli to Karl Marx, Mao Zedong, Hans Morgenthau and Henry Kissinger. But so too have some of the most charismatic and influential personalities in human history—from Gautam Buddha and Jesus Christ to Mahatma Gandhi—dwelt upon the renunciation of force and the possibility of eliminating it from human relationships. Modern international society is organised into units of nation-states. At any given time, most of the countries in the world are at peace. Yet most of them are also ready to go to war if necessary. Modern governments have not, therefore, been excused of the responsibility of preparing their countries against the eventuality of external attack.

War has traditionally performed certain functions in international relations from three points of view (Bull, 1977). From the perspective of states, it approximates the Clausewitzian dictum of being an instrument of policy, a means to a desired end. Thus in Vietnam during the 1960s, the one belief that the opposing sides shared in common was that war was the most effective instrument of solving the dispute. From the perspective of the system of states, war has been the basic determinant of the shape of the international system. It has been the arbiter of the creation, survival and elimination of actors in the system, of the ebb and flow of political frontiers, and of the rise and decline of regimes. From the viewpoint of international society, war has a dual aspect. It is a manifestation of disorder which threatens the survival of the society; hence societal concern to contain and regulate war. But it can also serve as the instrument of society if used to enforce community values and goals, for example punishment of illegal behaviour or enforcement of change that the society as a whole regards as just or desirable. In the first sense war is dysfunctional; in the second sense it would become the functional equivalent of the coercive authority of a municipal police force.

CAUSES OF WAR

Microtheories of violence trace the causes of aggression to individual behaviour: to particular personality traits, to the tendency to cognitive rigidity by key decision-makers in times of international crisis, to the displacement of frustration-induced hostility to foreign targets, to innate biological propensity to engage in aggressive behaviour, to socialisation into ritual aggressive behaviour; that is, to the greed, selfishness and stupidity that is inherent in human nature. Macrotheories of conflict postulate an even more bewildering array of causes of war: arms races, alliances, balance of power policies, military–industrial complexes, fascism, capitalism, communism, military dictatorships, militant religions, even the inexorable dialectic of an international crisis. The morphology of international crises is discussed by Victor Kremenyuk.

In a statement on violence in Seville on 16 May 1986, an international group of scientists rejected the contention that war is rooted in human nature. In particular, the group denied any scientific validity to five propositions condemning humans to the bondage of biological pessimism:

- that human beings have inherited a tendency to make war from animal ancestors;
- that violent behaviour is genetically determined;
- that aggressive behaviour has acquired an evolutionary ascendancy over other types of behaviour;
- that the human brain is violent;
- that war is caused by human "instinct" (Scientists, 1986).

At the microcosmic end of the explanation, it is of course true that biological mechanisms *enable* aggressive behaviour by the human species; but the *activation* of these mechanisms depends upon appropriate stimulation. The attempt to root war in human behaviour falls into the trap of psychologism. The leap from an analysis of individual behaviour—which exhibits good and evil tendencies—to an explanation of the group phenomenon of war is inferential rather than empirical, and what analysts make of the evidence depends on the theories that they hold. At the macrocosmic end, the most elegant explanation of warfare is international anarchy, that is the absence of restraints upon unbridled national behaviour. Or, putting it more provocatively, the *non-existence* of world government is *the cause* of war. While this is general enough to explain all wars, it is not altogether satisfactory. The cause of *every* air accident can be traced to the invention of the aeroplane; the invention by itself is therefore insufficient to explain the cause of *any particular* air accident. We look for more proximate causes: structural or design defect, pilot error, equipment or maintenance failure, or negligent traffic control. Both with air accidents and warfare, plurality of possible causes indicates multiplicity of possible remedies.

Social scientists study wars with the help of such variables as the parties to a conflict, the issue fields, the tensions and actions. Do dictatorships, for example, go to war more often? If so, then does the reason for their behaviour lie in their tendency to distract attention from domestic troubles by foreign adventures or in their tendency to perceive democracies as weak and appeasement-prone? Social scientists look at the outcomes of conflicts: were they forceful or peaceful; did they produce compromise or complete capitulation? They examine settlement procedures in order to evaluate the relative successes of bilateral negotiations, multilateral conferences and international organisations in facilitating particular types of outcomes. The objective of social science research is to tease out generalisations about patterns of violent international behaviour which can be tested, refined and become commonly accepted as valid.

Unfortunately, social science is still some distance away from the realisation of this goal. Geoffrey Blainey's chapter disposes of a number of shibboleths about the causes of war, positing them as explanations of rivalry and tension rather than war. He also argues that war and peace are not just opposites; they share so much in common that neither can be understood without the other.

The shortfall in the ambitious goal notwithstanding, social scientists have made some progress towards understanding aspects of violence in international relations. Furthermore, despite common mythology, the incidence of war per decade has been fairly stable since the Congress of Vienna (1815). While warfare has become more intense and destructive, it is not any more frequent. Indeed since there are several times as many independent actors in international relations today than was the case even up to the Second World War, the number of wars *per actor unit* in the international system has dramatically declined in the post-1945 era. The decline in the incidence of warfare is even more graphic in proportion to the number of conflictual relationships that are possible with greater number of actors in the system, that is, *per possible conflict dyad.*

NUCLEAR SPECTRE

The nuclear spectre haunting humanity today is the most urgent manifestation of the inadequacy of the institution of war. It is a sobering thought that an entire generation of people has grown up under the menacing shadow of the mushroom cloud. Though some perhaps may dream of the friendly blue skies which beckon beyond the clouds, for most people the nuclear spectre has been an inescapable element of the strategic landscape. For four decades, a majority of Americans and Europeans have accepted nuclear deterrence as a proper and dependable cornerstone of western security policies. Astonishingly, such a fundamental change in relations between different nations was put into place without serious public debate. Only in the 1980s has there been the sort of intensive and widespread call for justifying the strategy of nuclear deterrence that one would have expected at the start of the nuclear era. Today, not just a bunch of trendy intellectuals but a broad cross-section of concerned citizens have been scrutinising nuclear policies closely and demanding answers from their governments as to the ethics, military necessity and political wisdom of constructing defence policies around "the bomb."

The enormous destructiveness of nuclear weapons has produced four major changes in military strategy. First, modern delivery systems mean that there is no protection against nuclear bombs. The only defence against nuclear weapons is to be certain of destroying every enemy missile and bomber. Such certainty is not available today nor likely in the foreseeable future. Second, nuclear weapons have not just made old fashioned defence impossible; they have also destroyed the gallantry of olden days which pitted soldier against soldier and left noncombatants alone if not in peace. The historical trend towards blurring the line between military and civilian sectors, already in evidence in the two world wars, has been completed by nuclear weapons. It is now possible to destroy the enemy society without defeating or even engaging enemy forces. Third, the destructiveness of nuclear weapons and the speed of their delivery systems mean that wars will no longer be protracted affairs. Nuclear war could be over in days or even hours, denying leaders a chance to think again and change their minds. The final consequence results from the third fact as well. Because of the speed of nuclear war, a country can no longer afford to mobilise fully only with the imminent onset of hostilities. Nuclear forces have to be in a state of constant readiness at full strength.

Some analysts have argued that the cumulative impact of the four changes has been to make nuclear weapons devoid of any military use whatsoever; their only purpose can be deterrence. But here too strategists are confronted with a fundamental paradox. If one side seeks to deter war by creating the fear that it will use nuclear weapons, then it must convince the opponent of its determination to use them in certain circumstances. If however the weapons are used and produce a like response, then the side striking first is very much worse off than if it had abstained. Posing an unacceptable risk to the enemy therefore necessarily poses the same risk to oneself. To prepare to fight a nuclear war is to impose on a nuclear equation the logic of pre-nuclear strategy: the circle cannot be squared. As the disquieting implications of this paradox have begun to seep through to the public consciousness, people have made their unhappiness felt to their governments.

For all the destructiveness of nuclear weapons, nevertheless, and contrary to public mythology, wars have not been made obsolete. Indeed since the Second World War the number of people estimated to have died as a result of international conflicts and civil wars is in excess of twenty million. This belies the proposition that the advent of nuclear weapons means that war, far from being a continuation of policy by other means, is in fact the breakdown of policy resulting in mutual annihilation. Most international conflicts involve non-nuclear states, e.g. Iran and Iraq. Several of the more important conflicts of our time have seen non-nuclear nations fighting nuclear states, e.g. the United States in Vietnam and the Soviet Union in Afghanistan. The use of nuclear weapons in such wars is limited by the fact that their political and moral costs would be greater than the desired military and political objectives. Finally, in theory, even nuclear powers can engage in wars between themselves without using nuclear weapons. In practice however this has not occurred, not the least because of the danger that wars once started are difficult to keep limited to pre-determined levels of intensity—they tend to acquire a self-perpetuating logic of their own.

Despite the difficulties of military usability, therefore, nuclear weapons can still serve certain functions. The Harvard team (1983) identified seven goals of nuclear policy: basic deterrence; extended deterrence; crisis stability; war-fighting; war termination; counter-deterrence; and bargaining chip. Each of these purposes places its own requirements on type and level of nuclear forces. Not all the requirements can be fully met, and not all are consistent with one another.

Deciphering the strategic equation between the western and Soviet blocs is one of the great pastimes of our era. The actual numbers involved are not in serious dispute, and can be obtained with relative ease; but there is considerable controversy over how best to interpret the numbers. There are difficulties arising from the lack of symmetry between the elements which make up the strategic equation: weapons category, technological quality, geographic imperatives, and security interests. Because the two sides are not symmetrical, it is always possible to pick a category of weapons in which one side is superior to the other. All claims of superiority and inferiority should be treated with scepticism in any case: both sides have a huge margin of overkill. Similar caution is warranted in regard to the role of nuclear weapons in having kept the peace since 1945. How many of the modern-day great powers are likely to have gone to war against one another even in the absence of nuclear weapons? If the major cause of the two world wars was the problem of German power in Europe, then is the peace of post-1945 Europe attributable to the problem having been solved by the division of Germany? Perhaps peace has been a function as much of the progressive universalisation of the international system as of the nuclear factor?

TWENTIETH CENTURY ILLEGITIMACY

After the First and Second World Wars, peoples of the world were moved to demand that the institution of war be formally delegitimised. This was done, however imperfectly and however qualifiedly, in the Covenant of the League of Nations and the Charter of the United Nations Organisation. The Kellogg–Briand Pact of 1928 was another important milestone in the developing international movement to outlaw war.

Kal Holsti points out that by the standards of today, the costs of defeat in wars of the 17th–19th centuries were not disastrous. Regimes and states were not extinguished, the legitimacy of actors was not challenged, prolonged occupation was not attempted, civilians remained unaffected if they did not lie in the path of advancing (or retreating) armies. The total wars and the cold wars (both global and regional) of this century have not been similarly circumscribed by shared underlying values, limited goals, moderation in means, insulation of civilians and acceptance of enemies in battle as legitimate actors in international politics.

The nuclear dimension has given particular cogency and urgency to the progressive delegitimisation of war in this century. There is certainly growing questioning of the moral basis of the policy of nuclear deterrence. First, nuclear deterrence openly contemplates—indeed must be directly based on—the deliberate killing of people in the millions. In their pastoral letter of 3 May 1983, the Catholic Bishops of America expressed firm opposition to strategies of deliberate attack on large populations, and strategies that would result in catastrophic loss of life as an "unintended consequence" of weapons aimed at military targets. In the "butchery of untold magnitude" caused by a nuclear war, it would not be very comforting to know that one had died an innocent victim of "collateral damage." Second, most of the people killed would be innocent non-combatants. Western political rhetoric has it that citizens behind the Iron Curtain are persecuted victims of their own governments. That being so, is it not immoral to visit nuclear punishment upon innocent people for the sins of their totalitarian leaders? It is certainly immoral to destroy peoples in neighbouring countries through radiation, and arrogant of the human race to destroy other species because it could not manage its own affairs. Third, the only goal of nuclear retaliation when deterrence has failed would be revenge. Many religions and moral systems have difficulty reconciling vengeful killings with proper conduct; the disproportionate and indiscriminate scale of nuclear retaliatory vengeance cannot be reconciled with any self-respecting moral doctrine.

The above three are doubts about the morality of nuclear war. Interestingly, in their thoughtful and weighty effort to apply religious and moral principles to nuclear weapons, the Catholic Bishops condemned nuclear war yet gave "a strictly conditional moral acceptance of deterrence" in order to protect the independence and freedom of nations and peoples. The letter issued a profound challenge to US military policy and contributed to a delegitimisation of nuclear doctrines. Its conditional acceptance of nuclear deterrence was consistent with Pope John Paul II's statement to the United Nations in 1982: "In current conditions, 'deterrence' based on balance, certainly not as an end in itself but as a step on the way toward a progressive disarmament, may still be judged morally acceptable."

The conditions are more important than the fact of papal acceptability. Deterrence must be temporary and transient, pending but leading to progressive disarmament. It must also be "based on balance," that is on parity or "essential equivalence." This does not require equality, let alone superiority, in every weapons category; it does require willingness to concede parity to the adversary. Finally, the Pope argued that nuclear deterrence *may still be judged* morally acceptable—meaning that it is not automatically nor always so.

The Catholic Bishops in 1983 similarly qualified acceptance of nuclear deterrence as a necessary evil with significant conditions. In particular, even deterrence cannot evade the requirements of "just war" doctrines. Thus deterrence must satisfy the principle of *discrimination* between combatants and non-combatants: a smaller evil cannot be justified by a greater good. Secondly, deterrence must follow the rule of *proportionality*. The first requirement forbids the targeting of populations as nuclear hostages; the second places limits on the extent to which installations can be targeted, for even unintended damage may not justly exceed the evil to be avoided or the good desired to be achieved. Contemporary superpower targeting of "military related" enemy industry and utilities would inflict death and misery on millions of non-combatant citizens as "collateral" damage, and is therefore immoral.

Ali Mazrui poses the question as to the ethical difference between nuclear terrorism by states and terrorism by individuals and groups: is criminal activity done by officials on a large scale—terrorism against humanity—to be condoned while lesser mortals receive condemnation for relatively less significant acts of random terror? Those entrusted with the command of nuclear weapons must make compromises with their conscience in order to live in comfort despite holding the world to ransom. Nor are moral qualms stilled with the knowledge that the ruling elites of the nuclear powers build deep shelters and airborne command posts for themselves while offering their citizens as hostages. All this in the name of a policy supposed to guard citizens against enemy attack, a policy enunciated and devised by officials bearing the primary responsibility for protecting their citizens. What sort of morality can allow the privileged elite to be sheltered while leaving their wards unprotected?

Nuclear deterrence also poses a number of other moral challenges to our conscience. Deterrence rests on the threat to wage nuclear war. If a particular act is evil, then the threat to do it must also be immoral; if nuclear war is evil, then threatening and preparing for such war is also morally wrong. "Threaten No Evil" as a moral stricture is written into the United Nations Charter: "All members shall refrain from the *threat or use* of force" (Article 2.4; emphasis added). The United Nations may not amount to much as an organisation for world peace; its Charter however does express the global consensus about certain ethical values and norms of behaviour in international relations.

Deterrence based on hitting population centres ignores too the moral distinction between ends and means. We would rightly consider it immoral for the government to deter murder by threatening to kill any murderer's children. If this is not acceptable as proper public policy, why should nuclear deterrence be any more acceptable as proper foreign policy? A related means-ends dilemma concerns western society and people. The whole ideological conflict is supposed to be about freedom versus totalitarianism. The very destructiveness of nuclear weapons means that a garrison state will be created rather than risks accepted of such weapons falling into criminal hands. This being so, what are the values for the defence of which western society is being asked to make fundamental moral compromises?

Technological and military reality imposes yet another constraint on nuclear morality. Because the decision to retaliate must be instantaneous if deterrence has failed, there is no time for ordinary citizens or responible officials to make the transition from nuclear deterrence to war only after thoughtful moral reflection. In other words, deterrence places a premium upon immorally casual decisions in its time of greatest need, and therefore amounts to moral abdication. Given the steadily diminishing lead-times before retaliatory weapons must be unleashed under automated launch-on-warning strategies, one may well ask: what price such computer-based morality?

The above discussion presents the substantial moral doubts about nuclear weapons, war and strategy. Moral concern in itself must surely be applauded—there would be little cheering prospect left for humankind on the day that it lost its moral sensitivity.

Yet the moral dimension can be troubling in a second sense of being difficult to apply. The pursuit of morality, while wholly admirable in an individual, can still be less defensible in a statesman. The prophet can be wedded to absolute truth, the sage can devote his life to the search for ethical wisdom. The political leader however is required to act according to political wisdom. He must first accept the political realities of the world and of his own country, and then, within this framework, he must evaluate competing demands of moral and political choices. On occasions the moral issues themselves will be ambivalent and overlapping. Consider the distinction between nuclear war and nuclear weapons. Even if we are all agreed that nuclear war is evil, it does not follow that the nuclear weapons are themselves evil. (Can instruments ever be evil or good in themselves?) If nuclear war is evil, and if nuclear weapons on both sides help to deter their use in war by either side, then nuclear weapons and deterrence become strategies to combat evil. Fortunately, atomic weapons have been used only twice under conditions of war, at Hiroshima and Nagasaki. The interesting thing about both instances is that an atomic power used the weapons against a non-atomic country. Considerations of a new morality or international reaction were insufficient to stop the Americans from using this weapon of mass destruction; why should they succeed in imposing unilateral restraint in future? But if the Japanese had possessed atomic weaponry too, then the American government would have had greater cause to pause before escalating to the atomic level.

Determination of evil conduct must also take place in relation to intent. The goal of nuclear deterrence is not to wage war, but to avert war and deter aggressive behaviour by the other side. The intention is not, therefore, immoral, and the consequences are partly determined by the actions of the other side. Conversely, if total unilateral nuclear disarmament led to the use of nuclear weapons by the other side, then one could plausibly argue that disarmament led to evil results.

The argument can be extended to conventional warfare too. In all the conflicts and killings since the Second World War, the two superpowers have successfully avoided a direct war between themselves. It is possible that the fear of uncontrolled escalation to nuclear horrors severely inhibits adventurous tendencies to risk direct confrontation. Of the several million deaths in battle since the Second World War, not one has been caused by a nuclear warhead; every war fought since 1945 has been done so in the certainty that it would not become nuclear. The argument is developed by Blainey, who finds fault with both the uncritical pessimists and optimists of the nuclear era. Indeed he presents a historically sceptical analysis of the uniqueness of the nuclear age, suggesting a measure of continuity between the era of cavalry and ICBMs (intercontinental ballistic missiles) that may surprise. Today's weapons stockpile works out to 10 tons of TNT per capita; at the time of the First World War, there were 5 bullets per capita (Ziegler, 1987: 224): is nuclear overkill more heinous than conventional? It was suggested during discussions that the balance of nuclear peril notwithstanding, the governments and peoples probably feel safer today than in 1910. The mellowing of the Reagan administration, the accession of Mikhail Gorbachev, and the transformation of China under Deng Xiaoping have all contributed to the more optimistic outlook on international security in the past half dozen years.

Obviously I do not wish to argue that somehow nuclear weapons have made war more moral. Rather, I want to point out that there are genuine dilemmas for the moralist even in the nuclear realm. Killing is evil; yet most of us do not condemn all soldiers engaged in battle as necessarily evil. Similarly, nuclear deterrence too can be seen as a necessary evil. Because nuclear war is evil, it must be avoided; because nuclear deterrence is built around the strategy of fighting a nuclear war, we must strive to reduce reliance on it; but because it is necessary, we cannot abandon it carelessly. Perhaps, as Bishop Károly Tóth notes, the theory of the just war needs to be transformed into a theological doctrine of the just peace—an observation that reinforces Rajni Kothari's comment on the lack of an ideology of peace that could serve as the equivalent of the national interest–cum–national security ideology which sustains preparations for and engagement in wars.

SEDUCTIVENESS OF TECHNOLOGY

Bishop Tóth remarks too upon the lag between the ethical development and destructive technologies of the human race. Both superpowers are caught in the trap of a world of sovereign states having to cope with weapons of universal destruction. If drastically fewer nuclear weapons are indicated by considerations of human survival, then considerably fewer warheads are needed for purposes of deterrence. Soviet policy has been to strive for parity; Americans might be aiming at superiority, but certainly claim no less than parity. Yet deterrence requires neither superiority nor parity, but "sufficiency," which can be attained with a relatively small number of nuclear weapons invulnerable to enemy attack and capable of visiting "megadeath" upon the enemy. For example, deterrence based upon sufficiency is compatible with European nuclear disarmament, a nuclear-weapon-free zone in central Europe, and a policy of "no first use" by both superpowers.

A "no first use" policy is supposedly more difficult for the US because of western military inadequacies in vital regions, e.g. Europe. Yet there has never been any serious evidence of a Soviet intention to invade Western Europe. NATO policy has always been based upon the dictum of prudence that, given Soviet capabilities, preparations must be made against the possibility of Soviet aggression. Recent history also refutes the thesis that Soviet expansionism (e.g. in Afghanistan) is matched to the Soviet nuclear arsenal. The most spectacular Soviet territorial and political advances were made between 1945–1949, when the Americans had a monopoly of atomic weaponry. If American containment policy did not work in the era of US nuclear monopoly and superiority, there is even less reason to expect that it will work in the era of strategic parity.

The nuclear equation has been irrelevant in determining the outcomes of regional conflicts. Strategic parity stopped neither the Soviets from suffering a major political setback with the Israeli invasion of Lebanon in 1982, nor the Americans from suffering a major policy reversal with the disintegration of the Multinational Force in Beirut in 1984. In the final analysis, it takes two to make an act of intimidation succeed. Not all their military might enabled the Americans to deny communist victory in Vietnam; not all their concentrated firepower has allowed the Soviets to pacify Afghanistan in eight years of trying.

The nuclear weapons trap that the world finds itself in is the result of efforts to achieve security by means of technological solutions to the problem of violent disorder. Thus one scholar wrote in 1971 that "Until fundamental changes take place in the structure of world politics, a qualitative arms race may well be a most desirable form of competition between the Soviet Union and the United States" (Huntington, 1971: 401). The qualitative arms race has produced the ever-increasing destructive capacity of modern nuclear weapons (Figure 1.1). Such achievement is cause for shame not pride in the human race.

Star Wars

The shortcomings in the technological approach to national security are clearly evident in "Star Wars" or the Strategic Defence Initiative. The concept may well be translated into operational reality at some date, although the office responsible for conducting SDI research, the Strategic Defence Initiative Organisation (SDIO), announced in May 1985 that much of the concept was beyond America's technical reach for the foreseeable future. Ironically, Reagan's plans to put military technology into space mobilised a remarkable collection of people in support of the policy of nuclear deterrence. Even anti-nuclear groups, when confronted with SDI, began to see virtues in the logic of assured nuclear destruction—the foundation of stability between the superpowers for more than two decades.

Yet serious questions have been raised about SDI. Floated by President Reagan in March 1983, it is bedevilled by conceptual problems which have created difficulties with the American public, the Soviet Union and allies. Most experts seem to have proved even to the Pentagon that a leakproof, Bonn-to-Tokyo, all cities defence is extremely distant and doomed to imperfection. The Soviets could damage, destroy or elude the defence at a fraction of the cost of constructing it, and build their own defences to protect the targets of US missiles. The old adage demands that the Soviets pay more attention to American capacity than professed intent. They would therefore respond by matching the US defence technology at any cost, and by looking for offensive systems to guarantee penetration of

Figure 1.1: Area of Destruction by Nuclear Blasts

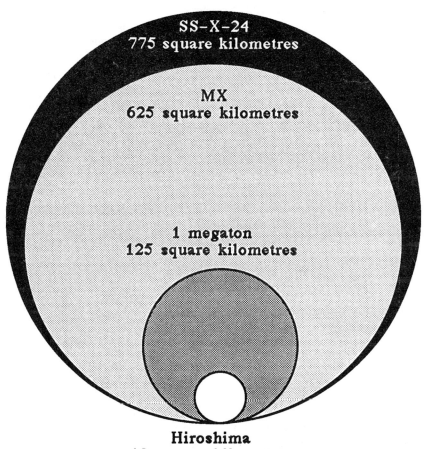

SS-X-24
775 square kilometres

MX
625 square kilometres

1 megaton
125 square kilometres

Hiroshima
10 square kilometres

any US shield. Americans have too often in the past underestimated Soviet determination, and miscalculated Soviet ability, to catch up.

SDI could also exact a significant political cost from US allies. In a notable speech on 15 March 1985, British Foreign Secretary Sir Geoffrey Howe questioned whether SDI could provide defences which worked, were survivable and cost-effective in comparison with a credible, sustainable and controllable mix of conventional and nuclear forces: "there would be no advantage in creating a new Maginot Line of the twenty–first century, liable to be outflanked by relatively simpler and demonstrably cheaper counter-measures" (*Times,* 22 March 1985).

Doubts about Star Wars are thus intense and widely-shared. A substantial body of scientific opinion is sceptical about the feasibility of SDI on technical grounds (the analogy with doubters about putting man on the moon is fallacious because the moon does not fight back); many strategists dispute its value because it conflicts with the logic of assured mutual vulnerability; US and allied public opinion remains unconvinced because it may escalate defence costs while undermining stable deterrence. The decision to develop, test and deploy Star Wars will therefore depend on fundamental political–strategic calculations and not just technology and research. In addition to feasibility, therefore, political leaders must also consider the wider issues of opportunity costs, likely offsetting developments on the Soviet side, and the survivability of SDI components against the countervailing Soviet measures. Because research can acquire an unstoppable momentum of its own, western leaders have to take care that political decisions are not preempted by the march of technology. It makes good sense to develop weapons systems in tandem with an assessment of their strategic implications.

Nuclear Winter

Technology as a problem rather than the solution is demonstrated also in the nuclear winter scenario. We should note that there is no consensus about the climatic after-effects of a nuclear war. Scientists disagree both on the probability of a nuclear winter, and about the threshold at which global climatic after-effects are triggered. In other words, (1) there is a difference of scientific opinion on the seriousness of the nuclear winter effect in terms of temperature change, time duration, and geographic extent; and (2) in terms of megatons or number of warheads exploded, the precise threshold for climatic effects will depend on how they are exploded, at what altitude, at what locations, on seasonal and weather considerations, and on the nature of the targets. By some calculations, the threshold ceiling of safety is between 500 to 2,000 strategic warheads. That is, the world could possibly survive a nuclear war in which the Americans and Soviets limited themselves to using only 250–1,000 warheads each. [The exact number depends on such factors as low or high yield bombs, and whether they are detonated in the air (airbursts) or on the ground (groundbursts).]

These uncertainties should not disguise the fact of growing acceptance by the scientific community that the probability of a nuclear winter is finite, that is greater than zero. In a nuclear war confined to the northern hemisphere, the "best case" scenario is that people would die in tens of millions, even minimal health care facilities for the survivors would be non-existent, and economies would be totally wrecked. Furthermore, while the nuclear winter would kill all growth, the post-nuclear summer would abort regenerative processes. The health and economic implications are severe even for non-combatant countries like New Zealand—a subject discussed more fully by Wren Green.

While the full range of implications of nuclear winter hypotheses for strategic doctrines will become clearer with official studies that have been initiated, some can already be identified. The most important appears to be that the possibility of a successful preemptive first strike recedes even further into the distance, for it will be an act of national suicide even without any retaliation. Logically, then, second-strike retaliatory capability need not be the only basis for deterrence; the nuclear winter scenario has now introduced an element of self-deterrence to enhance nuclear stability. From an overall political perspective, the nuclear winter scenario reconfirms the unacceptable nature of nuclear war, and sharpens our consciousness of the truth that we should be concerned not with the day after, but the day before.

It follows that any "first use" policy loses whatever dubious meaning it may have had once. "Rational" calculations of national security have led to the point where international security and species survival are threatened. To believe that a "first use" policy could successfully steer short of the safety threshold is to put great faith in the enemy's good sense and restraint. If that faith were to be transferred to the field of arms control negotiations, meaningful agreements would be much easier to achieve. Conversely, because "first use" guarantees self-destruction, it loses all credibility and therefore any value as a posture of deterrence.

Yet another consequence of the "nuclear winter" scenario may thus well be to stimulate a shift from nuclear to conventional forces as the "real deterrent" against Soviet aggression in Europe. Reliance upon nuclear weapons has made it more difficult to secure the political and financial support necessary to create an adequate conventional force. Sweden and Yugoslavia are neutral and nonaligned respectively. Both rely for their security *ultimately* on the US–Soviet nuclear deterrence, but neither has its own nuclear weapons. It has never been convincingly shown why Western Europe should not base its security upon the same equation: the peace of Europe is kept and could be kept by a more complicated set of circumstances than reliance on the European nuclear deterrent.

European history is a good illustration too of how the strategic certainties of yesterday are viewed as mere superstitions and myths today. Sweden and Denmark, or France and Germany, are some of the great historic enemies of yesteryears. Today, war between them seems inconceivable. Their once mutual fear has been submerged (to the point of extinction) in newly discovered common interests. There is therefore good historical precedent for striving for a similar transformation of the adversarial US–Soviet relationship into structures of common security. The existence of nuclear weapons themselves might be thought of as creating the most important common interest, namely survival. (It is pertinent to note here that in Eastern Europe, the Church and Marxism are ideologies in apparently irreconcilable conflict. Yet the need to subordinate the ideological conflict in the interests of the survival of both state and church has produced a pragmatic if watchful accommodation between the alternative centres of political power and social–religious power.) Blainey, Holsti and Mazrui in different ways demythify the era-centric view of war and conflict resolution which dominates the contemporary scholarly literature: in causes of conflict—conflict may be for ever, but issues come and go; in time-span of wars; in transience of dominant political cultures—empires rise and fall along with the technologies of warfare which sustain or destroy them.

CONFLICT MANAGEMENT

When faced with a military threat from an enemy, we can choose to respond by matching that threat. But there is an alternative, namely, to reduce and constrain the threat. Arms control measures are means of trying to constrain reciprocal threats without eliminating them. If we consider the motorway analogy, a generally obeyed traffic code ensures a smoother flow of vehicles with a diminished risk of accident. A highway code thus seeks to regulate traffic behaviour and make it more predictable, but does not prohibit it. Arms control regimes similarly seek to dampen the possibility of sudden dramatic changes in the relative military balance through weapons development in numbers or technology, but not to dismantle existing stockpiles.

Arms control measures can contribute to peace and security in many different ways. The most prominent suggestions in the 1980s have been, in Europe, for regional nuclear disarmament and, in the United States, for unilateral freeze on nuclear weapons. Other possibilities include partial agreements (e.g. no atmospheric testing), tacit agreements (e.g. acting as if SALT II, signed in 1979, were in force even without its formal ratification), and stabilising measures. A comprehensive test ban treaty (CTB) resolution was supported by a record 143 UN members in the General Assembly vote in December 1987. (France and the US were the only countries to vote against the resolution, with another eight countries abstaining.) This is an issue of particular concern to inhabitants of the Pacific, who are only too keenly aware of the truth that one nation's test is another peoples' ecocide.

Unfortunately, the typical modern government displays a marked imbalance in its bureaucratic allotments to military defence and arms control. For example, the annual budget for the US Arms Control and Disarmament Agency is less than the cost of two F-16 fighter aircrafts. The bureaucratic imbalance is further reinforced in the US by a constitutional one. An American administration, such as Reagan's, seeking increases in military spending, say for SDI research and testing, must carry a majority in Congress with it. An American president who negotiates a complex and difficult arms control agreement with the Soviet Union, for example the intermediate-range (500–5,500 km) nuclear forces (INF) treaty of December 1987, must have the treaty ratified by a two–thirds majority in the Senate. In effect then a Senate minority representing less than a third of US voters has the constitutional power to block ratification. Considering the diversity of interests represented in the American political process, obtaining a blocking minority in the Senate is not terribly difficult. Conversely, attempts to accommodate all such interest groups can seriously erode the credibility of arms limitation treaties. The history of US–Soviet arms negotiations since SALT I was signed in 1972 indicates that arms control efforts would have been substantially different in outcome had US presidents not been hampered by the pervasive fear of a Senate veto.

The potential for arms control agreements is limited by two factors, one technical, the other political. Because of the mutual suspicion and distrust between the two superpowers, only those agreements will be negotiated and ratified that are independently verifiable. Moscow and Washington will not rely upon each other's good faith; they require "hard evidence" that cheating is not possible. Development of sophisticated verification technology in the 1960s, e.g. photoreconnaissance satellites, made it possible to negotiate SALT I. The achievement of SALT I was in turn limited to the technology of verification, such as delivery vehicles big enough to be seen from space, e.g. ICBM launchers. Because of the importance of verification in sustaining confidence in the agreement, both sides promised not to interfere with each other's surveillance systems.

Technology marches on. Its march brings improved means of verification, so that weapons that lay beyond detection in the past will become verifiable in the future. But the march of technology has also meant that the arms race takes place in improving weapons sophistication rather than numbers, e.g. in accuracy. This complicates arms control negotiations by eroding the "firebreak" distinctions between tactical, theatre and strategic nuclear weapons, as well as between nuclear and conventional weapons with the development of "mini-nukes" or small nuclear weapons with yields around 1 kt (kilotonne). Let us take a specific example of verification difficulties. A freeze on all nuclear weapons systems requires procedures to verify the development, production, testing and deployment of about a hundred kinds of weapons and delivery systems, both offensive and defensive, across all levels of tactical, theatre and strategic forces. Such verification procedures must: (1) be devised; (2) be negotiated within the military–foreign policy bureaucracies of the two superpowers; (3) be negotiated between the two superpowers; (4) be ratified by them, which involves a major political battle to avoid a one–third Senate veto in the US; and (5) they must then come into force in time to stop the arms race. The last requirement is necessary to avoid the agreement being technologically obsolete at birth or in infancy, and places a premium upon quick negotiation; the first four requirements highlight the difficulties involved in securing an agreement, and indicate elaborate, extensive and time-consuming negotiations.

The political obstacle to arms control agreements is the state of superpower relations. Throughout human history, arms races have reflected as well as sharpened conflict between political systems. The SALT accord was made possible because of the prevailing climate of *détente,* and in turn contributed to a further relaxation of international tension. Unfortunately, the United States and the Soviet Union had different perceptions of and interests in *détente.* As the differences began to re-emerge in the late 1970s, relations between the superpowers once again cooled down.

In December 1987, in the words of the chief Soviet spokesman Gennadi Gerasimov, the world crossed the Rubicon of nuclear disarmament. The superpowers' INF agreement is the first disarmament agreement of the nuclear age: the US will destroy 859 INF missiles, the USSR 1,752. "Trust but verify," said Reagan in the context of the INF treaty. Indeed the treaty does not just permit verification; it requires it. It is unprecedented in the scope and rigour of its verification clauses and modalities.

The trust but verify slogan encapsulates the political reality that adversaries pay greater heed to each other's capabilities than intentions. Inability to attack is more readily believed than unwillingness to attack. This suggests that an arms control technique worth pursuing might be the strategy of non-provocative defence. If in force configuration, weapons systems and military deployments one side has clearly rejected offensive options in favour of "defensive defence," then the other side has cause to feel reassured rather than threatened. If a reciprocal cycle of fear is a cause of arms build-up and war, then a strategy of non-provocative defence helps to inhibit both.

We noted above the notion that arms races may be a cause of wars. The hypothesis immediately runs into two substantial objections, one definitional, the other causal. "Arms race" is one of those glib phrases that has gained wide international currency but is uncommonly difficult to define; rare is the user who attempts to pin down its precise meaning. The metaphor sits ill upon the facts. Historians seem to be agreed that there was a British–German naval race between 1898–1914, and a Franco–German army race between 1911–1914; but scholars disagree on the post-1945 US–Soviet rivalry. Rarely do the superpowers "race" each other in the numbers, quality or expenditures—three different metrics which may be divergent or congruent—of their armaments. The more important determinants of weapons stockpiles usually seem to be economic pressures or opportunities, political latitudes, regime needs, lobbying leverage of military–industrial–scientific complexes, etc. To be sure, there is increased proliferation of arms in absolute numbers. But there is no necessary increase relative to the number of expanded actors in the system, or to the gross world product, or to increased international trade flows. These particular ratios are not constant, but rise and fall over time, so that the metaphor "arms backstroke crawl" may be as valid at one point in time as an "arms race" at another.

Secondly, the argument that arms race (understood as an abnormal spurt in military expenditures by major powers in a system directly correlated to each other's armaments expansion) *causes* wars would not easily be sustainable on the historical record (Huntington, 1971). Indeed the conventional wisdom about the Second World War is that the *failure* of Britain and France to engage in an arms build-up in time was at least partly responsible for the onset of the war; that is, in this particular case it was a refusal to engage in an arms race that was a cause of war. Hence the claim *si vis pacem para bellum*—"If you want peace, prepare for war." If actions speak louder than words, then the vast majority of the world's countries would seem to subscribe to this theory.

Causality in social behaviour can be circular or mutual rather than unidirectional. That is, conflicts and arms races can have a mutually reinforcing effect on one another: tension can be as much a cause of an arms race as the other way round. Nuclear disarmament is no more a guaranteed path to the *nirvana* of peace than nuclear arms is a guarantee of nuclear holocaust being our *karma*. The empirical evidence suggests that three separate propositions are justified about the relationship between arms races and wars:

— an arms race can result in a war;
— an arms race can be terminated peacefully without resulting in war;
— wars may result even in the absence of any discernible arms race.

The first proposition leads to the policy prescription that disarmament needs to be pursued with unremitting vigour, although Inga Thorsson has rendered yeowoman service in pointing out that disarmament may require advance preparations in order to minimise social, political and economic dislocation: "If you want to disarm, first plan for conversion." Blainey adds the further warning against the perils of naive disarmament, which would precipitate the very calamity that it was designed to avert. Areas not presently militarised must be kept demilitarised by quarantining the virus of militarisation. This is particularly so because while, and possibly because, nuclear arms rule out nuclear war as a means of conflict resolution, they end up *perpetuating conflicts*. That is, as long as the instruments of warfare were not mutually suicidal, conflicts could be put to the test of arms and thus decided on the battlefield. But to rule out a test of arms because of the nuclear factor is to take away an important means of settling the conflict, and therefore to sustain conflict. Such prolonged conflict then becomes a partisan issue between rival competitors for power within countries.

The second proposition imbues efforts towards arms control and disarmament with hope: success is possible. The third proposition suggests that arms control and disarmament may be necessary conditions of peace, but are by no means sufficient. Like international mediation—discussed in this collection by Alain Brouillet—and peacekeeping, they are palliatives not cures: techniques of conflict management, not paths to conflict resolution. In view of their limited potential (since by their very nature they cannot address the institution of war but merely the means of its waging), the vast amount of intellectual and political effort invested in arms control and disarmament seems rather more surprising than the meagre dividends returned.

POVERTY AND ECOLOGY TRAPS

The diplomatic and arms control–disarmament paths to peace should be pursued in order to reduce the incentives to go to war, to limit the means of waging war, and to confine the damage caused by the outbreak of war. Conflict management techniques, such as mediation and peacekeeping, should be refined and made more effective within the existing institutional framework, in particular so as to narrow the development time lag between them and the instruments of warfare. International law, although unenforceable, is a vast body of rules which are accepted as having the status of law in relations between states (Bull, 1977). Its presence in the process of bargaining between states is indicated in the fact that countries do try to use it as an instrument to reinforce claims, or to try to evade it by denying its relevance to the facts or its applicability to the dispute in question. Bishop Tóth suggests that the Church, in addition to developing a doctrine of just peace, could play two further roles of exerting pressure on governments for peaceful conflict resolution, and acting as mediator if circumstances permit.

Yet the world may end with a whimper rather than a bang: with a total resource depletion, not with a general nuclear war. Ecological damage to the earth's life-support systems is a less spectacular but more basic threat to peace and survival. Pessimists conclude that the challenge of scarcity is more likely to precipitate conflict than compel collaboration, given the persistence of competitive national sovereignties as the organising principle of the international system.

If the problem of violence is more deep-rooted than war, then the solution too must be sought more fundamentally than in the mere elimination of the instruments of violence, be they nuclear or conventional. International politics will not come to an end, injustices will not disappear, conflicts will not fade away with the elimination of nuclear weapons. The technological approach to solving the world's problems has also come under question in the field of development, where it is seen as endangering the lives and lifestyles of millions of people. The technological quick-fix is insufficient to solve the problem of hunger. The major problem is not shortage of food, but lack of purchasing power. Hunger is thus part of the problem of distribution, and can be adequately addressed only through a transformation of social, political and economic structures alongside technological improvements in productivity and yield. The basic goal of development has shifted from modernisation to equity: peace based on an inequitable order can only be stultifying of the human spirit. The inter-relationships between peace, justice and environmental sensitivity are explored by Carl Friedrich von Weizsäcker.

The twentieth century has been an age of profound paradoxes. Standard bearers of the liberal democratic code act illiberally against democratic tendencies. Ali Mazrui remarks how the founding fathers of America separated its powers of government in domestic affairs as a bulwark against the tyranny of government, but failed to anticipate the abuses that its concentrated and enormously expanded power would produce internationally. But he notes too how the standard bearer of socialist emancipation has forged a hierarchical satellite system in Europe, precisely the continent which colonised the rest of the world in an earlier era. The luxuries of consumer societies in the industrialised West set in sharp relief the squalor and misery of an increasing majority of the world's population. The rural poor migrate to become the urban destitute. Great advances in art, science and agriculture compete for media attention with rapid growths in such epidemics as AIDs that symbolise the decay of civilisation, and in nuclear weaponry that threaten the very existence of civilisation. Technology has put humanity on the calamitous path to self-destruction.

We should bear in mind too the potential for tension between peace and development, the two great issues of our times. Peace seeks to preserve, and is fundamentally conservative; development aims to transform, and is fundamentally revisionist. (Similarly, development is an exploitative concept even in regard to man's relationship with nature.) The dangerous problem of war must therefore be viewed in the context of the more fundamental and more difficult problems of poverty and ecological degradation. Increasing numbers of human beings are marginalised and made expendable at the same time as insatiable man has gone on a rampage against nature. The logical elegance of strategic debates is not necessarily the most relevant frame of reference to the poor peasant anxious to feed his family for the night. To the dispensability of human beings and cultures must be added the catalogue of the ecological wars of great magnitude that have been and are being waged on the land, mountains, streams and agrosystems of the world: the common (wo)man has no defence against the erosion and plunder of resources that are the common heritage of (wo)mankind.

There is considerable discussion today of the relationship between nuclear weapons and world poverty. It has been argued that policies of nuclear deterrence have entailed such heavy expenditure on arms that they amount to stealing from the poor. The statistics on the arms race are staggering. The World Health Organisation spent less than $100 million in its ten–year campaign to rid the world of smallpox; the money would not buy even one modern strategic bomber. Alternatively, the price of one aircraft carrier would enable WHO to eradicate leprosy, malaria, trachoma and yaws. Funds are scarce to help 570 million malnourished and 1,500 million people who lack adequate medical services, but the world can afford $35 billion every year for trafficking in arms. The United Nations reckons that just one fifth of the world's annual military expenditures could abolish world hunger by the year 2000.

United Nations experts have identified military spending as an obstacle to economic growth. The arms race and development are therefore in a competitive relationship, an issue taken up by Inga Thorsson. Since 1945, 5–8 percent of the world's output has been allocated to the military. In addition to the 25 million regular military personnel, 20 percent of the world's scientists and engineers are engaged in research and development for military purposes. Yet the average military product is estimated as being twenty times as research intensive as the average consumer item for domestic use. A high defence outlay depresses economic growth directly by diverting investment funds, and indirectly by diverting research and development skills and efforts. This is particularly true for developing countries whose need for external inputs like capital, trade and technology is usurped by military outlays. There has even been a proposal to increase financial flows to developing countries by adopting a "disarmament dividend approach," under which budgetary savings resulting from disarmament measures would be placed in a special fund for development.

WORLD GOVERNMENT

Einstein's observation that atomic power has changed everything save our modes of thinking is frequently quoted. The lag in the nuclear revolution between its technological and political spheres means that we are caught in a drift towards unparalleled catastrophes. The political unit of international relations is still the sovereign nation-state, while the weapons of destruction that they possess are global and species-threatening. In other words, we are still trying to run an Einsteinian world along Newtonian—if not Ptolemaic—political principles.

For this reason, unilateral approaches will not be enough in the end. Instead we need concerted action following collective reflection. For all its shortcomings, the United Nations, or something very much like it, remains an indispensable instrument for the attainment of a civilised world community of peoples. One may also wonder how much of the United Nations deficiencies are due to wilful neglect rather than intrinsic defect. The organisation is located in New York city. The budget of the New York Police Department is larger than the annual regular budget of the United Nations. Indeed the UN budget is only one–fifth of the amount that Americans spend on pet food.

The United Nations remains in particular the best hope for the smaller and less powerful countries in their search for peace and security through effective arms control and disarmament, for social justice and human rights, for decent living standards through economic growth and development. The artificiality and unreality of self-imposed compartmentalisation by the human race is notably evident in the case of New Zealand. In terms of geographical space, it inhabits the South–East corner of the globe; in terms of political distances separating civilisations, it belongs to the West; in terms of economic divisions, it is grouped as part of the North. Little wonder that New Zealanders should be particularly sensitive to the growing loneliness and civic vacuum surrounding humankind today.

Humanity encourages us to uproot the fences which divide human beings into different nationalities; humility urges us to acknowledge the equal validity of alternative points of view. The nation-state is under attack from without: from technologies of destruction which no longer respect political frontiers, from transnational flows which defy national controls, and from global problems which demand collective resolution. But the nation-state is equally under attack in contemporary society from within, that is from sub-national groups seeking to preserve their autonomy and identity in the face of assimilative drives by national governments. The resurgence of provincialism and localism, perhaps unimaginable in the 1950s, has put the state and the world into a ferment. The ship of state is listing precariously, as it no longer seems adequate to the requirements of security, identity, and welfare in many parts of the world. Yet, paradoxically, the number of states since the Second World War has trebled, and the power and range of states has expanded enormously under the impulse of an interventionist ethic.

But the result of an expansive government is often to increase the distance between the state and the citizens. It would be enormously difficult to get people to identify affectively with the authority of a world-state. This suggests that world government is not necessarily the answer to the question of a just peace. Unless we are to fall victim to the fallacy of equating world peace with world government by definition, we have to recognise that the nation-state has not always guaranteed peace and order within its borders, and that the ideology of national self-determination has itself been one of the major causes of conflict in our times.

Continued survival of the species may come through the cohesive integrity of traditional civic society fulfilling basic needs, rather than through the homogenisation of an integrated nation-state or world-state. Any attempt to impose international order through world government would merely exacerbate the problem of peace in justice—yet Blainey believes that the surrender of freedoms to a world-state in return for freedom from insecurity is probable. What is desirable is international coherence within societal diversity: an organising principle for polities distinct from both the sovereign state and world government. The most urgent requirement for mankind is not a fanatic imposition of one's preferred moral–political system upon others, but rather peaceful coexistence based upon tolerance of different points of view, and an adoption of some concept of an international rule of law within a system of dispersed power. One suggestion that came up in discussions was the idea of geographically dispersed, functionally compartmentalised supranational governments for dealing with such subjects as ocean management and human rights, subjects that transcend national frontiers.

ATTITUDINAL TRANSFORMATION

If wars begin in the minds of men, then peace too must begin in the minds of men and women. The problem of war does not originate in nature and is not a necessary consequence of human nature. War is a particular type of social behaviour. But the organisation of human beings into social units is neither a necessary nor a sufficient condition of warfare. As a man-made institution, war can also be unmade by humanity. A necessary consequence of this seemingly innocuous proposition is that responsibility for transforming war into peace is vested in each and every individual human being.

It may be that the nuclear weapons trap, the poverty trap and the ecology trap are the results of a particular approach—the ideological underpinning of which was provided by a materialistic and unilinear theory of progress—which subordinates nature to competitive and exploitative human desires, instead of seeking to establish a harmony among nations, as well as between people and nature. The contemporary order, it is argued, is built on structures of domination and exploitation: of man over fellow man, of man over woman, of man over nature. Civil society has been transformed into the national security state, and international order has been metamorphosed into the balance of terror. Seductive as the ethic of consumption might be, five billion people cannot possibly emulate the wasteful lifestyles of the privileged few. This is why salvation must be located in a holistic framework and strategy: a balance between just peace and just change.

The idea of such a fundamental shift in attitudes is taken to its most radical conclusions in the gentlest of language by Willis Harman. System maintenance is impossible, system reform inadequate; what is needed, says Harman, is whole–system transformation. But before we decide that redemption lies in a total abandonment of the western mind-set, we might care to remember that such movements as for the protection of the environment and human rights (including civil rights of ethnic minorities) have their strongest bases in western countries too. Scientific inquiry has served to liberate us from the dogmas of religion, iniquities of tradition, and bondage to nature. And technical remedies combined with the competitive spirit have brought unparalleled levels of material prosperity to masses of people.

There is also a temptation, in blaming all ills upon the western mind-set, to resurrect a golden era of pre-European cultures and polities which does violence to the historical record. Wars that laid whole societies to waste were a recurrent pattern of behaviour of societies in complete isolation from European civilisation; cultures and peoples were enslaved, assimilated or destroyed by the aggressive–imperialist rivals of their day; scarred remnants bear silent testimony to the ravages upon nature by earlier societies uncontaminated by western science. Conversely, the most widely sought vehicle for cultural identity, expression and perpetuation is national self-determination, which fuses community with polity and has globalised the European nation-state system. Famine and starvation today in any part of the world mobilise international relief efforts on a scale without precedent in earlier eras. Major indicators of human welfare, such as infant mortality, life expectancy and literacy, demonstrate historically unparalleled progress even in the third world. How will the revolution of consciousness preserve the valuable heritage of the scientific–competitive drive while releasing us from its more unfortunate consequences? Beyond this, there is the further difficulty of the mechanics, modalities and stages of transition from the revolution of consciousness to the revolution of system. Harman himself spent some time on the subject of intermediate steps along the path to system transformation.

It is interesting that there has already occurred a fundamental shift in the attitudes of national security elites. The optimists of two–three decades ago put faith in the diffusionist munificence of technology and capitalism in spreading the fruits of wealth as the means of expanding the sum of human happiness. This has given way to a more pessimistic outlook on the world which no longer believes in five billion people copying the parasitic lifestyle of exuberance and affluence, and a more exclusioinst strategy which is obsessed with stability and preserving the *status quo* for the haves against the increasingly vociferous, assertive and indeed militant claims of the have nots. This is illustrated in the lifeboat ethics perspective developed by Garrett Hardin (1974), in which the 50 American occupants of a lifeboat with a carrying capacity of 60 are justified in rejecting the pleas of help of all one hundred swimmers floundering in the sea around them: deprivation degrades, opulence dehumanises.

With the crash of the stock markets in October–November 1987, many commentators noted the parallels with the crash of 1927 but remained sceptical of a repeat of the great depression. One of the reasons for their greater optimism is the belief that the world's leading economic powers learnt the important lesson in the 1930s that virulent protectionism of national economies caused the collapse of the international economy, and therefore of national economies. That is, the world economy is so integrated and interdependent that the health of *national* economies is inseparable from the viability of the *international* economy. The same consciousness needs to be awakened in the field of security: national security pursued in isolation from international security risks the destruction of both. While the policy implications of the dangers of protectionist dominoes seem to have been internalised by the key economic actors and decision-makers, the parallel policy implications in the realm of security have not. The concept of common security is not an ideal to be envisioned but the irreducible minimum for national survival.

No Annihilation without Representation

Conflict management techniques can be used and enhanced by governments, and continuing government-to-government dialogue is essential to suppressing anxiety levels by achieving transitional goals. But a basic shift in values and attitudes moving us towards a more ascetic world society, based on self-restraint and renunciation of force, requires the mobilisation of opinion elites and significant publics: those at the forefront of the environment, feminist, ethnic, civil rights and trade unions movements.

Nuclear peace is too important to be left just to the superpowers whose behaviour is guided by "apocalyptic theologies." They are apocalyptic in the strategic sense of peace being based on a theory of deterrence that threatens to blow up the world. They are apocalyptic also in the more fundamental sense of each superpower seeking salvation in the destruction of its wicked ideological opponent. The apocalypse, notes von Weizsäcker, is a message ultimately of hope, with world catastrophe being the means for the final triumph of good over evil.

The United States and the Soviet Union were both born of revolution, and are children of revolutionary doctrines rooted in Europe; both, notes Mazrui, have become fathers of imperialism. To an extent both had imperialism thrust upon them in the circumstances of the post-1945 world. Both were uncomfortable imperialists also because of the conflict with their founding ideologies, and guilt may have made their imperial behaviour even worse. Classical European colonialism carried with it accountability: planting the flag—which violated every American political sensitivity—meant accepting legal accountability for governance. Superpower imperialism by contrast has produced hegemony without responsibility. Both the US and the USSR are disliked as foremost powers within their regions; yet the hatred of *pax Sovietica* is more intense in Eastern Europe. Perhaps this is because Eastern Europe *vis-a-vis* the USSR fuses the two sets of relationships of Latin America (backyard) and Western Europe (loyal ally) *vis-a-vis* the USA: Eastern Europeans are doubly bonded to the Soviet sword. The ideology on which the USSR was founded emphasised the redistribution of economic power, yet the Soviet Union has been a force for redistribution of political power internationally. The US, founded on the redistribution of political power, has had its most profound international impact as an agent of economic change. The Soviet Union has not been discouraged from playing a politically liberating role outside Europe even in the face of prospective alignment with international capitalism by the liberated state. The US has preferred to become anti-liberationist if nationalism merged or was even tinged with communism.

The superpowers have the greatest stake in the preservation of world order, the greatest capacity to contribute to or destroy that order, and consequently the greatest responsibility in the management of world order. But the authority of the superpowers as defenders of the world order has been eroded somewhat in recent years because they have not been perceived by the rest of the world community as discharging their duty responsibly. Von Weizsäcker's diagnosis of the illness afflicting both superpowers is especially poignant in view of the tragedy that befell his own country when it was seduced into a power mentality earlier this century. Soviet–American dialogue and agreements in the 1960s–1970s built up a structure of cooperation which embodied the world's hopes for an avoidance of nuclear war. As the process of *detente* ground to a halt by the end of the 1970s and suffered reverses in the 1980s, the fruits of earlier cooperation began to decay and the superpowers abandoned their postures as responsible managers of the world order. There are of course other sources of disorderly tendencies. But it is also true that, as the superpowers reconstructed a structure of confrontation, they lost virtually all claim to be regarded as the nuclear trustees of mankind. It remains to be seen whether the INF agreement of December 1987 will reverse confrontation, reconstuct cooperation in preserving the nuclear peace, and enhance global perceptions of the superpowers as responsible managers of world order once again. Holsti's sketch of the superpowers' recent learning curve is certainly cause for optimism and hope.

Perceptions of the **United States** as the major belligerent power help to explain why the American government is the focus of so much attention from peace campaigners in the western world. Arguments that the Germans forced the US to develop the atomic bomb, the Japanese to use it, and the Soviets to keep it, have begun to ring hollow. The United States has initiated most of the major technological breakthroughs in the nuclear armoury, and remains the only country to have used such weapons in war. It is not entirely unreasonable to expect the United States, therefore, to launch the major initiatives in nuclear arms control and disarmament. Yet expectations of responsible American leadership and beneficial American statecraft have served to open a gap between America and its allies.

Jerry Hough has noted that the "vast majority of men of the Brezhnev–Gromyko generation were born between 1900 and 1910 and were almost all thrust into high positions in the wake of the purges of 1937–1938. Men of this generation remember World War I; their fathers may have fought in the Russo–Japanese War and reminisced about it; they, themselves, were high officials in World War II" (Hough, 1985: 45). According to another scholar of the **USSR**, "The coming to power of any new top leader in the Soviet Union changes, to a greater or lesser extent, the correlation of forces among the various institutional interests, opinion groupings and issue networks which exist within both the domestic and foreign policy making realms" (Brown, 1986: 1060). The case of Mikhail Gorbachev has proved no exception to this rule. He has seized the opportunity to try and reshape Soviet society both domestically and in its international relations.

A characterisitc Gorbachev approach seems to be to make the political environment more receptive to the possibility of fundamental change by engaging in bracing rhetoric at the declaratory level prior to policy innovations at the operational level. Gorbachev has already acquired a reputation as an impressive salesman of ideas who through a masterful campaign of public diplomacy can set the agenda for international affairs and force opponents into a reactive role. The Gorbachev style has been much in evidence in the arms control sphere: bold pronouncements, challenging visions and unilateral initiatives which not only made Soviet foreign policy uncomfortably unpredictable, but also created a superpower and international climate of opinion more conducive to concluding a historic nuclear disarmament agreement in December 1987, earlier false starts notwithstanding. On this "question of questions," Gorbachev was not interested in mere cosmetic changes at the margins of the nuclear balance; he wanted fundamental progress. He was not willing to negotiate away strategic parity with the USA; but he was prepared to contemplate strategic parity at a significantly lowered threshold.

In his notable Vladivostok speech of 28 July 1986, Gorbachev attacked what we might term the intellectual inertia which has produced a lag between the security requirements of the 1980s and the state of the world's nuclear arsenals. He called accordingly for a fundamental break with many conventional approaches to foreign policy, a break with the axioms of political thinking on the problem of war and peace, a break with the entrenched assumptions of individual and international security policies. In so doing, he acknowledged the special responsibility of the superpowers in the management of world order, which is the necessary corollary to their privileges flowing from that status. Furthermore, Gorbachev has been an evident believer in the linkage argument. There is an economic logic to the fervour with which he has pursued arms control and disarmament negotiations—even a superpower cannot live in security by military means alone.

If Gorbachev's initiatives are a bluff, then can they be shown up as such without being called? If they contain genuine offers of accommodation, then what responses should be forthcoming? How can the countries which are the objects of Gorbachev's courtship respond positively while minimising security risks to themselves? The whole subject of "New Thinking" under Mikhail Gorbachev is discussed by Timour Timofeev of the Soviet Academy of Sciences.

In the 1970s, the Sino–American *rapprochement* profoundly realigned the world's power relations. A normalisation of relations between **China** and the Soviet Union would usher in a similarly profound process of readjustment, not just regionally, but globally. The centrality of China to the entire Asian–Pacific region is attested to by the fact that it borders upon or is proximate to, and certainly relevant to, all the relationships of conflict in contemporary Asia–Pacific. The importance of the China factor is evident in the chapter by Jin Junhui. China under Deng and the USSR under Gorbachev seem less outwardly aggressive in their ideologies than America under the proselytising zeal of the Reagan administration—an apparent reversal of the situation in the 1950s.

The manner in which a mass movement in **New Zealand** has produced unilateral initiatives for nuclear disengagement by an American ally is an interesting case-study. ANZUS, the 1951 security alliance between Australia, New Zealand and the United States, came to be seen as having linked New Zealand to global American militarism, and this led to a questioning of the ANZUS arrangements as the institutional mechanism for the Americans to harness New Zealand resources to their war machine. The disconcerting realisation that New Zealand and the United States can differ in the identification of enemies and the choice of means to meet the threats raised calls to re-evaluate the logic of joint defence. New Zealand is a peaceable little country in the romantic South Seas. America appears at times to have taken on the attributes of a warfare state. In an eloquent address to the Dunedin branch of the New Zealand Institute of International Affairs on 30 April 1987, Prime Minister David Lange asserted that:

> ... nuclear weapons are themselves the greatest threat which exists to our future... far from adding to our security, they only put us more at risk....
>
> New Zealand cannot be defended by nuclear weapons and does not wish to be defended by nuclear weapons. We have disengaged ourselves from any nuclear strategy for the defence of New Zealand....
>
> When I think of the world's nuclear arsenals I know that what New Zealand has done as a measure of arms control [excluding nuclear warships from its ports] is a small step indeed. I also know that if we cannot take that step in New Zealand we cannot take it anywhere. If we cannot start in New Zealand we cannot start anywhere.

The Americans have remarked upon the contradictions in the Lange government's pursuit of foreign and defence policies. They have also been puzzled as to just what strategic or arms control objectives New Zealand, which is not a player in the nuclear game, hopes to achieve by its distinctive "anti-nuclear" policy. Yet it is also beyond dispute that New Zealand's stance has contributed to the global delegitimisation of nuclear weapons in the mid-1980s. The rationale for New Zealand's policy is provided by Russell Marshall, with Sir George Laking presenting a broader overview of the development of New Zealand foreign policy.

New Zealand, like every other country, does have the right, and indeed the responsibility, to make its voice heard on issues of global disarmament. The Americans and the Soviets have the power to destroy us all. We did not ask them to hold our fate in their hands; they have simply arrogated the power to themselves. Not having been consulted before being made hostage to their decisions on matters of life and death, we have every right to insist that there be no general annihilation without representation. Hiroshima was the first use of the atomic bomb; the international community *is* minding its business in trying to ensure that Nagasaki remains the last.

The perpetuation of the human race and the preservation of nature are too important to be left just to governments. System transformation will not be brought about by the managers and brokers of power, for the entrenched elites are the stoutest defenders of the established order based on divisions of inequalities. The future does not usually have a political constituency within the structures of government, with the result that governments can be unimaginative and short-sighted. They can also be remarkably adept at discovering difficulties in the way of solutions proposed by ordinary people. Therefore, global change must come from local action by the peoples of the world, by tapping the deep reservoirs of knowledge, wisdom, thinking and commitments that exist in them. Ali Mazrui remarks that powerlessness can corrupt as easily as power. The trappings of power can also blind politicians and officials, and the sophisticated complexities of theories blind scholars, to the simpler realities of basic choices confronting humanity in its moment of crisis. Power entraps the mind; powerlessness sets free the heart. Inga Thorsson puts her faith ultimately in the "power of the powerless" when mobilised in the great cause of peace. The great peace journey must march to the tune of *vox populi*.

CONCLUSION

The sayings of the Buddha begin with the words (Byrom, 1976: 3):

> We are what we think.
> All that we are arises with our thoughts.
> With our thoughts we make the world.

Having eaten of the fruit of forbidden knowledge, we have been cast into the nuclear world of eternal anguish: to know is to die.

Out of the despair of the present predicament must come hope for the future. To know that we will die if we choose to remain on our present path is to discover the reason for changing the course of human history: to know is to live. There is the story of two mortal enemies who come across one another on a narrow pathway. One must give way for the other to cross before they can both resume their journeys. The stronger man takes it as an issue of pride and honour and mutters "I do not give way to fools." His slender adversary replies "I do." It is the saving grace of such humility that the human race needs to rescue it from the predicament of its own making.

The phrase "I do" is in turn resonant of a certain vow which stresses bonds of love and togetherness, trust and fidelity between human beings—not in pain, but so as to experience life, joy and happiness to the fullest measure. It is also often the prelude to creation of new life. It has been said that each new baby that comes into this world is a reminder afresh that God has not totally despaired of humanity: hope springs eternal in the divine breast.

If we were given the knowledge that the last child of the human race was about to inherit the earth, and the power to order the affairs of the world, then what would be our approach to our daily behaviour? It is unlikely then that the selfish motives would predominate over the nobler sentiments. We seem to have lost faith in the belief that we are all descended from one common ancestry; perhaps we can be re-united in the belief that we are destined to share a common progeny. "Mother Earth" has nurtured the human race generously enough; do we have the right to deny the heritage of peace with nature due to the last child? In other words, in all our actions, we should always be guided by the thought of what it means for the last child—not necessarily the last child already born, but the last child of generations to come.

It may be that the last child perspective seems unduly pessimistic or fatalistic. There is an alternative approach which serves the same purpose of reminding us that we are itinerant guests upon earth and should not, in conformity with the norms of civilised behaviour, abuse the earth's hospitality. Rajni Kothari in his lecture spoke of the seventh generation perspective which informs the actions of North American Indians. All our important behaviour should be guided with the consideration of the world (in both its natural and social orders) that we would want our descendants seven generations hence to inherit and inhabit. In this we should be helped by the consciousness that our seventh generation ancestors preserved the world's harmony for us, including the gift of life. There is thus a fundamental continuity across generations of human beings to ensure the transmission of humanity's collective wisdom. The most important consequence of the last child–seventh generation ethic is that human beings are put at the centre of the decision-making process, and their welfare and contentment becomes the criterion by which to judge economic development and institutional restructuring. The conscious knowledge of this simple but eloquent fact might in turn ensure the continuity of the human race itself, not as masters over nature, but in peace with nature, in communion with creation as a whole, and at peace with itself.

PART ONE: NATIONAL PERSPECTIVES

2

Comprehensive Security

Russell Marshall

It gives me very great pleasure to contribute to this symposium on international conflict resolution. The University of Otago is to be congratulated on bringing together so many respected figures to analyse the dangers facing society, and try to formulate ways to meet the challenges of the final decade of this century. It is a formidable task.

It is with some diffidence that I offer a politician's view of the world we live in and the dangers we face: I am not an expert in the field of conflict resolution or security management.

Indeed, it could well be argued that politicians, especially those whose systems are adversarial, thrive on a measure of conflict, and are not averse either to exaggerating divisions or to creating the appearance of conflict solely for politicians' advantage. It was because I was troubled by the pervasiveness of conflict in many areas of our society that I promoted, in my previous position as Minister of Education, the development of peace studies programmes, which are more about conflict resolution than anything else. Ironically, perhaps predictably, those programmes themselves became a source of political argument and conflict.

Politicians, like academics, scientists and diplomats, have perceptions which can add to the total picture. In one sense politicians have an advantage. We need not feel constrained by the weight of traditional views. The perspective we have is not that of the bureaucrats who staff the international organisations. Nor is it that of academics or scientists. I am not denying their efforts. But we as politicians have different and special responsibilities. As politicians our duty is to those we represent. Our constituents look to us to protect their interests—economic, social, developmental. They look to us for security, in the widest possible sense.

It is our duty to ensure that in formulating policies on disarmament, on development, or on social issues, our governments pay due regard to those interests. Unless we do that, the people's confidence in us, their elected representatives, will have been misplaced.

It is the subject of security which I wish to address in this chapter. For security underlies so much of what this symposium is all about. Conflict results from irreconcilable views on security. Resolving conflict requires that people must recognise that their and their neighbours' security requirements can both be met.

At the governmental level, as at the personal, the same applies. No government can afford to overlook the fact that its prime responsibility is to ensure the safety and security of its citizens. But at the same time, no government can ignore the fact that now, as never before, all countries and regions are interdependent. What happens in Europe and Asia no longer leaves us in the South Pacific untouched. This interdependence is particularly obvious when one considers how nuclear weapons hold every one of us to ransom.

It can be argued that nuclear weapons have played an important role in the collective security arrangements which, for more than forty years, have helped to prevent global war. The many conflicts that have broken out have been local or regional in nature, and based on conventional weaponry.

But has the race to develop more modern and more powerful nuclear arsenals in fact made us more secure? I think not. Nuclear weapons now have the potential to destroy all life many times over. Such a risk is intolerable to every civilised person. Each individual, like the international community as a whole, has a duty to find other means to ensure humanity's survival.

The fact is that even on the widely accepted nuclear deterrent argument not all the arms now in existence are needed for security. That could be maintained with only a tiny fraction of the current weapons. This is recognised by all countries. But recognition is not action. The climate of tension and mistrust between East and West, and particularly between the superpowers, has meant that steps to end the arms race have not been easy.

A system of security which is no longer hostage to nuclear weapons must be our goal. The prospect of a nuclear-weapon-free world came a little closer when President Ronald Reagan met General Secretary Mikhail Gorbachev at Reykjavik in October 1986. The vision of such a world has lingered, long after the negotiations broke down.

Let us be realistic. It is not a vision that will be realised this year, or even this century. But the immediate challenge facing the international community is a more modest one. It is up to us here and now to determine how best to work for a nuclear-weapon-free world. It is up to us to take the first tentative steps in that direction. At the same time we must maintain the safety and security of each country and region.

Today the US and USSR are in the process of taking such a first tentative step. The elimination of all intermediate range nuclear missiles will, I fervently hope, become a turning point in the arms race. It will be concrete evidence of what we in New Zealand believe to be true—that safety and security can be maintained at a lower level of weaponry. That message is, in New Zealand's view, long overdue.

It is, however, only a first step. Next must come agreement on the immensely more disturbing and dangerous strategic weapons. Those countries which, like New Zealand, have applauded President Reagan and General Secretary Gorbachev for their political courage must now press for the reduction and eventual elimination of the strategic arsenals.

Agreement on 50 percent reductions in strategic nuclear arms, especially as part of a continuing process, would further emphasise that security can actually be enhanced by reducing the numbers of weapons. It would make easier the next 50 percent cut, and the next ....

If the safety and security of each country and region is to be maintained during the course of the disarmament process, then cuts in nuclear weaponry must be mutual. They must be balanced. They must be verifiable. It is encouraging that there is now something approaching common ground between East and West on these issues.

Equally encouraging is the apparent realisation that reductions in nuclear weapons cannot take place in isolation. Imbalances in conventional forces must also be taken into account. The deeper the cuts in nuclear weapons, the more important becomes agreement on levels of conventional forces. This is, plainly, of crucial significance in Europe. Western reliance on nuclear weapons in that theatre has been perceived as a necessary response to the larger conventional forces of the Warsaw Pact.

It is also of significance in North Asia. The removal of intermediate range nuclear forces (INF) must not be used by the Soviet Union as some sort of rationale for increasing its conventional forces in the region. New Zealand is concerned about security management in North Asia, and in the wider Asia–Pacific. In both areas the regional security situation is essentially different from that in the Atlantic–European theatre.

As the process of nuclear disarmament proceeds, regional security arrangements will have an increasingly important role to play in enhancing international stability. For all countries, whether related in adversarial terms or not, are now mutually dependent upon one another for their common security and survival. International security is today the sum total of all the bilateral and regional security commitments and relationships which link together in a global network.

Individual countries and groups of countries contribute to that network through those relationships in which they participate. But those relationships retain individual characteristics, reflecting the multifaceted nature of the global strategic framework.

In some regions, most obviously Europe, reliance on nuclear deterrence is at the forefront of strategic thinking. But there are those areas of the world where both global western interests and the security interests of the region in question are best served without the projection of nuclear force into the area.

That concept has been explicitly acknowledged in the Non-Proliferation Treaty (NPT). It has already been given practical (and legally binding) effect in Antarctica and Latin America. And the West has supported the case for similar arrangements in Africa, South Asia and the Middle East.

In New Zealand's view and that of its regional partners, the South Pacific is another such area. With members of the South Pacific Forum we have been active in promoting the adoption of the South Pacific Nuclear Free Zone Treaty.

That treaty seeks to preserve the region from rivalry involving nuclear weapons. It places prohibitions on the possession of nuclear explosive devices, their testing, and their stationing on national territory in the region. It was the unanimous view of the independent and self-governing states that adopted the treaty that, as in the case of Latin America, a nuclear-free zone in our part of the world would contribute to the security of each South Pacific country and the common security of all.

Neither the South Pacific Nuclear Free Zone nor New Zealand's national non-nuclear policy are intended to undermine the collective western security arrangements of which New Zealand has long been part. Nor do we believe that they have that effect.

On the contrary, New Zealand is determined to continue to meet its regional security commitments in conventional terms. That came out plainly in the 1987 defence review. At the international level, we have stood behind our policy that reductions in nuclear weapons can only take place under conditions which do not jeopardise the security of contracting parties. That, in our view, represents a valid and responsible contribution to the maintenance of effective collective defence.

However, security is much more than just military security, although there is a common tendency to equate the two. We must go beyond such a superficial analysis if security issues are to be addressed in a coherent and exhaustive way.

Threats to security come in many forms: military, economic, social, political, racial, religious, to name just a few. To respond to those threats in a constructive manner requires the development of a comprehensive security policy. That is what New Zealand is trying to do domestically, and what the South Pacific is trying to do on a regional scale.

Through the South Pacific Forum, countries in the South Pacific have determined on a strategy for the development of the region. That strategy addresses both the military and non-military aspects of the security equation. It is in its non-nuclear dimension that the strategy has attracted greatest international attention. But the truth is that its greatest emphasis is non-military. For it is a matter of record that in our part of the world, non-military factors are the greatest constraint on development.

Problems of isolation, remoteness, and a scarcity and non-mobility of natural resources are obvious. Less obvious, but just as real, is the tendency for our fundamental aspirations and priorities to be overlooked by outsiders. That tendency is understandable, given the small size and modest international influence of most Forum states. But our lack of clout is not an invitation to other countries to ignore the wishes and rights of the people of the South Pacific.

French nuclear testing is just one example of the sort of action taken by a major power without any apparent consideration for local sentiments. France is well aware that continued nuclear testing in our region is regarded as an action of gross arrogance, which causes grave offence, and that a cessation of testing would be welcomed as a positive demonstration of that country's willingness to treat its Pacific neighbours as equals.

The Pacific way is one of consultation, negotiation and consensus. That is how the South Pacific Forum operates. That is how outside powers are expected to behave if they want to play a constructive role in the development of the region.

In the past year there has been considerable progress made in this area. Through regional environmental and fisheries agreements negotiated with Forum members, major powers have demonstrated their sensitivity to South Pacific concerns. Complementing these agreements are the flows of aid to the less wealthy countries of the region. That aid originated from individual states both within and outside the region, and from multilateral bodies. Against a background of political stability, aid funds enable a country to set its course towards economic and social development. These measures, like the South Pacific Regional Trade and Economic Cooperation Agreement (SPARTECA), deal with particular non-military threats to security. Together with the region's non-nuclear stance they form the basis of a comprehensive regional security policy.

A regional security policy cannot of course exist in isolation. That is why we sought endorsement of the South Pacific Nuclear Free Zone Treaty (The Treaty of Rarotonga as it is sometimes called) by the nuclear-weapon states. Support for our region's non-nuclear aspirations would have been tangible recognition, by the major powers, of the right of small, non-nuclear countries to have a hand in their own destiny.

But the result has not been altogether satisfying. We have received some undertakings from four of the five nuclear powers to respect what the treaty sets out to achieve. China signed the relevant protocols to the agreement in an unequivocal and very satisfactory way. The Soviet Union, although a signatory as well, has qualified its signature in such a way as to cause considerable difficulty and disappointment for countries of the region.

It is deeply disappointing that the United States and the United Kingdom have refused to sign the treaty protocols. At the same time, however, they have indicated that their actions in the region are not inconsistent with the treaty. Finally, and I must confess, not unexpectedly, France has refused to be associated with the treaty. This is clearly the least helpful response. It is not at all what the countries of the region want to see as the final outcome.

In contrast to the less-than-positive response of most nuclear-weapon states has been the position taken by our Latin America neighbours. The twentieth anniversary of the signing of the Latin American nuclear-weapon-free zone treaty—the Treaty of Tlatelolco—was recently celebrated by OPANAL, the agency for the non-proliferation of nuclear weapons in Latin America. At its meeting, OPANAL expressed a desire for closer links with countries party to the Treaty of Rarotonga.

In Mexico in mid-October 1987 I met the Secretary General of OPANAL, who passed me a draft agreement, promoting cooperation between OPANAL and the South Pacific Bureau for Economic Cooperation (SPEC), the body which administers the Treaty of Rarotonga. I was asked to convey this draft to SPEC.

The draft agreement provides for regular consultations, the exchanges of observers, and scientific cooperation—the sort of practical and realistic measures from which both organisations will benefit. I see this as a major step forward in the disarmament field and in New Zealand/Latin American relations. I will be urging our South Pacific partners to look at it favourably.

OPANAL's initiative shows that New Zealand and its South Pacific neighbours are not alone in believing that nuclear-weapon-free zones can contribute to safety and security, and can further the international disarmament process. Joint South Pacific–Latin American cooperation in maintaining the non-nuclear status of our region will be a tangible expression of support for the disarmament measures now being contemplated by the superpowers. Reciprocal support for the sort of measures we are taking in the South Pacific would be much appreciated.

I have outlined New Zealand's perception of international and regional security requirements. To recapitulate:

— at the global level security has to be maintained at a vastly reduced level of weaponry, both nuclear and conventional;
— the ultimate goal must be the establishment of a climate for trust and confidence which will make possible the elimination of all nuclear weapons;
— the South Pacific must remain nuclear-weapon-free;
— security policies must be adopted which recognise all the factors contributing to insecurity, not just the military ones.

Over the past three years New Zealand has demonstrated a new independence of thought and action in its security policies. Our commitment to nuclear disarmament is well established. In the nuclear age, just where a nuclear war started would be practically irrelevant. We now know that even New Zealand would not be immune from the effects of even a limited nuclear exchange in the northern hemisphere.

The elimination of nuclear weapons is clearly the greatest measure the world could take to enhance its safety and security. But it is not enough to return to a world where mistrust and tension could result, once again, in the sort of conventional conflict which our older citizens recall with horror.

True peace is more than an absence of conflict. True peace will be achieved when all people and all states feel confident that their rights, their traditions, and their needs are not in jeopardy.

How these requirements can be met—whether they can be met—is the question this symposium has the opportunity to address. The solutions are not immediately obvious—witness recent events in Fiji for example. But the sort of analysis the symposium comes up with will provide an important resource on which individuals, governments and international organisations will be able to draw in the future.

Ordinary people everywhere look to groups such as this for a new direction. The responsibility is a heavy one to bear. On behalf of the people and the government of New Zealand I wish you well in your endeavours. The task is very tall, but it is not impossible—indeed it cannot be.

3

The Public Pursuit of Peace:
What Can a Small Country Do?

G. R. Laking

This chapter does not deal except incidentally with the resolution of global conflicts. It is rather a case study of a small southern hemisphere country seeking to chart its future in a world of rapid and accelerating change increasingly dominated by a fear of nuclear destruction.[1]

The chapter surveys in broad terms the development of a separate and identifiable foreign policy for New Zealand up to the 1970s; which marked the end of my direct association with the Ministry of Foreign Affairs. In doing so it pays special attention to the growth of public awareness of and involvement in the policy making process. It then looks at the impact of that involvement on more recent developments, particularly those which, since the election of a Labour government in 1984, have produced a reassessment of traditional strategic and defence concepts and in the process have brought New Zealand into conflict with three major northern hemisphere powers. It raises a number of questions about specific aspects of the new defence policy which seem to need answers if the public pursuit of peace on which the country has embarked is to be successfully sustained. Essentially it poses a question which confronts any government, and particularly the government of a small country, seeking to give priority to moral considerations in the development of its foreign and defence policies. One of the founding fathers of the New Zealand Ministry of Foreign Affairs, Sir Carl Berendsen, who had a major influence on the early stages of foreign policy development, is credited with the statement "I do not believe that anything that is morally wrong can ever be politically right." In these more critical times the question for the New Zealand government is how far it can be seen to forsake that principle in response to the realities of international politics without sacrificing the domestic public support on which its current policies are based.

DEVELOPMENT OF A FOREIGN POLICY

The notion of a completely independent foreign policy is unreal. Even the superpowers are obliged to accommodate themselves to the situation and actions of one another. But there are degrees of independence which can be measured by the extent to which the foreign policy of any country is concerned with the advancement of its own vital interests as opposed to those of others, or to the pursuit of ill-defined and unattainable general aims.

For countries which have moved from colonialism to an independent political status within a short space of time, there is usually a dividing line clearly marking the changeover from a situation in which responsibility for foreign policy is exercised by another state to one in which these matters come under the direct control of the country's own government. For New Zealand, which accepted its political independence only gradually over more than a century, the significant steps are not so plainly defined.

There has always been a sturdy streak of independence in the New Zealand attitude to the rest of the world, even during its long period of tutelage by Britain, but before the Second World War any initiative which seemed likely to have an adverse effect on British interests was seldom pressed beyond the point where the British government indicated that persistence could lead only to embarrassment or displeasure. That this should have been so is not surprising. The British Navy guaranteed the security of New Zealand and the British market provided almost the sole outlet for New Zealand exports. Britain was the source of the funds required for New Zealand's capital development and of most of the manufactured goods which New Zealand could not produce for itself. The relationship was one of mutual benefit and far outweighed the importance of any relationship with other countries (including Australia).

As late as the end of the nineteenth century, such was the assumed identity of interest between the two countries that the New Zealand government had no hesitation in offering, three weeks before war against the Boers was declared, to send New Zealand troops to South Africa. The New Zealand commitment to the support of Britain in the First World War was instantaneous and equally automatic. But from the end of that war, from which followed New Zealand's separate membership of the League of Nations, the country began increasingly to assume the responsibility of assessing for itself the nature of its vital interests and of pursuing them even though in particular instances this might be at some cost to the smooth conduct of the relationship with the British. The League in particular provided a forum for the expression of a New Zealand view on major international issues such as the principle of collective security and the Italian aggression against Ethiopia.

By the early 1950s the development of an independent stance consistent with New Zealand's interests was well under way. The process was sometimes painful, particularly in wartime situations where those interests had to be asserted in opposition to what British commanders saw as the larger tactical or strategic aims. There is as yet no public chronicle of the determined and successful efforts made by Prime Minister Peter Fraser in 1941 to oblige the British Navy to evacuate the beleaguered New Zealand forces from Greece despite the hazard to the ships involved; but the directness with which he spoke out against any disposition to disregard New Zealand's interests in a war which was not if its own making, but to which the country had committed a large part of its manpower, is well known. At the San Francisco Conference of 1945 which led to the creation of the UN, the vigour with which the New Zealand delegation advocated the development of a system of global security untrammelled by a great power veto was another sign of a growing independence of outlook. Perhaps even more significant, given the degree of potential embarrassment for the British government, was the leading role played by New Zealand in drafting the provisions of the UN Charter which set up a trusteeship system for dependent territories with the ultimate aim of self government or independence.

In the 1950s New Zealand was caught in a cross-fire of the deteriorating relationship between the US and Britain. Nothing could have been less comfortable than the situation of successive New Zealand prime ministers, representing an electorate still predominantly agrarian, with a deeply ingrained belief in the Commonwealth (if not the Empire) and in the all encompassing importance of the British market. The new element introduced by the Second World War was the seeming inevitability of our future reliance on the United States rather than Britain for our security. Initially that prospect was not too frightening because it seemed reasonable to assume that the so-called special relationship which had been developed between our two principal guarantors during the war would continue indefinitely.

Unfortunately for New Zealand's peace of mind, the rapid dissolution of Allied wartime alliances into a confrontation between East and West had its counterpart in the increasing strains and diversity of interest which showed up between Britain and the US. The unwillingness of the US to share the reality of its newly assumed leadership with any other country, the determination to put an end to colonialism, the breakdown in the arrangements for the sharing of nuclear knowledge and the pathological

American dislike of the British preferential tariff system—all these combined to erode very rapidly the facade Winston Churchill tried to maintain of a trans–Atlantic partnership of equals.

In these circumstances it was natural for successive New Zealand prime ministers to strive during the next decade to straddle these diverging stools, applying whatever degree of sophistication and foresight lay within their capabilities. These varied considerably but there was never any question for any of them that the future security of New Zealand would require continued involvement in some form of collective defence arrangement. A major objective was therefore to cultivate the best and closest possible relations with the US—on the face of it a simple enough concept but when considered against the background already outlined, capable of leading one into major pitfalls.

Even before the Second World War ended, New Zealand had learned that any assertion of independence which conflicted with the interests of the United States was likely to present hazards of a new and unfamiliar kind. Like Australia, New Zealand realised as the war reached its final stages that it needed to establish its right to a vote and voice at the peace table. Both countries saw themselves as entitled by reason of their war effort to share in the global decision making and to have particular attention paid to their views on the future of the South Pacific region. Responding to an Australian initiative New Zealand joined with that country in a regional security arrangement (the Canberra Pact of 1944) which was a bold declaration of their insistence on having a say in the post-war disposition of enemy territories in the South Pacific and in any proposed changes in the sovereignty of islands in the area. It went beyond a claim to consultation; it asserted a view that such matters should require the concurrence of New Zealand and Australia. Such a direct challenge both to British territorial interests in the Pacific and to the British and American perception of themselves as the agents of all the allied powers in determining the shape of the post-war world was bound to have a dramatic impact and to provoke a vigorous reaction. It is quite possible that the Australians at least were not unprepared for or unduly concerned at the likely British attitude, but both they and New Zealand must have found the weight of American displeasure a new experience. It was a baptism of fire which might have been even more traumatic if the climactic stages of the war had not engaged universal attention.

By the end of the Second World War the US was immersed in a series of massive and seemingly insoluble problems stemming from its reluctant leadership of the western world. Before the end of the decade, another issue had been added—the so-called 'loss' of China to the communists. The following year the US was immersed in the war in Korea.

The Americans at that stage felt themselves to be in need of friends and allies as they staggered under the weight of the problems they had inherited. They were receptive to any idea of intrinsic merit dropped in the right place at the right time. Despite the wartime differences and frictions, they valued their close cooperation with New Zealand between 1941 and 1945. Our representatives, now established in Washington, made for themselves a good reputation as sound and reasonable people. Moreover, New Zealand was considered (rightly or wrongly) to have influence in London which the Americans thought might be useful in helping to resolve some of their differences with the British, or at least to help their understanding of the British viewpoint.

There was an obverse to this coin. The British, who understandably regretted and even resented the transfer of the centre of power to Washington and the quite natural response of New Zealand (and Australia) to this development, vigorously resisted the growth of direct dealings with the Americans—a factor which needed to be taken constantly into account.

New Zealand's initial post-war concern was the possibility of a resurgence of Japanese militarism and through the Far Eastern Commission the government's representatives pressed hard and long for the conclusion of a repressive treaty similar to that imposed on Germany after the First World War. However, the dangers of trying to maintain a managed chaos in Japan persuaded the US administration of the merits of a much more liberal and far-sighted approach which eventually (and inevitably) carried the day.

Nevertheless, the New Zealand advocacy, with the Australians, of a different line was not without result. The Americans became impressed by our obvious concern for our future security and set about finding some means of relieving it. In 1950 they offered the ANZUS Treaty as a guarantee of Australian and New Zealand security in the Pacific. The initial reaction of New Zealand ministers was equivocal. They did not want to be involved in such a treaty without the British, but even more they disliked the idea of the reciprocal responsibilities which it envisaged. It was one thing for the Americans to guarantee us against aggression; it was quite another to suggest that New Zealand might be asked in some unpredictable circumstances to involve itself in military ventures in the Pacific. The various suggestions advanced from time to time that other countries such as the Philippines and even Japan should be parties evoked only expressions of horror from New Zealand ministers. It would have suited them if the US had been willing to give a unilateral guarantee to come to New Zealand aid if need be.

But the Australians, who were much further advanced along the road towards regarding themselves as a country with an independent future in Asia and the Pacific, wanted a cast-iron American guarantee and were quite prepared to pay the price of reciprocity. The New Zealand hesitations were eventually overcome and in September 1951 the ANZUS Treaty was signed in San Francisco at the same time as the Japanese Peace Treaty. The US made a separate security arrangement with the Philippines.

Ironically enough, by the time that ANZUS came into effect the nature of the presumed threat to New Zealand's security had changed. The country was already involved in the war in Korea, thus for the first time in its history sending New Zealand forces abroad in peacetime (other than to South Africa). It was a precedent made tolerable by the fact that the New Zealand contingent was part of a Commonwealth force and operating under the aegis of the UN, but even on that basis public hesitations about the government's decision were sufficient to serve notice that the view of the electorate in such matters was assuming increasing importance.

New Zealand had in the meantime turned its face against the recognition of the Communist regime in China—a decision made by Peter Fraser's government at the very end of its long term in office, on the simple basis that nothing should be done at that stage of events which might encourage the spread of communism in Asia. It was immediately endorsed by the incoming National government. That decision, which produced 20 years of sterile debate about the status of Taiwan and helped to seal off the Chinese mainland from any effective contact with the rest of the world, required the New Zealand authorities once again to choose between the British view in favour of recognition and the US view against it.

In the US the frustrations inherent in their involvement in yet another armed struggle in Korea, exacerbated by the hysteria of the China lobby, produced a chain of events which led through McCarthyism and eventually to the war in Vietnam. On the way the efforts of the administration to organise collective resistance to any further aggression in Southeast Asia produced the South–East Asia Treaty Organisation (SEATO), of which New Zealand, Australia and Britain all became members.

In some degree this eased the immediate discomfort in the relationship between New Zealand and Britain arising out of the latter's exclusion from ANZUS. Shortly thereafter it was agreed that the New Zealand commitment to supply substantial forces in the event of a major war should be transferred from the Middle East to Southeast Asia. New Zealand forces gave active assistance to the British in dealing with insurgency in Malaya and later in the confrontation between an independent Malaysia and Indonesia. Later still, both became parties, along with Australia, Malaysia and Singapore, in a Commonwealth Five Power Defence Arrangement for Southeast Asia.

In retrospect all these developments can be seen as part of a process of adjustment to a fundamentally new security situation. British interests in the Pacific area were contracting with the liquidation of her colonial empire. New Zealand, on the other hand, saw its future as being increasingly bound up with Asia and the Pacific rather than Europe. Probably the implications of this new situation were presented to New Zealand ministers in their starkest form during the Suez crisis of 1956. It was only in the face of the gravest reservations as to whether it served the New Zealand interest to do so that the cabinet finally gave public support to what proved to be one of the great diplomatic blunders of the century. It is not particularly surprising that a decade or more later the two countries should have seen their respective obligations in relation to Vietnam under the SEATO Treaty in different lights and that New Zealand should have involved itself more actively than Britain in support of the US and South Vietnam.

In the midst of this (sometimes excessive) preoccupation with military security, fundamental changes were taking place in other aspects of New Zealand life.

In the economic sphere the erosion of British financial and economic strength meant that Britain could no longer provide a market for all of New Zealand's exports or an adequate source of the investment capital which the country needed for its economic growth. After 16 years of hesitation New Zealand accepted membership of the World Bank and the International Monetary Fund, and began to seek development loans in New York and elsewhere. The country found itself obliged to broaden the base of the economy in order to provide employment for a rapidly increasing population and at the same time to find new markets for a growing range of exports. Even the rise of a forestry industry, the first such major development in the field of primary exports since the advent of refrigerated shipping in 1882, served notice that henceforth New Zealand would need to think of its trading arrangements in global terms. The British may have needed New Zealand lamb but they did not need New Zealand trees or timber products. Moreover, by 1960 it was evident that British membership in the European Community (EC) was inevitable and that with it would come the eventual disappearance of New Zealand's preferential trading position in the British market. New Zealand has reason to be grateful that a combination of General Charles de Gaulle and the Little Englanders allowed the country a breathing space of 10 years in which to adjust to this new and awesome prospect.

It was probably this factor more than any other which introduced into the formulation of New Zealand foreign policy an element which had previously been lacking—a direct connection in the public consciousness between domestic and external issues. Leaving aside New Zealand's involvement in two world wars, it could be said that before this link-up occurred there was minimal public interest in foreign policy issues. They were considered to be the province of the Minister of Foreign Affairs and his advisers. What went on in the UN stirred scarcely a ripple in New Zealand waters. Parliamentary debates on foreign affairs were almost invariably dreary and pedestrian. In the mind of the average New Zealander diplomacy was concerned with matters of high policy which had little or no relevance to bread and butter issues such as trade and the raising of external loans. For too long little serious thought was given, for example, to the possibility that New Zealand's inability to expand its trade with mainland China might have some connection with the country's failure to enter into governmental relations with Peking and even more with our continuing attachment to Taiwan; or to the possibility that by sustained effort undertaken jointly by government and private enterprise the political influences which were thought to make the US market unattractive might be exploited to New Zealand's advantage.

This growing public awareness of external issues was highlighted by the controversy over New Zealand participation in the war in Vietnam which became a party political issue, destroying for the time being the traditional bipartisan attitude to external questions. In fact by the late 1960s and early 1970s New Zealand foreign policy development could be said to have arrived at a major watershed. The storm warnings of 1960–1961 about British entry into the EC had grown to a loud roar and the question became a major national preoccupation. The seeming intractability of the situation in Vietnam gave rise to public questioning of the country's whole relationship with the US. SEATO became a convenient whipping boy and the validity of the ANZUS relationship, hitherto accepted as a cornerstone of New Zealand security, was called into question. Growth of feeling about French nuclear testing in the Pacific inspired the third Labour government which took office in 1972 to strong action. It sent a frigate to Moruroa as a gesture of protest and joined Australia in an action before the World Court which brought an end to atmospheric testing. That controversy produced a reaction in New Zealand both against France and against the US and served to increase New Zealand awareness of its growing involvement with the newly independent states of the South Pacific. In other ways also this

Pacific awareness impinged increasingly on the New Zealand consciousness as the numbers of immigrants from the South Pacific entering New Zealand continued to grow and to demonstrate in yet another direction the connection between domestic and external issues. Added to this was the sudden assault on the temples of the New Zealand Rugby Football Union launched from the UN in New York. A seemingly domestic preoccupation about sporting relations with South Africa was turned into an international controversy involving a large part of the Third World. It obliged New Zealand to acknowledge that it had become a target for some of the indignation previously directed against other countries for their racial policies. Finally, when it became obvious shortly after Richard Nixon's election to the presidency that the situation *vis-a-vis* China was about to change it suddenly seemed possible that New Zealand, after many years of sturdy support for Taiwan, might be left as its last, loneliest and loveliest supporter. Immediately after the general election of 1972, the newly elected Labour government moved to recognise the regime in Peking. Had the National government been re-elected it would have taken the same course. The public reaction to the change was minimal. It clearly had wide support.

This development, coming after so many years of desultory debate, was further evidence of the continuing efforts being made to identify New Zealand's vital interests, and to test the validity of her foreign policy attitudes against the reality of her situation in the world and her ability to promote those interests. In particular the notion that external trade policies which except in times of war have always been the major preoccupation in public attitudes towards the rest of the world, can be pursued independently of other policies had largely been dissipated. One result has been greater cohesion in policy development, wider acceptance of the inter-relationship among various facets of policy and better coordination of activity among the interested agencies in New Zealand. On the other hand, as recent events suggest, other new factors have entered into the process of policy formulation.

In the forty years which followed the end of World War II the principal crisis with which New Zealand was called up to deal was not one of any threat to its territorial security but the equally fundamental threat to its economy posed by the inevitable entry of Britain into the European Economic Community. When the threat became overt in the late 1950s it marked for the New Zealand public the end of an age of innocence which had assumed the indefinite continuation of an almost total dependence on Britain both as a market and as a source of development capital. It provided the impetus for a major effort to broaden the base of the economy, to diversify export markets and to encourage investment from sources like the

United States, Western Europe and Japan. The events of the past three or four years have shown the extent of the problems remaining to be solved—many of them generated by the changes which have already taken place—but the transformation of the economy between 1960 and 1980 can legitimately be recorded in the New Zealand context as an example of successful crisis management. It was due primarily to the breadth of public support for the government's actions which was generated between the first British approaches to the community and its final entry. In my rather long exposure to the parliamentary and government scene in New Zealand, that was a rare experience and is epitomised by an incident in which I was involved as head of the Prime Minister's Department during the changeover from the defeated National government to the incoming Labour government at the end of 1972. At the time the arrangements being negotiated to protect the New Zealand position for primary produce in the British market were in their final critical stages. As the official responsible for arranging the changeover from the outgoing to the incoming Prime Minister, I was invited by the former to brief his successor and to seek his agreement to messages being sent to the New Zealand negotiators in Europe. When I made the approach to Norman Kirk his response was that he saw no need for consultation. He was satisfied that what was being done was in the best interests of the country and that no better arrangement was practicable.

NUCLEAR FREE NEW ZEALAND

The recital of these events is relevant to the developments which have taken place since a Labour government was returned to office in 1984. It was committed to a further restructuring of the economy and also believed and asserted that it had a mandate to implement its policy of making New Zealand "nuclear free." This included not merely a prohibition on the acquisition of nuclear weapons or their presence on New Zealand soil but also a prohibition on visits by nuclear-armed or nuclear-powered vessels in New Zealand waters, the establishment of a South Pacific Nuclear-Weapons-Free Zone and the prohibition of dumping of nuclear wastes and the testing of nuclear weapons in the Pacific. It contemplated a change of direction which would be feasible only with major public endorsement.

The extent to which the voting in the 1984 election was materially influenced by the expectation of significant action on the nuclear front is a matter of dispute. There are those who would say that the overriding concern of most voters was the urge to free the country from the straitjacket of an interventionist government too long in office and that despite the campaign rhetoric, foreign policy issues played little part in the decisions made by voters. Such discussion, however, became irrelevant following the election of the Labour government for a second term in 1987. That result, reinforced by other surveys of public opinion, justified the government in its view that in its determination to make New Zealand and the South Pacific "nuclear free" it has wide voter support.

The policy on ship visits which was given immediate effect in 1984 has since then been enshrined in legislation. However, it is questionable whether, even if the government had not been returned in 1987, another government would have found it politically feasible, either domestically or internationally, to return to the *status quo*. The impact of the government's public attitudes and actions on the country's defence relationships since 1984 had already been so significant as to exclude that possibility.

The strong and immoderate reaction of the United States to the knowledge that its naval vessels would no longer be free to visit New Zealand ports effectively made ANZUS inoperative as a tripartite arrangement. Access to United States intelligence was severely restricted as was New Zealand participation in long established joint naval and military exercises. In its relations with the United States, New Zealand was downgraded from ally to friend. The "security guarantee" to New Zealand under ANZUS has since been withdrawn.

The immediate impact of these measures was undoubtedly to strengthen public support in New Zealand for the government's position. They were interpreted as an oppressive tactic unfairly employed by a major power to browbeat a small country. When the British also made public their displeasure with the New Zealand policy, which applies equally to their vessels and aircraft, that feeling was reinforced. It needed only the bizarre terrorist incident instigated by the French against the *Rainbow Warrior* to put the seal on a sense of outrage at what were seen to be attempts to intervene in the affairs of a sovereign state.

It was inevitable that in the search for a new foreign policy and defence posture, the discussion in New Zealand, once projected into the public arena, should be dominated by the most dramatic manifestation of radical choice—the rupture of an alliance which for more than thirty years had been accepted as the cornerstone of the country's security. In the meantime the repercussions of the policy changes introduced by the government have spread much wider than this one issue. Internationally New Zealand has attracted a degree of attention which it has never previously known. Its anti-nuclear stance has found substantial support among influential non-governmental groups in both hemispheres. In New Zealand, the cumulative effect of these events has been to strengthen the sense of national identity.

That in turn has set in motion strong currents of opinion which not merely support the actions of the government but to some extent drive the development of its anti-nuclear policy and limit its freedom of action in its dealings with countries most directly concerned with the consequences of it.

There is no more difficult area in which to apply the Berendsonian principle than in the realm of national security, the maintenance of which is the prime obligation of any government. Where conflicts of interest arise as between sovereign states, accommodation, as has already been said, is unavoidable. Where that conflict occurs between major powers on the one hand and a small power on the other, the burden of accommodation falls heaviest on the latter as shown by the resolution of the *Rainbow Warrior* affair.

In the present situation what is new in the New Zealand experience is the degree of public involvement in policy formulation which on the one hand has made change possible but on the other has introduced problems of management. If the public perception of what is happening changes, either because the assumptions underlying the policies prove to be unsound or because the evidence to support them has not been explained sufficiently to resist the pressure of external events, then the difficulty of retaining the moral high ground is immeasurably increased.

The Report of the Defence Committee of Enquiry set up by the government in 1985 to report on the attitudes of New Zealanders to defence and security issues analyses this problem of management as applied to "the first duty of any government, [which] is to provide security for the citizens."

> However, if in a democracy a Government decides to consult individual members of the community, many factors enter into the equation and affect the perception of cost benefit. For people are not calculating machines: defence and security are only part of their lives and preoccupations....
>
> The weight of particular elements in an individual's total perception of the cost/benefit balance varies from person to person and, for some, from time to time; thus the politics of a defence strategy may change. There are those for whom a principle or moral imperative is over-riding: for example, the security of the country, or the need to resist aggression anywhere, or loyalty to old friends; or—from a different perspective—the immorality of nuclear weapons, or the need to prevent the destruction of the human race, or "independence" and "sovereignty." Others though they might prefer to follow a principled course, see a need to be prudent. These seek to balance several elements with the aim, for example, of protecting the national economic or other interests, or promoting national unity. The balance they establish may be influenced by the

type of threat they consider faces the nation and by its immediacy or remoteness. A sense of imminent threat to one's country or a friend's country may reinforce support for collective security and the complex of loyalties and obligations bound up with that concept. But if nuclear war is perceived as the most immediate threat to oneself, or to all humanity, then the sense of an imperative need to prevent it may dominate the balance. One set may evoke support for one set of principles, another may bring a call for reliance on a different set (Report, 1986: 13).

The results of the series of polls conducted by the Committee, while they have been subjected to conflicting interpretations, reflect very clearly the main elements exposed in this analysis. According to the Committee, "the two major objectives of the majority of New Zealanders" are that New Zealand should remain in alliances (72 percent), and that New Zealand should have a nuclear free defence policy (73 percent).

In response to specific questions on ANZUS and visits by nuclear ships, "the most preferred option ... was for New Zealand to be a member of ANZUS without allowing nuclear ship visits (44 percent)."

The Committee then addressed a further question to the 44 percent (mentioned immediately above) as to whether if forced to choose, they would favour New Zealand's remaining in ANZUS and allowing visits by nuclear vessels. Relating this to the results of the original poll on these options, the Committee concluded that 52 percent of New Zealanders would choose this option as against 44 percent who would not support it. This interpretation was to emerge as a major point of disagreement between the Prime Minister and the Committee.

On a broader issue the Committee concluded that:

More people were worried about nuclear war than any other threat to New Zealand. The poll produced clear evidence that New Zealanders viewed nuclear weapons and other weapons of mass destruction with considerable disquiet. There was an overwhelming rejection of the stationing on land in New Zealand of nuclear weapons and all other weapons of mass destruction (Report, 1986: 42).

Against this background the government commissioned a review of defence policy. Its order of reference required it to "take account of the Government's firm policy to exclude nuclear weapons from New Zealand" and also the need to adjust resources to meet defence needs. The conclusions reached by the review panel were largely accepted by the government and now form the basis of its defence policy.

The review established that the central defence objective is "to develop greater self reliance and work closely with Australia to meet the defence needs of the South Pacific." The options of armed and unarmed neutrality were rejected. The review went on to note that this primary concern for our own region "means a change of emphasis. Viewing our security as entirely dependent on a role within an alliance that is global in scope is a form of thinking that belongs to an earlier era and is no longer appropriate."

Despite this emphasis on regional security in the South Pacific, the more detailed statement of defence objectives which follows includes a number which are much wider in geographical extent (Defence, 1987: 31):

— "To continue to meet ANZUS obligations in conventional terms";
— "To contribute to the maintenance of peace and stability in Southeast Asia by continuing to maintain an active role in the Five Power Defence Arrangements";
— "To promote peace and international security through contributions to United Nations peacekeeping operations."

This chapter is not concerned with an examination of the defence capabilities which the defence review considers necessary to meet these defence objectives or of any restructuring of the defence forces which may follow. It is concerned rather with prior questions which are more likely to affect the public perception of the significance of the changes in promoting the acknowledged central objective of defence policy—"the preservation of New Zealand's security and that of the Island states for which we are responsible" (Defence, 1987: 5).

It is apparent from the conclusions reached by the Defence Committee of Enquiry into what New Zealanders want in matters of defence and security and from the absence of any bipartisan approach to these issues that the degree of consensus which has existed in the past on comparable issues (involvement in the First and Second World Wars and the repercussions of British entry into the EC) is not present in this instance. For the 73 percent who want a nuclear free defence policy, the primary concern is obviously fear of nuclear disaster. Abandonment of the United States' nuclear umbrella is seen by them as one way to limit the possibility of New Zealand becoming a target in any nuclear exchange. The South Pacific is seen as an area of stability and New Zealand's geographic isolation (surrounded by "the biggest moat in the world") as offering a unique protection against the likelihood of conventional assault on its security.

On the other hand the 72 percent who consider that New Zealand should remain in alliances, while presumably sharing anti-nuclear sentiments to a greater or lesser extent, clearly have some reservations about the validity of the assumptions on which the anti-nuclear policy is based.

To remove those reservations would seem to require more detailed argument than can be found in the defence review or in governmental statements on several basic questions:

1. In what sense is the strategic situation in the South Pacific as it affects the security of New Zealand different from that which existed immediately before the events which led to the nullification of ANZUS?
2. Is it possible any longer to regard the geographic isolation of New Zealand as a significant element contributing to its security?
3. To what extent can reliance be placed on the traditional stability of the South Pacific in the face of:

   (a) the creation of a number of small weak states each seeking to assert and maintain its independence, often through non-traditional alignments or internal change;
   (b) the growth of international interest in the resources of the sea and of the Antarctic continent;
   (c) continuing French intransigence over nuclear testing and the future of New Caledonia?

4. Is it possible, as the Defence Review proposes, to contemplate New Zealand involvement in meeting "low-level" threats to the security of the South Pacific without at the same time accepting the possibility that they will develop in ways which sooner or later affect the interests of other Pacific powers such as Australia and the United States? In that event what options are open to New Zealand as a basis of cooperation with those countries?

There are signs that an effort is now being made on both sides to limit the damage to the broader relationship between New Zealand and the United States. If hopes of a mutual accommodation are to be realised, then a new focus of cooperation outside of ANZUS may need to be found. A treaty, based on shared assumptions not only about the security interests common to the parties but also about the need for collective action to maintain them and the measures to be employed to that end, ceases to have any great significance in the face of fundamental disagreement on those basic ingredients. There have been differences of interpretation in the past but for the most part they have been resolved in private discussion and they did not in any event strike at the roots of the tripartite understandings in the same way as the current issues.

It may be that the day of formal alliances such as ANZUS has passed. A recent survey of major power relations in Northeast Asia sponsored by the Asia Society of New York (Scalapino, 1987) reached the conclusion that:

> One major trend of recent decades has been the decline of ideology in virtually all of the major Pacific Asian nations, as leaders increasingly grapple with problems on a pragmatic, experimental basis. Alliances, many of which bound their members together through the common ground of ideology, have similarly been affected, so that today alignments tend to be preferred over alliances. No development is of greater importance to an understanding of international relations at the close of the twentieth century than this trend towards alignments, with all the fluidity, complexity and uncertainty that accompanies it.

CONCLUSION

In the context of a symposium on conflict resolution these may appear as parochial concerns. The fact remains that at a critical time in the development of the country's independence, a New Zealand government has embarked on a new path which it believes will advance the cause of global peace. It has done so in a way which has attracted international attention. Its efforts to keep faith with its policies in the face of external pressures, including unpredictable developments in the South Pacific, will inevitably be the object of continuing scrutiny and add to its problem of both domestic and external management.

The first stage in the implementation of the new policies may be said to have ended with the passage of the legislation which makes New Zealand "nuclear free." As this chapter is written, the second and more difficult stage is beginning. The need now is to move the debate on to a different level, to seek a resolution of the conflicts over security issues which have arisen with other countries and to do so without sacrifice of principle.

In the case of Australia and the United States, the breadth and importance of the New Zealand relationship with both those countries make it inevitable that in time the current differences on these issues will be resolved. That may be possible within the ANZUS framework, but more probably will need to be found outside it. However, it is unlikely that such an outcome can be achieved in the near future unless it is precipitated by a deterioration of the security situation in the South Pacific, which might lead to a more visible and contentious presence in the area by countries such as France, the Soviet Union and the United States. If that were to happen, it could prove to be a crucial test for the New Zealand government as to how to adjust to that situation without undermining public support for its non-nuclear policies.

In the longer term there is a larger question. It concerns the perception which many people in the northern hemisphere now have of New Zealand (and which a majority of New Zealanders still have of themselves) as a western-oriented society uniquely placed by reason of its geographical isolation to sustain innovative change while remaining basically unaltered. That view is being challenged by those who would say that New Zealand is in the process of profound and even revolutionary change which goes well beyond restructuring of the economy and is only marginally responsive to governmental action. It is a product of demographic change and other related factors which are rapidly diluting the traditional view of the New Zealand connection with the northern hemisphere. The spearhead of that change is the resurgence of a sense of their separate identity and culture among the Maori people, which is now receiving official if belated acknowledgment. It is reinforced by the rise in the number of other Polynesian people now permanently settled in the country. Added to that is the experience of at least two generations of New Zealanders born and raised in the South Pacific who identify most closely with that region of the world and who for more than forty years have not been conscious of any serious threat to the security of the country other than the menace of nuclear war or disaster. Against that background one can have at best a clouded picture of the likely nature of New Zealand society by the end of the twentieth century or of the view which such a society will have of its relations with the rest of the world. What will be seen in that context as "morally wrong" must be even more speculative.

NOTES

1. Parts of this chapter draw upon G. R. Laking, "The Evolution of an Independent Foreign Policy" in *Beyond New Zealand: The Foreign Policy of a Small State,* edited by J. Henderson, K. Jackson and R. Kennaway (Auckland: Methuen, 1980).

4

Should Deterrence Fail:
Consequences of Nuclear War for Non-Combatant Countries

Wren Green

Driven for decades by deep mistrust for each other, the two superpowers have been building up enormous arsenals and ever more sophisticated weaponry in a never-ending race, without awareness of the potentially very severe environmental consequences arising from the use of these weapons.... One must both hope and fear for the future of mankind (Crutzen, 1985: 36).

The purpose of this chapter is to show why recent improvements in scientific understanding of the consequences of nuclear war have profound implications for nuclear war policies and the quest for genuine global peace and security. Military planners have long devised strategies of deterrence and of fighting nuclear war with incomplete and misleading understanding of the likely consequences of their actions. Those complex doctrines are now called into question and the moral argument against their continuation is strengthened.

This chapter will not contribute directly to the major symposium theme of resolving international conflicts by peaceful means. That task is left to the other participants who have distinguished credentials for doing so. Instead it looks at the consequences of the failure of deterrence in both global and local terms.

First, I update the present scientific understanding of the global disruptions to climate and agriculture that could follow nuclear war. Second, I summarise the results of a recent study of the likely consequences of nuclear war for New Zealand.

61

GLOBAL CONSEQUENCES OF NUCLEAR WAR

The opening quote to this chapter is from Paul Crutzen, an atmospheric chemist, whose work with John Birks in 1982 on the amount of smoke that might be produced after nuclear war was the breakthrough that led to the concept now referred to as "nuclear winter" (Crutzen and Birks, 1982). Further developed by Turco and others (Turco *et al.*, 1983), the concept of "nuclear winter" subsequently became the focus of intense international scientific study.

The basic concept is straightforward. In a major nuclear war thousands of intense firestorms would be started in cities, industrial areas, forests and wildlands. These fires would produce enormous quantities of smoke, including soot, mixed with dust from the explosions. The smoke, and particularly the soot component, would strongly absorb the sunlight that normally warms the earth. Although soot and smoke particles would block incoming sunlight, infra-red radiation from the earth would pass through these particles and return to space.

The net result would be a significant heat imbalance. The outcome would be a rapid cooling within a few days over northern hemisphere countries that had been bombed. Smoke clouds would spread within 2–3 weeks over most countries between 30°–60° North and reduce light levels by 90–95 percent for the first few weeks. Temperatures would fall sharply, especially for a spring–summer war in the northern hemisphere.

The implications of these studies prompted the International Council of Scientific Unions to request their interdisciplinary committee, called SCOPE (Scientific Committee on Problems of the Environment), to undertake a major study. The result was two and a half years of work by 300 scientists from 30 countries, culminating in the release of their findings in September 1985 (Harwell and Hutchinson, 1985; Pittock *et al.*, 1986). The major findings of this massive cooperative effort are covered very briefly in the next section.

Disruptions to Global Climate

Authors of Volume 1 of the SCOPE report used complex, three-dimensional, general circulation computer models to test the hypothesis of major disruptions to global climate following massive clouds of smoke and soot rising into the skies. The early speculations of "nuclear winter" were largely confirmed and extended much further.

Nuclear war during a northern spring or summer was found to be particularly devastating. At that time the solar energy would lift smoke well above the area of "rain out" and into the upper atmosphere. The temperature might drop over northern continents (30°–60°N) by 20°C for some weeks, and be several degrees below normal for a year or longer.

A proportion of this smoke could be actively carried into the southern hemisphere skies within a few months of a summer war. Light levels at the latitudes of Australia and New Zealand would then drop by about 20 percent. Temperatures would fall perhaps by up to 3°C in New Zealand. Recovery to normal temperature would be slow and spread over 1–2 years.

Nuclear war during a northern winter is predicted to have much smaller effects. The reduction in incoming solar energy would lessen the amount of smoke that was lifted into the upper atmosphere. More would be rained out in the following months from the lower atmosphere and the amount available for transport into the southern hemisphere would probably be much less.

Rainfall patterns could be drastically affected in the northern hemisphere with less severe effects in southern countries. The computer models suggested that very stable weather patterns could develop over large areas. The outcome could be little or no rain for months and elimination of the monsoons in Asia and tropical Africa for 1–2 years. This outcome has not been given the media prominence of "nuclear winter," yet lack of monsoons would devastate food production for many nations. Tropical forests could also be severely affected by drought and by any short-term freezing episodes.

In fact, "nuclear winter" is a convenient but inadequate metaphor for the pervasive and complex climatic and biological disruptions that could follow a major nuclear war. Urban firestorms would be filled with toxic pollutants from burning petroleum products, synthetic and natural chemicals. Freezing toxic inversion fogs would probably form in valleys in combatant countries. The acidity of the resulting rain water could increase tenfold, devastating surviving forests and other terrestrial ecosystems in Europe, USSR and North America. Run-off of pollutants into lakes, rivers and estuaries would seriously damage all these biological systems.

Levels of radioactive fallout between 30°–60°N could be lethal not only to people, but also to other mammals, birds and some plant species, especially conifers. The SCOPE study estimated that from 6–20 percent of the total land area of NATO and Warsaw Pact countries would receive levels of fallout in the first few days that would be lethal for unprotected humans.

Nuclear explosions would reduce levels of atmospheric ozone, the natural screen against ultraviolet (UV) radiation. As the smoke clouds cleared, the levels of UV radiation would rise to damaging levels. Tropical forests, fresh water and marine systems, and food crops would be especially stressed. Recovery to normal levels of UV would be uncertain and could take up to 10 years.

Disruptions to Agricultural Production

Volume II of the SCOPE report broke new ground. It showed the jeopardy into which the United States and the Soviet Union have placed the citizens of combatant and non-combatant countries alike. In doing so, the report moved the primary focus of nuclear war consequences from the direct effects of nuclear explosions to the indirect effects on the global environment.

First, research showed that the world's major food crops (including wheat, rice, corn) are very sensitive to small drops in average temperature. There are historical examples for this effect. The "Little Ice Age," from the late sixteenth to late seventeenth century, was about $1\,^{\circ}C$ cooler on average throughout the summers. The growing season in Europe was cut by about a month, which caused significant drops in grain yield and led to starvation and epidemics in some regions. A $3\,^{\circ}C$ drop in average summer temperatures would probably eliminate the Canadian wheat crop.

The SCOPE study showed that grain production could be reduced to virtually zero in the northern hemisphere for at least one summer following a major nuclear war (Harwell and Hutchinson, 1985). These conclusions would hold for *small* average temperature drops that would be well within the temperature drops currently predicted for northern latitudes. Other climatic stresses (drought, radiation, pollution) would add additional stresses and have their own significant impacts on crop yields.

Northern food production would also be severely reduced by the massive disruptions to energy, chemical, seed and human inputs to complex agricultural systems. These disruptions, coupled with an assumed loss of effective international trade for a year, could reduce food production to insignificant levels in many countries for a year, *independently of temperature effects.*

Second, the research showed that natural ecosystems could only support about 1 percent of the planet's five billion people. The other 99 percent are dependent on complex, but vulnerable agricultural systems.

Further analysis showed that the vast majority of countries have less than one year's supply of food available at any point during the year.

The indirect outcome of a major nuclear war would therefore be starvation, especially for many of the 85 percent of the world's population who live north of the equator. Nuclear war impacts would thus extend to non-combatant countries, not by blast and fire, but through starvation on an unprecedented scale. There could be 250–1,000 million possible victims of direct effects of exploding warheads (WHO, 1983). In contrast, starvation could kill an additional one–three billion people, according to the SCOPE report. Fatalities in India from starvation could exceed the number of fatalities in the Soviet Union and the United States caused directly by nuclear explosions.

The "Nuclear Autumn" Sideshow

Despite the rigour of the SCOPE study and the demonstrated vulnerability of major food crops to small decreases in average temperature, to international trade and to other disruptions, media interest was aroused during 1986 by peripheral diversions. Some scientists promoted "nuclear autumn" scenarios (Thompson and Schneider, 1986) which led to media speculation that the substantive hypothesis was no longer valid (Seitz, 1986). These arguments received wide media exposure which singularly failed to address the substantive conclusions of the agricultural scientists in Volume II of the Scope report (Harwell and Hutchinson, 1985). The straw man that was held up as the central tenet of "nuclear winter" research was the validity of the temperature drops that had been postulated in the initial, simple computer models (Turco *et al.*, 1983). These had indeed been subsequently modified, but not on the basis that the underlying principle was invalid. Unfortunately, the outcome amongst the general public was to raise doubts about the basic validity of the hypothesis and to create the impression that scientists no longer agreed on the major points.

The Bangkok Accord

To see if there were any genuine grounds for disagreement over predictions from climate models, to exchange new findings between physical and biological scientists, and to develop the concept of national case studies, SCOPE held an international conference in Bangkok in February 1987.

A statement published in *Environment* (Warner, 1987) summarised the consensus that was reached by the participants. Taking into account all the climate modelling studies that had been done, participants concluded that no changes to the substantive conclusions of the 1985 SCOPE report were required. In particular, the biological and agricultural conclusions remained unaltered. The major impact would still come from disruptions to agricultural production, massive crop losses, and the resulting starvation of hundreds of millions of people. As one leading participant had written earlier, the appropriate image of the aftermath of nuclear war for most of the world's population still remained starving people in Ethiopia rather than the experiences of Hiroshima and Nagasaki (Harwell and Grover, 1985).

The Bangkok conference also recognised the importance of moving beyond the general, global-level studies to a series of national case studies. These would be able to examine regional differences in effects, especially between northern and southern hemispheres, and between combatant and non-combatant countries. Country-specific studies would also make it possible to study the impacts on societies as well, a topic the SCOPE researchers did not explore. A national case study on New Zealand that included these wider impacts was underway at the time of the Bangkok conference. The findings of that study are summarised below.

NEW ZEALAND NUCLEAR IMPACTS STUDY

New Zealand is widely regarded as a country that should survive nuclear war relatively unscathed physically, providing it were not a target. The SCOPE report predicted that island countries in southern oceans would be subjected to much smaller temperature drops than northern continents. Other climatic effects New Zealand might experience—drought, pollution, higher UV levels, radioactive fallout—would be considerably lessened by distance from the major areas of conflict.

Food production is well in excess of the local consumption needs of New Zealand's 3.3 million people. (Dairy, meat and horticultural products are major exports.) The SCOPE report concluded that even if New Zealand lost 50 percent of agricultural production through climatic disruptions, production levels would still exceed local demands. On that basis New Zealand was seen as a likely "surviving" nation.

But rather than engender complacency, the SCOPE report stimulated New Zealand scientists into proposing that the wider consequences for New Zealand be examined in a more comprehensive study. The level of analysis in the SCOPE study (Harwell and Hutchinson, 1985) was clearly inadequate with respect to the full range of societal impacts that New Zealand would be likely to experience. An earlier, pre-nuclear winter study had emphasised that disruptions would follow if export trades were lost (Preddey, 1985; Preddey *et al.*, 1982).

The government's initiatives during 1984–1985 on disarmament and the banning of nuclear weapons from New Zealand territory had made many more New Zealanders aware of the importance of and difficulties associated with preventing nuclear war. It had also made clear the stark truth that prevention of nuclear war was ultimately the responsibility of nuclear-weapon states and that such prevention could fail.

This was reflected in a 1986 Defence Committee of Inquiry which stated the need for "a realistic assessment of the risks, consequences and measures required in the event of a nuclear conflict" (Report, 1986: 57). The study that eventuated was a six-month, preliminary investigation into the likely effects of a large-scale nuclear war in the northern hemisphere on the society, economy and environment of New Zealand. The government funded the study with $125,000 from reparations paid to New Zealand as a consequence of the bombing of the Greenpeace vessel *Rainbow Warrior* in Auckland in 1985. One of the tasks of the study team was to report on issues that would require additional study. Many such policy issues were identified in the study team's report (Green *et al.*, 1987).

Study Assumptions

The major assumptions used in the study were:

1. Bombing is confined largely to the northern hemisphere and New Zealand is not a target;
2. Current conditions and existing levels of preparedness apply;
3. All trade between the northern and southern hemispheres ceases for the foreseeable future;
4a. Three Australian–US communication facilities at North West Cape, Pine Gap and Nurrungar are destroyed by separate nuclear strikes. Reduced trade with Australia is possible; *or*
4b. These facilities are destroyed as well as other military targets and two major cities in Australia. In addition, both Australia and New Zealand are affected by the electromagnetic pulse from a high altitude (400km) nuclear explosion. Trade with Australia collapses;
5a. New Zealand experiences no significant changes in temperature. (Corresponds to war during a northern winter); *or*

5b. Average temperatures fall by 3°C throughout the New Zealand spring, by 2°C throughout summer and by 1°C for the next 18 months.

Major Findings

...even without direct physical impacts, a major nuclear war would fundamentally disrupt New Zealand society. The effects would be widespread, some sudden, some longer lasting (Green *et al.*, 1987: 146).

The impacts on New Zealand of nuclear war would be pervasive, complex and highly disruptive to all aspects of society. New Zealand might not be a nuclear target, but the extent of the upheavals, even under the most optimistic of outcomes, would make a "return to normal" most unlikely. The psychological trauma of surviving a war which had abruptly killed so many millions, including friends or even family members in the northern hemisphere, would be the first impact. Many others would follow quickly.

Four main inter-related points emerged from the study. These were the extent of New Zealand's dependence on international trade (and the consequences of its abrupt loss), the increasing vulnerability of the technologies used in key systems, the strong interdependencies between sectors and the lack of contingency planning by the government for such major disruptions.

New Zealand, more than many other countries, is dependent on external trade for its economic activity and the well-being of its society. Eighty percent of trade is with northern hemisphere countries. The abrupt loss of that trade would cause enormous disruptions.

Simple estimates of the consequent effects on employment suggested that employment might fall by about 40–50 percent. Financial disruption and chaos could be severe, especially if the government had no plans for coping with the initial upheavals and uncertainties. Loss of imports would cripple manufacturing, since so many basic items (from ball bearings, to machinery, to electric motors and vehicles) are imported, usually from northern countries.

Health care is totally dependent on imported medicines, medical and dental supplies. Medicines would need to be rationed or else they would be used up within six months. The other requirements for health, such as clean water, operative sewage systems, refuse collection, disinfectants and a healthy diet could all be less available with rising unemployment, social breakdown, inadequate maintenance of machinery and loss of imported chemicals. Trying to develop effective rationing systems after nuclear war would be difficult, perhaps impossible.

Communication, transport and energy systems would become increasingly exposed to breakdown and failure as supplies of imports were used up. Local supplies of diesel and petrol would be halved with the loss of imported crude oils for refining in New Zealand. Almost all lubricating oils are imported with sufficient stocks for only two to three months. Rationing systems would be needed, alternative fuels (such as methanol) would need to be developed and used widely and the energy sector kept operating. Unprecedented stresses on society, coupled with enormous physical and organisational difficulties, could make these objectives impossible to achieve. The result would be major failures in this and other key sectors.

The second point that emerged was the increasing vulnerability of imported technologies to major disruptions in supply. The price of technological sophistication for consumer countries is a growing dependence on manufacturers for equipment, maintenance and spare parts. Those manufacturers are predominantly in northern hemisphere countries.

This vulnerability occurs in New Zealand at many levels, from the imported electronic telephone systems to a complex synthetic petrol facility and the country's single oil refinery. Problems with imported equipment would inevitably occur in the months and years after nuclear war. Breakdowns would be sudden and unpredictable. Some problems to major energy facilities would be well beyond the capacity of local engineering skills and resources to resolve. The capacity to resurrect older technologies and to develop alternatives which could be sustained by local skills and resources would be crucial. Yet much useful knowledge, human skills, and old equipment is being lost every year. Steam locomotives rust away, mechanical printing presses are junked in favour of imported electronic equipment and the skills to manufacture manual telephones and exchanges pass into history.

There is no economic rationale for resurrecting and reverting to such "obsolete" technologies now, nor is such a course advocated by the study (Green *et al.,* 1987). What is raised as a policy issue is the need to identify important vulnerabilities and examine the options and costs of improving self-reliance. Merely retaining the capacity to resort to simpler, but locally sustainable, technologies could become crucial for New Zealand in the event of nuclear war. National security after nuclear war assumes much wider dimensions than those of military security.

The third major point to emerge was the strong interdependence between sectors which would compound the problems faced by a post-nuclear war society in New Zealand. The health system depends on trade, energy, maintenance of urban systems and transport. For example, failure of urban pumping systems would lead to contamination of water supplies by sewage and possible epidemics of disease.

The sub-sectors of energy (electricity, natural gas, liquid fuels, coal) are deeply dependent on one another and on transport and communications. Loss of the country's major natural gas field, through the breakdown of the off-shore platform, would render the synthetic petrol plant inoperative, cut all gas for electricity generation and drastically reduce gas supplies now used directly for vehicles and heating. With liquid fuels severely cut, transport of food to large urban areas could become much more difficult, industries even more difficult to sustain, and the viability of cities would be further stressed. Interdependencies emphasise the value of identifying ways to increase self-reliance. Reducing the vulnerability of one sector would improve the viability of those to which it is linked.

Finally, the report noted the lack of contingency planning for the multiple crises that would confront the government and people of New Zealand should nuclear war occur. While the direct impacts on New Zealand would probably be relatively minor, the overall consequences would depend crucially on how well prepared New Zealanders were. At present, they are ill informed and ill prepared. Indeed, the report does not venture a prediction as to whether New Zealand society would survive as a cooperative, democratic, functioning system in face of the enormous shocks and problems that it would experience. The potential for social unrest, economic collapse and decline into a brutal, fractionalised society would be considerable.

This grimmer outcome would be more likely with disruptions caused by two additional factors, refugees and an electromagnetic pulse (EMP) effect. The number of refugees likely to arrive in New Zealand, either as starving desperate civilians, or as aggressive military forces, could not be estimated with any precision. Many different outcomes would be possible. The study concluded that relatively *small* numbers of refugees would impose severe demands on basic services and a social system struggling to cope with local needs. Refugees could well be carrying infectious diseases, given the high probability of disease epidemics occurring in northern hemisphere countries after nuclear war (Abrams, 1982). Plague, typhoid fever, cholera and typhus might get established in New Zealand several months after nuclear war via refugees, when existing vaccines supplies could be low and ineffective.

While refugees would impose an uncertain threat, the consequences of an EMP over New Zealand would be devastating. EMP effects are a likely component of nuclear war, given the disruption to military command and control systems caused by the huge surge of electromagnetic energy. The scenario leading to an EMP affecting New Zealand and technical aspects are given in the report (Green *et al.,* 1987). The energy from an EMP would be picked up by any conducting metallic "antenna," including power and telephone lines, aerials and other wiring. Most easily damaged are sensitive electronic items using microchips—computers, microprocessors, control units, electronic ignition systems, etc.

New Zealand's national electricity grid would not withstand the surge in voltage and current; the result would be a total blackout. Some repairs would be possible, perhaps to 30–50 percent of the system, providing a work force was available. Destruction of computer control systems would make the synthetic petrol facility and the oil refinery inoperative. Repairs would be unlikely. Natural gas production would be crippled, liquid transport fuels would probably run out in weeks. The results of an EMP for communications systems would be disastrous, with the telephone system completely out of action and the likely loss of radio, television and newspapers. People would know only what they could find out for themselves. The government would have very limited information and be unable to communicate effectively with the public. Financial systems would probably collapse along with the pre-war social, political and economic systems.

The consequences of a high-altitude nuclear explosion, leading to a significant EMP over New Zealand, could be a nation suddenly forced into the conditions of subsistence living practised by their ancestors a hundred years ago. However, the people in post-nuclear war New Zealand would be without the skills, equipment or social structures that were appropriate in that earlier age.

IMPLICATIONS

This preliminary study of the likely impacts on New Zealand of nuclear war has shown the catastrophic long-term disruptions that could occur after nuclear war in a non-combatant country far from the war zones. Neither nuclear warheads nor nuclear winter need to be invoked in reaching that conclusion. That, perhaps, is the most important message from this analysis. The indirect, global effects of nuclear war may vary widely between non-combatant countries, with particular circumstances and locations producing other unexpected outcomes.

There is considerable merit in further national case studies in a wide variety of non-combatant countries throughout the world. I suspect that they would reinforce the points that could be taken from the New Zealand study. First, the more effort that is applied to studying the consequences of nuclear war, the more catastrophic and pervasive those consequences are found to be. Second, indirect effects of nuclear war are as significant for human survival as direct effects, although major variations between regions are likely. As a consequence all states, not only nuclear powers, have substantial obligations and substantial rights, on behalf of their citizens, to involve themselves in initiatives that will reduce the nuclear threat which hangs over the planet.

Clearly the stakes are unacceptably high both for combatants and non-combatants. The onus is on all of us to find new ways of resolving conflict, at the personal as well as the international level. The Russell–Einstein Manifesto of 1955 eloquently stated the choice we still face and still have not made:

> There lies before us, if we choose, continual progress in happiness, knowledge and wisdom. Shall we instead choose death, because we cannot forget our quarrels? We appeal, as human beings, to human beings; remember your humanity, and forget the rest.

5

China's Role in the Search for Peace in Asia

Jin Junhui

PRESENT SITUATION IN ASIA

It is characteristic that in recent years there have existed simultaneously favourable and unfavourable factors in the development of Asia. The favourable factors are mainly the following. First, the development of Asia, or broadly speaking, the development of the Asian–Pacific region, is infused with dynamism and vitality. The economy of this region has developed for quite a long period at a rate higher than that in other regions. Various countries in Asia in order to overcome temporary difficulties and promote economic development have been engaged in successful economic policy adjustments or structural reform. Economic cooperation among countries in this region has also been enlarged and strengthened. We are justified in believing that economic development in Asia will certainly have an even brighter future, and that the share of the Asian economy in the whole world economy will be further enlarged.

Second, in adapting to the needs of speedy economic development, certain countries in this region either have taken the initiative or have been forced by circumstances to adopt some important measures in the field of political reform which broadens democracy in the society. Therefore the political stability of these countries has been basically maintained.

Third, more and more countries in this region are pursuing an independent foreign policy against hegemonism and power politics of the superpowers, especially in their new round of arms race and against the foreign invasion of any country or interference in other countries' internal affairs. This fact shows that the great majority of the Asian countries have become an important force in the cause of safeguarding world peace.

On the other hand, there also exist several unfavourable factors. First, along with the increasingly important role that Asian countries play in the world, the rivalry between the two superpowers in Asia has also been intensified. Their armed forces in this region have been greatly strengthened, and both the Soviet Union and the United States have deployed ever more sophisticated weapons in the Asian–Pacific region.

Second, regional wars in Afghanistan and Kampuchea are still intensively dragging on. The invasions of these two nations by foreign aggressive forces not only brought heavy losses in indigenous human lives and material resources, but have also seriously threatened the security of the respective neighbouring countries. Especially the Gulf war between Iran and Iraq now is showing a dangerous tendency of further expansion and even internationalisation along with the increasing involvement of the two superpowers.

Third, because of ethnic and communal contradictions, boundary disputes or other unsolved questions inherited from the history among various countries in this region, there has often occurred bloodshed or armed conflict within the countries themselves or between them. These incidents and conflicts naturally cause turbulence and instability in this region.

China is a socialist developing country. It has been pursuing all along an independent foreign policy of peace, which in the process of implementation has also been undergoing appropriate adjustments in accordance with the development of the international situation. One important principle of this foreign policy is that China will never attach itself to any big power or power blocs or submit to their pressure. Premier Zhao Ziyang has pointed out that "we take a principled stand in handling our relations with the United States and the Soviet Union. We will not refrain from improving relations with them because we oppose their hegemonism, nor will we give up our anti-hegemonist stand because we want to improve our relations with them, nor will we try to improve our relations with one of them at the expense of the other."

Another important principle of this foreign policy is that China wishes to establish normalised state relations with other countries according to the Five Principles of Peaceful Coexistence (i.e. mutual respect for sovereignty and territorial integrity, non-aggression, non-interference in each other's internal affairs, equality and mutual benefit, and peaceful coexistence). China also believes that it is necessary to solve the problems with other countries inherited from history through negotiations on the basis of upholding principles, respecting the history and the reality, exercising mutual understanding and mutual accommodation. The outstanding examples in this respect in recent times are the successful settlements of the Hong Kong and Macao issues according to the principle of "One country, two systems." Upholding this same principle, China will strive unremittingly for the peaceful reunification of Taiwan with the mainland, and is confident that this lofty goal will certainly be achieved in the future.

As an Asian country, China closely watches the trend of development in the Asian region. Guided by its independent foreign policy of peace, China is now working enthusiastically for the maintenance of peace and stability in this region as well as in the whole world.

CURRENT ASIAN CONFLICTS

As to the attitudes towards regional conflicts or "hot spots," it is of the utmost importance that China never supports any aggression or interference. At the same time China approves of political solutions to international disputes. However, all such solutions must be fair and reasonable if they are to be viable, and they must ensure the independence, sovereignty and territorial integrity of the countries which are the victims of foreign aggression or interference.

China has consistently maintained that the key to the solution of the Kampuchean question lies in Vietnam's cessation of its aggression and speedy withdrawal of all its troops from Kampuchea. Under the pressure of international public opinion, the Vietnamese authorities have over the years talked a lot about a "political settlement" but have in fact failed to show any sincerity. Their stubborn position of aggression and expansion has remained unchanged. Furthermore, they brazenly try to disguise themselves as an outsider, insisting that Kampuchea's "national reconciliation" come before their troops' withdrawal. All in all, what the Vietnamese really want is to prop up a Vietnamese-controlled "government" and protect the Vietnamese vested interests that were gained through aggression and expansion.

China seeks no self-interest in Kampuchea. It believes that the eight-point proposal on a political settlement of the Kampuchean question put forward by the Coalition Government of Democratic Kampuchea headed by Prince Norodom Sihanouk is fair and reasonable. China believes that after the withdrawal of all Vietnamese troops from Kampuchea under international supervision, the Kampuchean people can effect true national reconciliation and choose their own government through UN-supervised free elections so that Kampuchea under the leadership of Prince Norodom Sihanouk will become an independent, peaceful, neutral and nonaligned country. This will be in the interest of peace and stability of that region as well as of the rest of Southeast Asia.

As to the question of Afghanistan, China maintains that as long as the foreign aggressors do not withdraw, the war of resistance to aggression will not stop. It is clear that "guarantee first, troop-withdrawal afterwards" are nothing but excuses for delaying the withdrawal of troops from Afghanistan. If the Soviet Union really wants a political settlement, it should without any hesitation withdraw all its troops from there as soon as possible. This is the key to the settlement of the Afghan question and the only way to heal the "bleeding wound." It is the sincere hope of China that Afghanistan will regain its status as an independent, sovereign, neutral and nonaligned country at an early date.

Here I would like to add that China sincerely hopes to improve Sino–Soviet relations, so that the two countries may be good neighbours. Although in recent years much has been accomplished in the improvement of economic, commercial, cultural and scientific–technological relations between the two countries, due to the three obstacles—with the Soviet support of the Vietnamese occupation of Kampuchea being the most important and urgent among them—the political normalisation between China and the Soviet Union has not yet been achieved.

China's stand on the Gulf war is also clear and reasonable. It has all along taken a position of neutrality and of promoting reconciliation between Iran and Iraq, and urged them to bury the hatchet as soon as possible, engage in peaceful reconstruction and strive for further development rather than wearing themselves out in the war. Resolution 598 adopted unanimously by the Security Council through concerted efforts of all its member states reflects the strong desire of the international community for a speedy end to the Iran–Iraq war, and has provided a good basis for a peaceful settlement of the conflict. China has made, and will continue to make efforts to promote a comprehensive implementation of the resolution. It is not only necessary for Iran and Iraq to stop immediately all their military actions, but also very important for all parties concerned to exercise restraint and ensure free and safe passage of the international waterways in the Gulf. China has appealed to the big powers to stop their military involvement in the Gulf so as to avoid escalation of the conflict, leaving the littoral countries of the Gulf to solve the Gulf problem by themselves through consultations.

As to the question of the Korean peninsula, China considers that tension in this region can be eased only through reduced military confrontation and increased contacts and dialogue between the two parts of Korea. The Government of North Korea has recently put forward successive proposals such as phased disarmament by both parties, withdrawal of the US troops and tripartite talks at the foreign minister level.

China as a close neighbour of Korea is concerned at how the situation there will develop. It is to be hoped that the constructive proposals mentioned above will receive a favourable response from the parties concerned.

DISARMAMENT

Let us first of all take a look at the reality of the nuclear armaments in the world today. The most important fact is that the two superpowers possess the largest and most sophisticated nuclear arsenals, amounting to over 97 percent of the total nuclear weapons in the world. Their nuclear weapons have long reached the level of over-saturation and overkill. The grim realities are that whatever their intentions are, only these two have the strength and capability of launching a nuclear war.

Therefore, China is of the view that the two superpowers should take the lead in halting immediately the testing, production and deployment of all types of nuclear weapons. Furthermore, they should drastically reduce and destroy all types of nuclear weapons that they have deployed anywhere inside and outside their countries so as to create conditions for other nuclear states to take part in nuclear disarmament.

It is good news that the United States and the Soviet Union will formally conclude an INF (intermediate range nuclear forces) treaty in the near future. China hopes that after its conclusion it will be thoroughly implemented and all their long range and short range INF missiles deployed in Europe and Asia will be totally destroyed. Although this is only the first step towards nuclear arms reduction, China sincerely welcomes it.

Obviously, it is absolutely necessary that conventional armaments be reduced drastically along with nuclear disarmament. Conventional armaments of any country should be used only for self-defence. It goes without saying that the superpowers and their military blocs which possess the largest and most sophisticated conventional weapons should take the lead in drastically reducing their conventional armaments. This is of crucial importance to the maintenance of world peace.

Outer space is the common heritage of mankind, and its development and utilisation should bring benefits to mankind. It is against the will of mankind if any country should develop, test, produce or deploy outer space weapons in any way. It is hoped that an international convention on the complete prohibition of outer space weapons can be concluded at an early date.

China also maintains that all countries, big or small, strong or weak militarily, should have the equal right of participating in the discussion and settlement of the disarmament question which should not be monopolised by a few big powers. No disarmament agreement should be reached at the expense of other countries' interests.

Now, here I would like to say a few words about the steps taken by China in the field of disarmament.

As early as 1964, China declared explicitly on the very first day when it came into possession of nuclear weapons that at no time and under no circumstances would it be the first to use nuclear weapons. China has also undertaken not to use or threaten to use nuclear weapons against non-nuclear states or parties to nuclear-free zones. China has successively signed the relevant protocols to the Treaty for the Prohibition of Nuclear Weapons in Latin America (the Treaty of Tlatelolco) and the South Pacific Nuclear Free Zone Treaty (the Treaty of Rarotonga). China does not advocate or encourage nuclear proliferation, nor does it help other countries to develop nuclear weapons. China supports whatever actions and initiatives that are conducive to the realisation of disarmament and elimination of the threat of nuclear war. China has taken a number of steps to cut its military expenditures on its own initiative. The important decision made by the Chinese government to reduce China's armed forces by a million men is being implemented smoothly. China has not carried out any nuclear test for years. Furthermore, it declared last year that it would conduct no more atmospheric nuclear test in the future. All this has fully demonstrated China's sincerity for peace and disarmament and its determination to take concrete steps in this regard.

Everyone knows that China's productive forces are comparatively weak and that its economy is relatively backward. China is still at the initial stage of socialism. During this fairly long historical period, its main task is to expand vigorously the productive forces so that China will gradually lift itself out of poverty, backwardness and under-development. To this end, on the one hand it must persist in reform and opening up at home and to the outside world, on the other hand it will also remain unchanged for a long time in pursuing an independent foreign policy of peace. By pursuing this policy, China aims at both securing a lasting international environment of peace for its socialist modernisation drive, and fulfilling its responsibilities and obligations to world peace and development in tune with international trends. Consequently, only in this way would it be possible for China to develop faster and contribute more to mankind.

6

New Thinking and International Changes

Timour Timofeev

In our dynamic, rapidly changing and interdependent world the links between internal and international processes are growing stronger. From this point of view the Soviet Union considers the entire scope of problems of restructuring, of new thinking both in its economic and political aspects. These issues are not approached in a narrow way.

The wider meaning of "restructuring" is that it concerns not only the USSR: the world could do with a restructuring, especially considering that the planet is saturated with nuclear weapons, and beset with serious economic and ecological problems, with poverty and diseases. When underlining the importance of combining national and international interests, many political figures note that the world is tired of existing tensions and striving for a better life, for mutual understanding.

Today, in the nuclear age, international and national security have become particularly interconnected. Global problems have assumed enormous significance, and the contemporary world is interdependent as never before. It has therefore become all the more imperative to search for ways and means of reaching responsible solutions to major national and international issues.

This calls for joint efforts—the efforts of the entire world community—if we are to utilise the real potential of the United Nations Organisation for the purpose of strengthening peace and international security—both political and economic.

This idea has been repeatedly developed by Soviet leaders. Thus, in an important address to the Secretary General of the United Nations Organisation, Mikhail Gorbachev said that today, as never before, it was necessary to state openly and loudly, that the main objective set in the UN Charter has still not been achieved—there are still no guarantees of stable peace. Today, as never before, joint efforts by states and peoples are needed to ward off the threat of nuclear catastrophe from mankind.

What is needed above all for this purpose in practical terms is to put an end to the arms race on earth and keep it out of space.

What is also required are fresh efforts to calm regional sites of tension and to remove the last vestiges of colonialism in all its manifestations. The United Nations has many other pressing tasks: to facilitate, through real disarmament measures, the release of resources for the purposes of development, and the overcoming of backwardness, hunger, disease and poverty. The reshaping of international economic relations on a just and democratic basis and ensuring genuine human rights and liberties, most notably the right to a peaceful life, should also serve these purposes. The prime attention of its member states should be directed at making UN activities still more effective and fruitful (Gorbachev, 1986: 99–100).

The Soviet Union contributes and will continue to contribute in every possible way to the successful fulfilment by the United Nations of its lofty mission. This is urgently necessary today for developing constructive interaction between states and peoples on the scale of the entire planet, the more so as the necessary prerequisites exist, both political and socioeconomic.

Such interaction is essential, first and foremost, in order to avert a nuclear catastrophe, in order that civilisation could survive. It is essential also in order to solve—together and in the interests of everyone—other urgent problems common to all mankind. Of fundamental significance in this connection are the conclusions drawn in the Political Report to the 27th Congress of the Communist Party of the Soviet Union (CPSU) regarding the contradictions of a global scale, affecting the very foundations of the existence of civilisation. Reference is made, first of all, to pollution of the environment, the air and oceans, and to the exhaustion of natural resources. The need for effective international procedures and mechanisms, which would make for the rational use of the world's resources as an asset belonging to all humanity, is becoming increasingly apparent.

> The global problems affecting all humanity, cannot be resolved by one state or a group of states. This calls for a cooperation on a worldwide scale, for close and constructive joint action by the majority of countries. This cooperation must be based on completely equal rights and a respect for the sovereignty of each state. It must be based on conscientious compliance with accepted commitments and with the standards of international law. Such is the main demand of the time in which we live (Gorbachev, 1986a: 362).

The principles of new political thinking whose implementation in international relations is vigourously favoured by the Soviet Union are based not on some temporary or time-serving considerations but on a profound philosophical foundation. They reflect well-thought out positions, a deep conviction in not only the necessity, but also the real possibility of creating conditions for the survival of mankind. The official documents of the CPSU proclaim that the real dialectics of contemporary development consists in a combination of competition between the two systems and in a growing tendency towards interdependence of the states of the world community. This is how Soviet people see the present world—controversial but interdependent, and in many ways an integral world. The main direction of struggle in contemporary conditions is to create worthy, truly human material and spiritual conditions of life for all nations to ensure that the planet should be habitable and to deal with its reaches rationally. This view of the global problems facing mankind increasingly finds its many-faceted reflection in the works of a number of Soviet specialists in the political, economic, philosophical and other sciences, such as Eduard Shevardnadze (1986) and Anatoly Dobrynin (1987).

NEW POLITICAL THINKING

Transition to new political thinking—the imperative of nuclear age—is important for a correct analysis of the problems of international conflicts. A very controversial situation has developed in this sphere during the last few years.

On the one hand, all recognise the topicality of such problems. True, some in the West assess somewhat pessimistically the possibilities of the more or less reliable study of the deep-going causes of various conflicts, revealing their interconnections, effective investigation of their typology, ways and means of their resolution, etc. Here is one of the discourses by a prominent European scientist delivered at a very representative symposium jointly convened by UNESCO and the Pugwash movement of scientists:

> The dynamics of the arms race has been the subject of much debate. Is technological progress the driving force, or are the military applications of science and technology motivated by political conflicts? Is the arms race a primary source of conflict or is it a consequence of a strategic confrontation rooted in political and ideological differences? .... These questions belong to the "chicken or egg" type of problem, a category that is hardly useful to address in general terms, but which nevertheless underlines a fundamental problem (like morphogenesis) requiring a lot of research before it can be properly formulated, let alone solved (Calogero, 1982: 13).

On the other hand, simultaneously with the development of such—often predominantly "methodological"—debates (on the origin and significance of crisis situations), a number of concrete regional conflicts are becoming more acute. They are fraught with serious dangers, result in many casualties and stand in the way of achieving healthier international relations.

There are some people who still underestimate such dangers. Such an underestimation is rooted, first and foremost, in an insufficient realisation of the possible consequences of conflict situations as well as in failing to understand the specific features of the development of international relations in general. Here it is appropriate to quote recent assessments and thoughts of George F. Kennan, a prominent American foreign policy expert and historian. In the foreword to a new and interesting book by Norman Cousins, he writes:

> When the first nuclear weapon was exploded over Hiroshima, and in the years immediately following, a number of weighty and impressive voices could be heard, pointing out that the emergence of destructive power of this magnitude invalidated the greater part of traditional thinking about the relationship of war to national policy and calling for the adoption of a new mind-set—a new way of looking at things, one based on the recognition that war was no longer a rational option for great industrial powers and that other means would have to be found to resolve the conflicts of interest that would always be bound to arise among them (Kennan, 1987: 9).

The great intellects of that day demanded this. In addition to Albert Einstein and Bertrand Russell, there were a number of military leaders like Generals Douglas MacArthur and Dwight Eisenhower, and others. They realised the suicidal quality of nuclear weapons and the danger in allowing it to become the basis of defence postures and the object of international competition. They spoke with a sense of urgency and went to their deaths hoping that their warnings would surely not fall on deaf ears and that a new generation of leaders would recognise that this is the world of new political realities and thus would draw the necessary conclusions.

Alas, this has not happened. Kennan points out that for thirty years past their warnings have been ignored in many respects by influential circles in the West. There has been no new mind-set. There has been no recognition of the uniqueness of the weapons of mass destruction, no recognition of the dangers of their unlimited development. On the contrary, nuclear explosive has come to be treated as just another weapon, vastly superior to others, of course, in the capacity for indiscriminate destruction, but subject to the same rules and conventions that had governed conventional weaponry and its uses in the past ages.

> The suicidal quality of these devices has been ignored. They have been made subject to the primitive assumption that the value of a weapon is simply proportionate to its destructiveness and that the more you have of any weapon, in relation to similar holdings of your adversary, the more secure you are .... And all those psychological distortions that had been allowed to accompany armed conflict in the pre-nuclear age have come to be applied to the competition in the development of this form of weaponry. People have gone on, in other words, behaving as though this were 1916 instead of 1986 and as though the nuclear weapon were only some new species of artillery. This was, of course, precisely what the Einsteins and the Eisenhowers and the others had tried to warn about (Kennan, 1987: 10).

But during the last seven decades the world has changed, and the changes taking place in it can contribute to consolidating positive trends in international relations. Profound political and social shifts have been clearly revealed during our epoch. After October 1917 a fundamental qualitative change emerged in international life, with an intensification of the processes contributing to its democratisation. The influence of popular masses and public opinion on world politics increased as never before (Timofeev, 1987: 195–207).

Under these conditions the idea of setting up a comprehensive system of international security began to emerge as an increasingly realistic goal. New important ideas began to influence also the sphere of scientific analysis of crisis situations, and efficient ways of resolving them (including regional conflicts). During the last few years there has been a further development of research in this sphere by scientists from several countries.

A very important stimulus for in-depth study of such problems and the development of research in this sphere is a striving for a more precise formulation of approaches to them based on the principles of new political thinking. This was clearly revealed in the recent article "Reality and Guarantees for a Secure World" by Mikhail Gorbachev. While emphasising the fact that the world community cannot stay away from inter-state conflicts, he, among other things, supported the proposal to set up under the United Nations Organisation a multilateral centre for lessening the danger of war. There was also expressed the idea of creating a mechanism for broad international monitoring of the implementation of agreements aimed at alleviating international tensions, limiting armaments and controlling the military situation in conflict regions. It was emphasised that at all stages of a conflict it is necessary to use all means of peaceful settlement of disagreements and disputes between states, and to initiate proposals aimed at mediating and assisting in achieving the settlement of conflicts. The ideas and initiatives concerning non-governmental commissions and groups engaged in the analysis of the causes, circumstances and methods of settling various conflict situations also deserve attention.

Of considerable significance is how to apply practically the conceptual principles of the new thinking in today's and tomorrow's reality. It can and must be implemented—both on the regional and national scale, and in international forums (which are very important in themselves: there is reflected in addition to everything else, the growing activity of the diverse spectrum of peace-loving forces, the increasing influence of the world public opinion). The new political thinking needs development of new efficient approaches—for the purpose of making decisions on the most important problems—both global and regional.

We proceed from the fact that there exists a growing mutual link between these and other problems. Indeed, many regional conflicts and their consequences often influence the international atmosphere as a whole. If constructive steps aimed at their settlement are not taken, they may result in collisions of far greater dimensions fraught with grave danger. At the same time the majority of global problems involve the destinies of the peoples of each country of the world.

It should be emphasised that in the Soviet Union the philosophy of the new thinking permeates all the most important political publications and documents. This is formulated in a concise form in the resolutions of the CPSU, in the works and speeches of the General Secretary of the CPSU Central Committee, Mikhail Gorbachev, as well as other Soviet statesmen. These questions have been developed and represented in broad outline in new books for the officials of foreign policy departments which are being published at present; in the speeches and articles by the secretaries of the CPSU Central Committee, by the leading figures of the Ministry for Foreign Affairs and other organisations.

How do they interpret principal questions connected, for instance, with the assessment of the prerequisites, character, real and potential consequences of various international conflicts? As an example let us take the study "New Thinking and Diplomacy" written quite recently by Anatoly Kovalev (first deputy Foreign Minister of the USSR) and published in October 1987. It is intended to be a new chapter in the book *The Basics of Diplomacy*. This book is being put out by International Relations—one of the most prestigious publishing houses in Moscow. The author reminds the readers that in a number of regions of the world in the past regional conflicts broke out and escalated as a result of the interference, and sometimes direct armed interventions by forces from other regions. In the list of the actions performed by imperialist politics there exist, as he points out, many actions involving the bayonets of the marines, soldiers of "rapid deployment" forces and sometimes mercenaries. But it would be wrong, the author emphasises, to miss the significance of contradictions accumulated in various regions of the globe in the course of decades and centuries. Thus not only the continuous attempts to look at the world as its backyard and the arbitrary proclamation of the zones of their "vital interests," but also other attributes of the policy of "neo-globalism" engender such regional conflicts. There, in these regions exists its own political fuel, not only that which was brought from outside. It permeates the problems (often inherited from the period of colonial domination), public consciousness (particularly in their national and religious spectrums); with it are filled the mechanisms of state power, parties, sects, people. And it would be wrong to forget that such "home-made" fuel is capable of spontaneous combustion.

The approach of the Soviet Union lies in disengaging conflict situations, where they exist, in implementing prophylactic measures aimed at preventing "spontaneous combustion" and what is even more important—preventing the temptations of military adventures from the outside in the regions fraught with the danger of explosion. And he, emphasises the author, is very far from considering regional conflicts as a zone of rivalry between two or more large powers. Primitivism in assessing the causes and moving forces lying behind regional conflicts, the superficial view of the soil engendering them, is, at the very least, non-productive; sometimes it is fraught with dangerous consequences. A cautious, responsible approach to these problems, and not the policy of brute force and constant threats to resort to force, is the only realistic one. The Soviet Union proposes to other interested parties: let us search for their resolution, let us act jointly. This applies to the Middle East, to the Iran–Iraq war, to the crisis in Central America, to the Afghan problem, to the situation in South Africa and Indochina. The most important thing here is to consider strictly the rights of the peoples themselves to select their own road into the future, not to interfere in the internal affairs of other states. "The just political settlement of regional conflicts is dictated by the same logic of the interdependent and integral world which requires the solution of other, global problems ..." (Kovalev, 1987).

Meanwhile some western politicians strive to set off major international problems (for instance, the problems of progress towards limiting armaments), against the questions of resolution of regional conflicts. Their logic goes like this: first build confidence by solving regional conflicts, and only after that tackle the progress in the sphere of disarmament. But in the Soviet view it is necessary to advance along the broad front, resolving these questions simultaneously, i.e. when the settlement of one problem contributes to the solution of the other.

RECENT INITIATIVES

Recently there began emerging certain shifts in international affairs. An increasing number of countries are now in favour of negotiations and improvement of the situation around the hotbeds of conflict. Actively contributing to promoting this process, the USSR structures its foreign policy in the light of the interests of consolidating peace. Nuclear war cannot be a means for achieving any reasonable objectives in the international arena; in the existing situation the arms race cannot be won. Also no state can feel secure without equal security for all other states. Each nation, irrespective of the fact whether it is big or small, has the sovereign right to select its own economic and social system and its way of development. Indeed, with the growing interdependence of states, the differences in economic and social systems, ideologies and world outlooks must not be considered as obstacles to mutually advantageous cooperation between all countries.

The application of the new thinking to the concrete conditions of the Asian–Pacific region has produced a programme which Mikhail Gorbachev set forth in his Vladivostok speech in July 1986 and which he further elaborated in his interview with the Indonesian newspaper *Merdeka* on 21 July 1987.

These are the main components of this programme:

- elimination of regional hotbeds of tension by means of political settlement;
- a halt to the nuclear arms race;
- reduction of armed forces and conventional armaments;
- creation of nuclear-free zones;
- dismantling of military bases on foreign territories;
- confidence-building measures in the military field;
- arrangement of equitable and mutually advantageous economic cooperation between all the countries of the region;
- efforts to set up a new international economic order;

— preparations for the eventual convocation of an all–Asia conference for a joint search for constructive solutions.

The Delhi Declaration on Principles for a Nuclear-Weapon-Free and Non-Violent World is an example of the politico–philosophical approach to the vital problems of inter-state relations. The document goes beyond bilateral and regional frameworks.

It is necessary to point out the Soviet Union's readiness to dismantle all its medium-range missiles not only in the European but also in the Asian part of its territory which is a major step towards the wishes of the Asian countries. Shorter-range missiles are also to be dismantled.

The USSR favours the start of negotiations on reducing the activity of naval fleets in the Pacific, whose contacts may lead to confrontation and generate the danger of conflicts. There could also be a limitation on the areas of navigation by nuclear-armed warships so that they should not approach the shores of the other side within the range of operation of their onboard nuclear weapons.

The Soviet Union will spare no effort in striving for a full-scale agreement on halting nuclear tests. It also attaches great significance to reducing armed forces and conventional armaments.

The Soviet Government has issued resolute calls for an end to the fratricidal Iran–Iraq war which already has taken more than a million human lives and has ceased to be a bilateral affair. All warships not belonging to the countries of the region should be withdrawn from the Persian Gulf. Just as resolutely the Soviet Union condemns the attempts on the part of the United States and some of its allies to internationalise this conflict. The Soviet Union wants to reduce the military confrontation to a minimum.

Attention should be drawn to new initiatives set forth by Mikhail Gorbachev. For instance, in his recent speech in Murmansk he outlined a number of sweeping new proposals to make a number of regions, including the north of Europe and the Arctic, a zone of peace and international cooperation. He suggested that these countries should embark on talks and scaling down of military activity in the North as a whole, both in the eastern and western hemispheres. The General Secretary of the CPSU Central Committee pointed out that if, for instance, northern Europe became a nuclear-free zone, then the USSR would remove its nuclear missile submarines from the Baltic fleet. He also urged consultations between the Warsaw Pact and NATO to restrict naval and air activity in the Arctic.

The USSR called for an international conference in 1988 to coordinate scientific research and cooperation in environmental protection, and also underlined its readiness to discuss any counter-proposals and ideas.

At the same time it is important to increase efforts at helping the UN to take positive decisions and ensure that the discussions on the concept of international economic security as a part of its system of world security be continued in a business-like spirit. Considerable attention has been given, for instance, to the debates on the questions of stabilising the world economy.

In this connection the following should be noted. On the one hand, in the course of broad discussions of the economic development trends in various regions, the inclination to analyse the state of the world economy taking into account the increasing interdependence of the economies of various countries is becoming stronger. Moreover, lately a number of economists note a definite growth of synchronisation in the development of crisis phenomena and the aggravation of contradictions of reproduction in various links of the world capitalist economic system.

On the other hand, there is a growing understanding of the fact that the burden of serious economic difficulties could be alleviated if tangible results were achieved on the way to disarmament. Undoubtedly these problems claim attention in connection with disarmament and development, and in particular the idea of setting up a fund for the development at the expense of disarmament.

The urgency of these problems is also felt in the industrially developed countries. A number of proposals and projects have been put forward by leading economists in various countries. They deal with the problems of weakening the economic burden of the arms race, and with the questions of transition to an "economy of peace." These projects are at present in the focus of attention. They naturally figure increasingly at various international forums–both at conferences convened by the UN and at numerous meetings sponsored by non-governmental organisations.

I can refer, for instance, to recent statements made by outstanding political figures who attended the important meetings held in Moscow and devoted to the 70th anniversary of the Great October Socialist Revolution. The General Secretary of the CPSU Central Committee Mikhail Gorbachev in his report [and also in his new book: *Perestroika and New Thinking for Our Country and the Whole World* (1987a)] pointed out that the Soviet Union has come out resolutely for strengthening the prestige of the United Nations, for the full and effective use of the powers conferred upon it and its agencies by the international community. The Soviet Union is doing its best to enable the United Nations, a universal mechanism, to competently discuss and ensure a collective search for a balance of interests of all countries, and to discharge its peacemaking functions effectively.

The most important thing is that the Soviet concept and its firm dedication to peace are reflected in practical action, in all international moves, and in the very style of its foreign policy and diplomacy which are permeated with a commitment to dialogue—a frank and honest dialogue conducted with due regard for mutual concerns and for the advances of science, without attempting to outmanoeuvre or deceive anyone.

And so, now that more than two years have elapsed, we can say with confidence that the new political thinking is not merely another declaration or appeal but a philosophy of action and, indeed, a philosophy of a way of life. In its development, it is keeping pace with objective processes under way in our world, and it is in fact already working.

The October 1986 meeting in Reykjavik ranks among the events which have occurred since the new stage in international affairs began, which deserve to be mentioned on this occasion and which will go down in history. The Reykjavik meeting gave a practical boost to the new political thinking, enabled it to gain ground in diverse social and political quarters, and made international political contacts more fruitful.

It is true that, gauged against the scope of the tasks mankind will have to tackle to ensure its survival, very little has so far been accomplished. But a beginning has been made, and the first signs of change are in evidence. This is borne out, among other things, by the understanding that has been reached with the United States on concluding in the near future an agreement on medium and shorter-range missiles. The conclusion of this agreement is very important in itself: it will, for the first time, eliminate a whole class of nuclear weapons; be the first tangible step along the path of scrapping nuclear arsenals; and will show that it is in fact possible to advance in this direction without prejudice to anyone's interests.

That is obviously a major success of the new way of thinking, a result of readiness to search for mutually acceptable solutions while strictly safeguarding the principle of equal security.

However, the question concerning this agreement was largely settled back in Reykjavik, at the second of the US–USSR summit meeting in the 1980s. In this critical period the world expects the third and fourth Soviet–US summits to produce more than merely an official acknowledgment of the decisions agreed upon a year ago, and more than merely a continuation of the discussion. The growing danger that weapons may be perfected to a point where they will become uncontrollable is an urgent reminder of the need to waste no time.

That is why the USSR will work at these meetings for a palpable breakthrough, for concrete results in reducing strategic offensive armaments and barring weapons from outer space—the key to removing the nuclear threat.

The Soviet leadership has pointed out that there are serious reasons for optimism, for regarding comprehensive security as being really attainable (Gorbachev, 1987b: 55–76). And during the celebration of the 70th anniversary of the Revolution, the Soviet Union examined again different aspects of the prospects of advancement to durable peace. The new way of thinking has helped to conclude that a comprehensive system of international security in the context of disarmament is needed and possible.

7

Past and Future Wars

Geoffrey Blainey

If this were a specialists' symposium on the prevention of malaria, we would probably reach an early agreement on the causes of the disease even though we then disagreed on the action plan. But a symposium on how to prevent nuclear war runs into the immediate hurdle that there is little agreement on what causes war. After centuries of debate, and after the writing of tens of thousands of learned articles in this century alone, specialists on war still do not agree on the causes of the disease. Most of their remedies are therefore unlikely to be effective. One remarkable aspect of the diagnosis of war is that contradictory theories about its causes are usually allowed to coexist peacefully. Instead they should be forced to fight each other.

My own views on the causes of war and peace I have held for sometime. They are set out in the book of 1973, *The Causes of War,* and a summary of my arguments is appended to this chapter. Central to my way of interpreting the causes of war is my belief that any plausible explanation of war must also be capable, if turned upside down or tilted, of explaining peace. I believe that any explanation of why some wars are long and some wars are short should logically be related to an overall explanation of the causes of war. To express it another way, any factor which shortens a war must by definition be a cause of peace. I believe that in trying to analyse why wars occur and why peace occurs, the more revealing and illuminating time is often the outbreak of peace rather than the outbreak of war. In keeping with my assumptions, an explanation of 1918 is as vital as an explanation of 1914. Indeed the end of a war, being laced less with emotional propaganda, and being startlingly clear-cut as a mirror of the distribution of military power, is easier to analyse effectively.

I also think, on the basis of the existing evidence, that a study of the history of wars before the invention of the atomic bomb is still a vital guide to the causes of wars during our nuclear era. Admittedly, many political scientists see the nuclear era as unique and declare that 1945 is a deep chasm isolating most lessons that might have been culled from the earlier era of conventional weapons. I find myself reluctant to accept too readily the verdict of those scholars who, while rarely studying history, insist that the nuclear era is unique. To say that any era is unique is to issue a profoundly historical statement, and such statements should not be accepted lightly from those scholars who do not study history. I tend to see far more continuity than chasm when comparing war and peace in the years before 1945 and the years after 1945. We are inclined to forget, in this overpowering nuclear era, that each military generation since the 1860s has been inclined to see itself as so revolutionary in its military techniques that it believes that it can learn little from the past. I do not wish to be unduly emphatic in stressing the continuity, since 1945, of military history and of the politics of war-making and peace-making. Continuity is a matter of degree; as a break with the past the year 1945 is probably of greater magnitude than any previous break, but the continuity is still apparent in the field of war and peace.

NUCLEAR PESSIMISTS

Can mankind avoid another major war? Can a nuclear war be averted? I ask these questions only in relation to the next 50 years. To try to predict events 50 years ahead is an awesome task. To try to see even further ahead is more hazardous because the most devastating military weapon, a hundred years hence, will not be a nuclear warhead but a military device of which we now know nothing. It would not be realistic to think that nuclear weapons, as we know them, represent the last phase in military innovations. Remarkable as gunpowder was, it gave way in the second half of the 19th century to dynamite and cordite, and later to nuclear power. Remarkable as were the artillery of the Crimean War, the machine gun of 1900, the submarine and the Dreadnought battleship of 1918, and the armoured division of 1940, they have been surpassed by missiles and other projectiles.

It is a frequent assumption today that the nuclear era will go on and on. In warfare, however, it is highly probable that the nuclear era, like every other era which has been flavoured by a particular technology, will ultimately give way to another era. I confine my comments to the nuclear era.

Opinion polls emphasise that in the western world, young people are especially fearful of nuclear weapons. Indeed there is a strong tendency to see the post-1945 generations as especially unlucky, being the first in mankind's long history to face an uncertain future. But an uncertain future has been more normal than we realise. In many centuries since the birth of Christ the imminent end of the world was a widespread fear. Thus in the 16th century, Martin Luther thought that the world would probably come to an end before 1600.

Most critics would now dismiss Luther and other prophets as the victims of outmoded superstitions, and yet it could be argued that today's predictions of a nuclear holocaust could well be based partly on superstition as well as on reasoned argument. We should be very alert to the dangers of a nuclear war: those dangers are real. But several of the most frequent predictions made about the nuclear era are shaky.

The dangers we now face and the options we possess as human beings are obscured by myths or, at best, quarter-truths. For example, it is widely said that an arms race inevitably leads to war and it is sometimes said that we are in the grip of such a race. This theory arose originally out of the events leading to the First World War. I examined the evidence in my book, *The Causes of War,* and was surprised to find that the theory did not sufficiently match the facts in the period 1894–1914. In that arms race some of Europe's big powers were actually spending a lower proportion of their budget on arms as the so-called arms race gathered momentum. An examination of Soviet and American spending in the years 1952 to 1976 has also cast doubt on the modern concept of an arms race in which each spurt in expenditure on arms by one superpower is the result of the previous jump in expenditure by a rival superpower. A. F. K. Organski and Jacek Kugler, in their book *The War Ledger* (1980), give strong but not watertight reasons, using statistical evidence in support, for their proposition that there was not an arms race between the superpowers in that period. They argue that changes in the American and Soviet expenditure on arms can be explained more satisfactorily in terms of internal factors in each nation rather than as a series of urgent responses to the armament expenditure of the rival.

I do not mean to suggest that an arms race can never be a prelude to war and never be a cause of war. Sometimes, however, an arms race is more a reflection of a period of swift innovation in weaponry, and the innovation makes old weapons obsolete and leads to a spurt of spending on the new weapons. Some arms races are marked more by confidence in the minds of the rival nations while other races, perhaps more dangerous to the peace, are spurred by tensions. Sometimes an arms race is a substitute for war, and can be seen as a series of effective threats which, being effective, make war less likely. Peace can often be defined as a time when nations' threats to one another are taken seriously and so do not have to be implemented: the war breaks out when the threats cease to work.

The idea that arms races inevitably lead to war carries the corollary that disarmament agreements must promote peace. Gradual disarmament is often seen as the panacea for war. There is a powerful case on economic grounds for arms control and for international disarmament, but we should not be carried away by the idea that disarmament usually promotes peace. Hitler's rise to world power in the 1930s was aided enormously by the arms reduction agreements signed amidst cheers a decade earlier by the victors of the First World War and by the very considerable decline in defence expenditure by the superpowers of that era, especially in the years 1929–1934. The world depression brought disarmament on a useful scale but the disarming did not help the peace of Europe. I do not wish to be dogmatic on this issue. I merely wish to suggest that warnings of the grave dangers of arms races and the benefits of plans for disarmament are not always as persuasive as they seem.

Some of the popular and gloomy theories about nuclear war tend to be theories of inevitability. Devastating nuclear warfare will certainly occur, it is argued, if the two superpowers should fight. I myself am not convinced that a superpowers' war, if it occurs, will necessarily be a nuclear war. Whereas it is widely assumed that a powerful weapon, once in existence, must be used, I am not so sure. Perhaps the most formidable of the new weapons at the end of the First World War was chemical warfare, and it was seen as a decisive weapon of the future. Gas can be devastating, as the Italians showed against the Ethiopians in 1936, the Japanese against the Chinese on the Yangtze River in 1941, and as Iraq and Iran appear to have shown in the Gulf War in the 1980s. But like germ warfare, gas warfare has been used with remarkable restraint, and the fear of retaliation almost certainly banned it during the Second World War. The same fear of retaliation as well as the weight of international opinion have, so far, probably helped to curb the use of nuclear weapons. Remarkably, they have not been used in a war since 1945. I am not insisting that nuclear weapons will not again be used: rather I am challenging the assumption that they will automatically be used on the large scale if another major war or world war should occur.

It is widely argued that if, in a crisis between the superpowers, the first nuclear missile is fired, it will lead automatically to a clockwork succession of strikes. It is widely assumed that a war, once that first nuclear missile is fired, will be unstoppable, will be incredibly devastating, and will be over in a few hours or days. This tragic scenario is possible. To me, however, it is not the most likely course of events.

Even in our computer era, warfare remains one of the least predictable of human activities. Wars rarely go according to plan. Rarely does the most powerful weapon of an era—and in our era it is the nuclear missile—determine the course of the war in the way actually predicted. Nor is it true that all-powerful weapons make inevitably for a short war. One strong conclusion does emerge from a study of wars in the last 200 years. In nearly every era, the major European wars involving the superpowers and their allies have tended to be long wars, lasting much longer than two-nation wars. While they were expected to be short, they were almost invariably long wars. The evidence inclines me to the view that a major general war, if it comes in the next 50 years, will probably not be dominated by nuclear weapons and will not necessarily be short.

NUCLEAR OPTIMISTS

While I have mainly criticised those who, in my eye, are too pessimistic, I should also touch on the optimists. There is a widely held theory that nuclear weapons generally promote peace and that the present long period of relative peace amongst the technologically advanced nations comes mainly from the fact that all-out war is now self-defeating. The cost of war, it is said, now exceeds the likely prizes of victory. I myself think that nuclear weapons so far have probably promoted peace amongst the big powers. But our present period of peace is not unique and so it does not need a unique explanation.

The world since 1945 is very different from the world preceding it. The number of independent nations has multiplied, and so the number of potential international wars has multiplied too. It is very difficult, in comparing the world of say the period 1845 to 1945 with our post-war world, to make any useful calculation of whether the world as a whole is now more prone or less prone to indulge in international wars or in civil wars. But it is possible to look at the major powers—and they are the ones which employ the deadliest military technology—and to make useful comparisons about their tendency, over time, to engage in major wars against each other. If we designate today's major economic and political powers, not necessarily in order, as the United States, the Soviet Union, France, Britain, Germany, Japan and China, then we can observe that since 1945 not one of these powers has fought the others—with the unusual exception of the Korean War where China briefly was on the opposite side to the United States. In various other wars, not least Vietnam, the two superpowers fought each other partly through proxies but they did not directly fight each other. The four decades since the end of the Second World War can thus be labelled as relatively peaceful, by this important definition. As these seven big powers include the main possessors of nuclear armaments, they constitute a crucial category for analysis.

The fact that since 1945 the seven big powers have avoided a major war, and the fact that Europe—the seat of the two world wars—has been remarkably peaceful since 1945 entitles observers to extract some optimism from the nuclear era, even if many other parts of the world have created bloodshed on a large scale. These optimists are inclined to attribute the peace, amongst the big powers and in Europe itself, to the invention of nuclear weapons. They see nuclear weapons as an unusually strong promoter of peace. I have some sympathy with their argument. My own study of history persuades me—and will continue to do so until evidence to the contrary is found—that war becomes less likely if in the minds of nations' decision-makers the losses from fighting seem likely to exceed the gains. Certainly nuclear weapons have tended to make war appear to be a suicidal rather than a triumphant activity: I do not wish, however, to be too dogmatic on that point. History can produce many examples from the pre-nuclear era of leaders who initiated a suicidal war, believing it would be a triumph. It is possible then that eventually the nuclear era might produce another example of a similar grand delusion.

There has been a tendency to be carried away by the lack of a major-power war since 1945 and to see it as unique. A unique occurrence, of course, usually receives a unique explanation, and in this instance the unusual peace is attributed to the unusual weapons. But Europe experienced two very long periods of relative international peace between the end of the Napoleonic Wars in 1815 and the outbreak of the First World War in 1914. One period ran from 1815 to 1848, a peace of 33 years, and another ran from the end of the Franco–Prussian War in 1871 to the outbreak of the first Balkans War in 1911 or, some would argue, to the outbreak of the Great War in 1914. In the light of these facts we should not become too eager to see the international peace in Europe since 1945 as unique, nor is it necessarily an augury for the whole world. Europe is now less dominant; for the first time in hundreds of years Europe is the home of only one of the two great military powers and is the home of no more than two of the four great economic powers in the world.

I offer another reason against seeing nuclear weapons as the only cause—or even the main cause—of the relative peace between the world's big seven powers during the four decades since 1945. If we examine the great powers of the century running from 1815 to 1914, we find that they enjoyed an even longer period of peace. Designating, for most of that period, the world's great economic and military powers as Britain, France, Russia, Austria-Hungary, Prussia-Germany and the United States, we find that they fought each other rarely in that relatively peaceful period of 99 years. Britain and France as allies fought Russia on the shores of the Black Sea from 1853 to 1856; and Prussia briefly fought Austria in 1866 and France in 1871, both being wars of astonishing speed. These three wars were remarkably self-contained, being fought over a reltively small area; they did not entangle, as in 1914–1918, a wide range of other nations; and two of the three wars were short: indeed the Austro-Prussian War was called the Seven Weeks' War. The relations between the great powers as well as Europe's relative freedom from international wars gave the 99 years from 1815–1914 a feeling of unprecedented peacefulness to most of those who lived in the later part of that period and who knew enough history to interpret it in the wider context of European history. By 1900 there was a widespread feeling amongst intellectuals and many liberal churchmen and politicians that war as an institution was in sharp decline, and the 1910–1911 edition of the *Encyclopaedia Britannica* contained an article on "Peace" which made the brave assertion—rather exploded some three years later—that "war is coming, among progressive peoples, to be regarded merely as an accidental disturbance of that harmony and concord among mankind which nations require for the fostering of their domestic welfare."

The nuclear era has been infinitely less disastrous than the pessimists in the era's first twenty years had predicted. But the optimists should also be cautious. They are not yet in a position to affirm that the era since 1945 has been uniquely peaceful, and they will probably not be in such a position of judgment until perhaps the year 2020 or later. They therefore should be wary of largely attributing to nuclear weapons a period of peace which had parallels even before nuclear weapons were invented.

I offer one comment on the peace movement. Those who warn about the dangers of war usually carry out a valuable service. The peace movement also has a therapeutic quality—in part it is an alternative religion which helps the young to confront the danger of nuclear war. But a peace movement, if it is based on dubious theories about the causes of war, can actually promote war more than peace. It is not unfair to quote Bishop Mandell Creighton's statement, made—rather too emphatically for a bishop—in the late 19th century: "No people do so much harm as those who go about doing good." Peace is too important an issue to depend partly on people whose heart might be in the right place but whose brain is not. Unfortunately we do not yet know enough about the causes of international peace. Without more knowledge, an agreed formula for preserving the peace will be risky and could even be self-defeating.

FUNCTIONS OF WAR

It may sound cynical to say so but it would be more cynical, really, not to say so: war has traditionally fulfilled an important function. In the absence of sound and trusted organisations for solving international disputes, war was the method used by independent nations to solve their disputes and, if possible, to maintain their national sovereignty. Another perceived function of international war in the nineteenth and twentieth centuries has been to reallocate natural resources and living space, often taking them from a declining nation and allocating them to a rising nation. Sometimes this process results in a rough natural justice but sometimes it defies justice.

During a long period of peace the international boundaries and the resources they enclose remain frozen but increasingly an expanding nation—expanding in determination, energy, and perhaps population—is pressing on some of those boundaries. Usually the boundaries of nations represent the final results of a previous war: they represent the hierarchy of national power of a past era, now frozen. But over time the superior power of the nation, which had drawn those boundaries at the end of a victorious war, may diminish. The loser of that past war will then, perhaps with the aid of allies, try again to redraw the boundary.

It was war which reallocated the vast resources occupied by relatively few people in the North Americas and much of South America, as well as in Australia and New Zealand, transferring them—with accompanying human tragedy—to European peoples who were more capable of developing them and populating them. An American Indian or a Maori of New Zealand will understandably lament the series of wars, campaigns and skirmishes which transferred their territory; but it was unmistakeably in the interests of the people of the world as a whole. Tens of millions of people gained the right to live through those events, and to share in the resultant increase in the world's annual output of food, minerals and energy. The same functional argument for the greatest good of the greatest number is increasingly used against South Africa.

Sometimes war is simply a way of executing a long-standing grievance. It is through war that ethnic groups, who believe that their nation should embrace kinsmen across the international border, try to achieve their goal. It is through war that big nations try to maintain what they have. War is still the nations' accepted mechanism for trying to retain what they possess, and the accepted mechanism for trying to gain what another nation possesses—whether natural resources, ports, living space or places rich in historical and cultural associations.

We cannot easily justify the resort to war in an era when war as an instrument is so sharp and deadly and, sometimes, suicidal. But the fact is that war has fulfilled these functions, and is still believed by many national leaders to fulfil them. The big advantage of warfare is that, in the eyes of those who deliberately choose it as the means of achieving their ambition, it will give them what no other method can assure them—it can give victory. Again and again such a hope is falsified. Nonetheless most nations in modern times have gone to war with hope, believing that they will gain more by fighting than by not fighting.

The nuclear era makes this form of problem-solving far less efficient, but in a sense we are still on the threshold of the era of nuclear warfare. Perhaps the world will become more sympathetic to new means of solving international disputes when it experiences a major nuclear war and realises how archaic and inefficient warfare has become as a problem-solver. Unfortunately, most national leaders are not yet convinced, when they decide to fight a war, that war itself creates more problems than it solves.

International war has been the most acceptable way of solving serious disputes between independent nations. War is now less acceptable because of the brute power of modern military weapons, but it will remain somewhat acceptable until opinion leaders realise that war has fulfilled a function and that more effective ways of fulfilling that function must be devised. At present hardly a nation which values its independence is willing to submit unconditionally to the adjudication of a vital dispute submitted to the United Nations or to an international court. You may say, "this is outrageous," but it is still a fact. One weakness of the international peace movement is its reluctance to face fully this fact. War will more easily be banned or regulated if there is another resort of final appeal. War will remain the final court of appeal until we successfully ask: what is an alternative court of appeal which nations are likely to accept?

CONCLUSION

One solution to international war is a world government. Such a government was unthinkable even in 1900 but now, for the first time in world history, it is a possibility because of dramatic changes in communications and surveillance. In the next fifty years a world government, if it does arise, is more likely to emerge through conquest than through consent. Even if it initially comes through the consent of most nations, it is unlikely to remain a democratic government. It is more likely to be authoritarian and its success in keeping the peace—if it does succeed—is likely to stem partly from its suppression of liberty in many parts of the world.

In conclusion, I am not as pessimistic as the typical young person about the dangers of a nuclear holocaust in the next fifty years. I think a nuclear war involving hundreds of missiles and creating colossal death and devastation is unlikely: I would place the odds as perhaps 5 to 1 against such a devastating event. I think slightly more likely is a major war which uses few or no nuclear weapons. Since it will probably not be a short war, it will be devastating. I am also inclined to think that someday a world government will emerge and that it will not be palatable to those who value freedom but far more palatable to those who value freedom from international war.

Appendix 7.1: Summary of Arguments on the Causes of International War

Source: Geoffrey Blainey, *The Causes of War* (London: Macmillan, rev. ed. 1988); reprinted by permission.

FLAWS IN CURRENT THEORIES OF WAR AND PEACE

1. Most of the popular theories on international war—and the explanations by many historians of individuals wars—blame capitalists, dictators, monarchs or other individuals or pressure groups. These theories, however, explain rivalry and tension rather than war: rivalry and tension between countries can exist for generations without producing war.

2. Governments' aims and ambitions are vital in explaining each war, but to emphasise ambitions and to ignore the *means* of implementing ambitions is to ignore the main question which has to be explained. For the outbreak of war and the outbreak of peace are essentially decisions to implement aims by new *means*. To attempt to explain war is to attempt to explain why *forceful means* were selected.

3. The evidence of past wars does not support the respectable theory that an uneven "balance of power" tends to promote war. If the theory is turned upside down, however, it has some validity.

4. The evidence of past wars does not support the scapegoat theory and its assumption that rulers facing internal troubles often started a foreign war in the hope that a victory would promote peace at home.

5. The evidence of past wars does not support the 'one pair of hands' theory of war: the belief that a nation busily making money will have no spare energy or time for the making of war.

6. The idea that the human race has an innate love of fighting cannot be carried far as an explanation of war. On the statistical evidence of the last three or thirteen centuries it could be argued with no less validity that man has an innate love of peace. Since war and peace mark fluctuations in the relations between nations, they are more likely to be explained by factors which themselves fluctuate than by factors which are "innate."

7. War-weariness in a nation often promotes peace and war-fever promotes war, but there have been notable instances where war-weariness promoted war.

8. The Manchester theory argues that increasing contact between nations—through common languages, foreign travel and the exchange of commodities and ideas—dispels prejudice and strongly promotes peace. The evidence for this theory, however, is not convincing.

9. No wars are unintended or "accidental." What is often unintended is the length and bloodiness of the war. Defeat too is unintended.

10. Changes in society, technology and warfare in the last three centuries spurred some observers to suggest that international relations were thereby so revolutionised that past experience was largely irrelevant. There is much evidence, however, to suggest that there is considerable continuity between the era of cavalry and the era of intercontinental missiles.

A FRAMEWORK OF CAUSES

11. In their origins, war and peace are not polar opposites, and the distinction between a war-maker and a peace-maker is often a mirage.

12. The idea that one nation can be mainly blamed for causing a war is as erroneous as the idea that one nation can be mainly praised for causing the end of a war. Most current explanations of war, however, rest on these errors.

13. If it is true that the breakdown of diplomacy leads to war, it is also true that the breakdown of war leads to diplomacy.

14. While the breakdown of diplomacy reflects the belief of each nation that it will gain more by fighting than by negotiating, the breakdown of war reflects the belief of each nation that it will gain more by negotiating than by fighting.

15. Neutrality, like war and peace, depends on agreement. Sweden and Switzerland, for instance, have remained neutral for more than a century and a

half not only because they chose neutrality but because warring nations permitted them to remain neutral.

16. War and peace are more than opposites. They have so much in common that neither can be understood without the other.

17. War and peace appear to share the same framework of causes. The same set of factors should appear in explanations of the :

— outbreak of war;
— widening of war by the entry of new nations;
— outbreak of peace;
— surmounting of crises during a period of peace;
— and, of course, the ending of peace.

18. When leaders of rival nations have to decide whether to begin, continue or end a war, they are, consciously or unconsciously, asking variations of the same question: they are assessing their ability or inability to impose their will on the rival nation.

19. In deciding for war or peace, national leaders appear to be strongly influenced by at least seven factors:

i.   military strength and the ability to apply that strength efficiently in the likely theatre of war;
ii. predictions of how outside nations will behave if war should occur;
iii. perceptions of whether there is internal unity or discord in their land and in the land of the enemy;
iv. knowledge or forgetfulness of the realities and sufferings of war;
v.   nationalism and ideology;
vi. the state of the economy and also its ability to sustain the kind of war envisaged;
vii. the personality and experience of those who shared in the decision.

20. Wars usually begin when two nations disagree on their relative strength, and wars usually cease when the fighting nations agree on their relative strength. Agreement or disagreement emerges from the shuffling of the same set of factors. Thus each factor is capable of promoting war or peace.

21. A change in one factor—for example the defection of an ally or the eruption of strife in the land of the enemy—may dramatically alter a nation's assessment of its bargaining position. In the short term that factor could wield an influence which seems irrationally large.

22. When nations prepare to fight one another, they have contradictory expectations of the likely duration and outcome of the war. When those predictions, however, cease to be contradictory, the war is almost certain to end.

23. Any factor which increases the likelihood that nations will agree on their relative power is a potential cause of peace. One powerful cause of peace is a decisive war, for war provides the most widely-accepted measure of power.

24. Even a decisive war cannot have permanent influence, for victory is invariably a wasting asset.

25. A formula for measuring international power is essential: ironically the most useful formula is warfare. Until the function of warfare is appreciated, the search for a more humane and more efficient way of measuring power is likely to be haphazard.

PATTERNS OF FIGHTING

26. To precede war with a formal "declaration of war" is usually regarded as normal behaviour, but the evidence since 1700 suggests that it was abnormal. The Japanese surprise attack on Pearl Harbor in 1941 belonged to a strong international tradition.

27. Wars confined to two nations were fought usually on the geographical fringes rather than near the core of world power.

28. A general war or a world war began usually as a war between two nations and then became a series of wars which were interlocked and were fought simultaneously. An explanation of a general or many-sided war should therefore be structurally similar to the explanation of several two-sided wars.

29. A civil war was most likely to develop into an international war when one side in the civil war had ideological, racial or other links with an outside nation.

30. A general war was usually, by the standards of the age, a long war. Even in the era of nuclear weapons a general war—if it occurs—will possibly be a long war.

31. It is doubtful whether any war since 1700 was begun with the belief, by *both sides,* that it would be a long war.

32. The idea that great advances in the technology of warfare inevitably led to shorter wars was held by many generations but falsified by many wars.

33. In human behaviour few events are more difficult to predict than the course and duration of a war: that is one of the vital unlearned lessons of warfare.

MYTHS AND PERILS OF THE NUCLEAR ERA

34. The idea that a nuclear arms race will usually lead to war should be viewed warily.

35. The long period of peace between the superpowers is not primarily the result of the nuclear terror, but nuclear fears will be increasingly important if that peace is to be considerably prolonged. Whereas a forty–year peace is not unique, an eighty–year peace will require the presence of unusual peace-making factors.

36. The nuclear era seems to follow the same basic rule of earlier eras: that peace will prevail if nations believe they lose more than they gain by resolving their disagreements through fighting.

37. While it is widely feared that nuclear weapons will soon be used on the large scale, there are historical precedents for major military weapons and crucial military tactics lying unused for very long periods.

38. The idea that a nuclear war will be short rests on the dubious theory that the prevailing military technology largely determines whether a war will be short or long. On the contrary, a nuclear war could be of long or short duration.

39. The peace movement is increasingly important but it is a double‑edged sword and is capable, even with the noblest intentions, of promoting war rather than peace.

8

Paths to Peace? Theories of Conflict Resolution and Realities of International Politics

K. J. Holsti

Studies of conflict resolution and crisis management have proliferated in the literature of international politics and peace science over the past three decades. This literature has the well-meaning purpose of exploring those sorts of situations and kinds of governmental or international organisation activity that can help prevent crises from breaking out into war or, somewhat less dramatically, that can bring to an end those conflicts that have already involved contests of arms. The reasons for the proliferation of this literature are not hard to locate. Despite great hopes at the end of both world wars that such experiences would not be repeated; and despite the creation of international and regional organisations designed to prevent war through collective security and to ease peaceful change through mediation, conciliation, and arbitral procedures, wars and crises have continued to plague mankind. The literature explosion reflects disillusionment with diplomatic realities.

Let us review the dimensions of the problem. One would think by the sheer volume of peace literature that we are on the verge of an apocalyptic conflagration, that the world is headed for certain destruction, and that senseless spending on arms will result inevitably in a catastrophe of unprecedented proportions. Much of this view is based on extrapolation of trends—particularly defence spending and development of new nuclear weapons technologies in the Soviet Union and the United States. But war is not just a problem of the superpowers, nor were international organisations created primarily to constrain their activities. War and crises are problems endemic to the international system as a whole, and not just to two of its members.

The Correlates of War project at the University of Michigan provides us with the data necessary to chronicle the trends of international conflict and crisis since the end of the Napoleonic Wars. For the entire period

1816–1980 there have been 67 inter-state wars, 51 extra-systemic (imperial) wars, and 106 civil wars (Small and Singer, 1982).[1] The majority have occurred in the twentieth century. The incidence of war has increased over the years, but this should not be entirely surprising as the number of states has increased from about 23 in the 1820s to over 160 today. Using the analogy of traffic, we would expect that as it thickens there is a higher probability of accidents. When the number of wars is adjusted by the number of states in the system, then, the incidence of wars has actually been declining over the past century. For example, the number of wars begun in the period 1816–1848, divided by the number of nations (28.8 average for the period) was 0.70. In contrast, the figures had declined to 0.23 for the post-World War II period until 1980 (Small and Singer, 1982: 131). On the other hand, wars have tended to last longer and involve more battle deaths, so that the optimism generated by the declining incidence of war, adjusted by the number of states, has to be tempered by a recognition that the human and material costs of war have increased.

The literature on conflict resolution is not related solely to war, however. There is also the problem of potentially lethal crises, those recurring situations that international organisations were supposed to handle in such a manner as to preclude violence. What has been the record on crises, both those that terminated short of war, and those that did not? Are we not becoming increasingly war-prone, if not engaged in more wars? Zeev Maoz has identified 827 international conflicts between 1815 and 1976 that involved the threat, display, and/or use of military force, their location, participants, and outcomes (Maoz, 1982). Of the 827, 210 occurred in the nineteenth century with the remaining 617 in the first three-quarters of the twentieth century. For the entire period there was an annual average of 5.2 war-threatening or war-producing conflicts. Of the 827, 67 ended with wars (8 percent). The most peaceful period followed the Napoleonic Wars, while the period since 1945 has seen the highest number of crises. In an absolute sense, the world today is significantly more "war-prone" than it was in previous eras—although there has been a slight decline in the number of crises that actually end with war. But again, we have to adjust for the historically unprecedented explosion of new states that has taken place during the last forty years—itself a major cause of war. Maoz's figures show that the most conflict-prone era was between 1910 and 1920 (an artifact of World War I) while the period since 1950 has been comparable to the 1850s and 1860s. Put in statistical terms, in an average for five year periods, there has been about 1.2 war-threatening conflicts per state in the system between 1950 and 1976, while the figure for the relatively peaceful 1830s and 1840s is about 0.8. Overall, the twentieth century has been somewhat more conflict-prone than the preceding eras, but not startlingly more so.

We should add, finally, that the states most likely to participate in conflicts are the great powers, led by the United States which for the period 1815–1976 was ivolved in 120 war-threatening conflicts, 50 of them as initiator. It is followed closely by England, Russia/USSR, and France. An interesting shift has taken place since World War II, however. If we look at the annual frequency of conflict-involvement rather than total involvements over time (which skews the figures for states that have been long-time members of the "family of nations"), the most conflict-prone have not been the traditional great powers, but rather Israel, nonaligned India, Vietnam, and Uganda (Maoz, 1982: 57).

However we interpret these figures, the magnitude of the problem remains great. The costs of war in terms of lives, property damage, social dislocation—the staggering international refugee problem, for example—and economic woes have become largely intolerable. War has become the mega-problem of the twentieth century, even if the incidence, given the increased number of actors, has been declining. But that decline has not been precipitous, as one might have expected given: (1) the existence of numerous international institutions designed specifically to resolve and abate international conflicts; (2) the "lessons learned" from World War II; (3) the significant changes in public attitudes towards the use of force in international relations; and (4) the growth of economic interdependence. We could also have anticipated, as the nineteenth century liberals argued, that as publics become more literate and involved in politics, they would constitute an important constraint against those who would use force. Finally, we have seen over the past forty years a great outpouring of scientific studies of wars, crises, and techniques of conflict resolution. Our knowledge of the subject is vastly expanded. None of these developments, however, seems to have had an appreciable impact on the overall incidence of conflicts, crises, and wars. This constitutes the puzzle which I will explore in this essay.

In searching for possible explanations, I want to examine the "ideology" of conflict resolution. By ideology, I do not mean faith and symbols, but rather the intellectual foundations and assumptions upon which contemporary scholarly and diplomatic approaches to conflict resolution are based. I will argue that these approaches make incomplete diagnoses of the etiology of international conflict and that, therefore, their prescriptive elements may be only partially helpful, or helpful only for particular types of conflicts. First, let us establish briefly the social setting in which conflict resolution, peace research, and peace science have evolved. Our next task is to delineate the major intellectual approaches to the problem of conflict resolution. Third, I will demonstrate how some types of international conflict are inconsistent with the assumptions of the literature. I then provide some evidence from practice to show to what extent international institutions have been able or unable to fulfil their mandates for the pacific settlement of international conflicts (or, as is more often the case, the non-pacific, non-settlement of disputes). This record underlines some of the limitations—more intellectual than diplomatic—of the conflict resolution approach to peace. The essay concludes with an examination of the cold war, a particular type of conflict for which the literature seems to have only limited applicability.

CHANGING ATTITUDES TO USE OF FORCE

In the seventeenth and eighteenth centuries war was commonly viewed as a heroic enterprise reflecting upon *la gloire* of the king and dynasty. Although the public of peasants and tradesmen ultimately paid for the "sport of kings," campaigns, sieges, and conquests were often spectacles popularly launched, and popularly celebrated by Te Deums and other forms of festivities when they came to an end. By the nineteenth century, after the sufferings inflicted by and upon the Napoleonic armies, more sober views came into prominence, including those espoused by the early predecessors of our contemporary peace movements. Martial spirits, jingoism, and some public adulation of the military continued to characterise literature in late nineteenth century Europe but as a counterweight, there were the novels of Emile Zola, the peace and anti-slavery movements, the founding of the Red Cross, and the growing campaign for arms limitation and the creation of an international tribunal. However, the conventional wisdom for the majority was that the use of armed force was the prerogative of the sovereign, and a legitimate means of dealing with threats to security—real or imagined—slights upon national honour, and the manifold purposes of national expansion.

The decision-makers of Europe in August 1914 nevertheless had a premonition of the catastrophic consequences of what was about to befall the continent. Whatever the braggadocio, posturing, and blustering of the kaisers and publicists who argued that armed violence separated the strong and fit nations from the weak, many diplomats understood that a general war would involve much more than a few manoeuvres, some sieges, and honourable surrenders. The costs and futility of World War I and the repeat performance twenty years after the Treaty of Versailles indicated to even the most stout-hearted militarist or social Darwinist that the ultimate objective of arms must be to preserve peace, and not to wage war. By 1918, the nineteenth century conventional attitudes towards international violence had been completely repudiated—only to be resurrected to new heights of popularity in Japan, Germany, and Italy by militarists and the fascist dictators. The lessons of 1914 had to be learned all over agian.

The Nuremberg and Tokyo trials established that wars of aggression are parallel to "crimes against humanity." The theory of collective security enshrined in both the League of Nations and the United Nations justifies the collective use of force, as well as self-defence, but condemns it for other purposes. By the 1950s, the national ministries of defence defined their tasks in terms of deterrence rather than war. For the peace movement and some of the academic literature on war, international violence came to be commonly portrayed as a contagious disease, a pathological consequence of sovereignty and nationalism, a tragedy resulting from misperceptions, faulty decision-making, and poor communications, and a remnant of martial habits that are hanging on inappropriately during the age of interdependence.

Whether adopting a legalistic approach, as in studies of conflict-resolving procedures in international organisations, or a broader sociological approach that seeks to locate the causes of conflict and their amelioration in all social contexts, much of the literature has a didactic purpose. The need for practical knowledge, given the record of international conflicts and crises, is obvious. The academic study of conflict can help practitioners fashion strategies and institutions that can prevent wars and, should this fail, to bring wars to an end more rapidly than would be the case through the playing out of military combat. Some of the literature sees conflict in generic terms; its properties are essentially the same no matter what the context. Hence, we can learn something about the strategies and tactics of conflict resolution at the international level by examining inter-personal relationships, labour-management negotiations, and laboratory simulations involving undergraduate students (an example of the transferability of concepts and analyses between different social levels is the fine study by C. R. Mitchell, 1981). The experiences of international mediators and peacekeeping forces serve as further mines of information that can be transferred to new situations as they arise. The study of conflict resolution thus has brought together people from diverse intellectual and career backgrounds spanning academia, trade unions, the peace movement, experimental psychology, economics, the military, and diplomacy.

My purpose is not to review or summarise its major landmarks, much less to suggest better tactics for interjecting third parties into international crises. (For some representative samples of the literature, see Bercovitch, 1984; Burton, 1969; Coser, 1961; Frei, 1982; *International Journal,* 1985; Lall, 1986; Young, 1967.) I prefer to address the puzzle raised by the antinomy between our attitudes towards and knowledge of the etiology and characteristics of international conflicts and crises on the one hand, and the persistence of the phenomena on the other. I raise more speculative issues about the relationship between what we *think* about international conflict, and what the historical record demonstrates. Given the record of diplomacy within international and regional organisations, do we have realistic expectations regarding the practical value of the theoretical literature?

MEANING OF CONFLICT RESOLUTION

The term "conflict resolution" is by no means lacking in ambiguity. Conflict offers few problems, but resolution raises difficulties, only two of which will be discussed here. What forms can "resolution" take? And what is the distinction between resolution and management?

Let us assume that a conflict involves a claim, demand, or move by party A against the interests of party B (and perhaps others as well). The issue(s) under contention need not concern us at this point. We can assume that the likelihood of the use of force increases to the extent that the parties attach significant value to their respective positions: A to change the *status quo,* B to maintain it. The options in this setting are: (1) A forces B to move back from its initial position by conquest or the successful threat of violence (coercion); (2) A can somehow persuade B through peaceful negotiations to alter its commitment to the maintenance of the *status quo* —this may be done through various forms of exchange, promise, reward, or some combination of them; or (3) A can withdraw its demands, claims, or actions and thus restore the *status quo.* All of these will resolve the conflict, the latter two by peaceful means. The problem is that a conflict can also be resolved by option (1), by the surrender of party B. It basically meets all of A's demands or acquiesces in A's "occupation" of a new position; thus war is avoided or terminated. Such was the case of Munich. Capitulation can include a formal treaty or other instrument of settlement, thus giving the outcome a patina of legitimacy.

Clearly, however, the term "resolution" in the literature implies outcomes other than surrender or systematic appeasement. Otherwise, we would fall into the trap of accepting conquest and successful bullying as legitimate means of resolving international conflicts. Under the Charter of the United Nations, they are clearly unacceptable. Thus, "conflict resolution" really implies procedures and terms of settlement associated with various forms of compromise or withdrawal. A further possibility is that a creative solution may bring net benefits to both parties, although in the short term it is often difficult to convince parties to a conflict that this is possible.

If some sort of compromise or creative settlement is the hallmark of successful conflict resolution, then it assumes that the parties maintain only *conditional* commitments to their demands, claims, and positions, and that both parties can be convinced that they will prefer a compromise outcome (or withdrawal) to a test of military strength. Unfortunately, this is not the case in many conflicts.

A second problem with the literature relates to the distinction between conflict management and conflict resolution. Using the origins of World War I as the paradigmatic example of crisis pathology, the literature suggests that many, perhaps most, conflicts are the result of misunderstanding, misperceptions, faulty decision-making processes, and poor predictions about the results of the use of force. Although there were a few in the German military who sought an opportunity to break up the *Entente Cordiale* by military means, and undeniably the Austro–Hungarian authorities sought to humiliate Serbia, most decision-makers in the European capitals had a pretty realistic view of the consequences of war and were committed to finding a peaceful solution to the Sarajevo crisis. The argument is that in this case the timetables for mobilisation structured the decision-making in such a manner as to preclude delays necessary for negotiations and possible mediation. This was the war that nobody wanted, yet it happened. Various studies have documented the misperceptions, lost opportunities, and constraints imposed by time (O. R. Holsti, 1972).

The intervention of third parties into these sorts of situations, the literature suggests, can help avert war. Mediators and other go-betweens can convey messages, provide unbiased information, alter the calculations of costs, risks, and benefits by pointing out the consequences of an armed contest, and provide many other services that will inject notes of objectivity and sobriety into the decision-makers' calculations. The purposes of these activities are really in the realm of conflict abatement or war-avoidance rather than conflict resolution. But even if successful, the gap between war avoidance and conflict resolution remains. This raises no problems—particularly if we are talking about a crisis involving the potential use of nuclear weapons. But what of the situation where an armed conflict may be a necessary prelude to a compromise outcome? In many conflicts, commitments become conditional only *after* a test of arms. There may be, in other words, an inconsistency between the goals of war avoidance and conflict resolutions. War avoidance can actually prolong a conflict.

Moreover, granted that third party intervention into crisis decision-making may reduce the possibility of war, are we to assume that the "lessons" of World War I are applicable to all crises? Does the view of war as a consequence of misunderstanding, misperception, and faulty information match the historical record? Such characterisations of and assumptions about international conflict are not incorrect. But they are incomplete. They are limited because they derive their views of international politics from a tradition that portrays most conflicts as *bargaining situations,* often resulting in wars only because of decision-making pathologies reminiscent of World War I. The unspoken view of conflict in the literature is that adversaries can reach agreements short of the use of force if they get to know each other, eliminate their mutual misunderstandings, and acknowledge each others' needs. Violence is always destructive; it can never be constructive in helping to bring lasting settlements. These views of international politics have come down from the tradition of the *philosophes,* Jeremy Bentham, the nineteenth century peace movement, the idealism of Woodrow Wilson, and today much of the academic literature on conflict resolution. The problem is that they represent more a prescription for conflict resolution than a comprehensive diagnosis of various kinds of conflicts.

Historically, it is clear that demands, claims, and aggressive actions are not always based on misperceptions; nor are they always raised in order to be compromised or withdrawn. A significant portion—unfortunately we do not have the data to establish how pervasive—of the wars of the last three hundred years have involved issues of fundamental importance to dynasts, governments, and societies as a whole. Many crises and wars have resulted from the incompatible positions two or more parties have taken on issues that represent the core values of a regime and/or society. Some crises, such as the Agadir incident or the Quemoy–Matsu brinkmanship episode, may be fabricated for symbolic purposes, but many involve essentially irreconcilable values. The Thirty Years' War divided the Catholic and Protestant political units of the Holy Roman Empire. The questions that gave rise to war in addition to the restoration of ancient "liberties" in some realms of the Empire, involved matters fundamental to the faiths, including the upbringing of children and freedom of conscience. These are not matters that can be compromised easily. The War of the Spanish Succession was perceived by the enemies of Louis XIV as involving far more than the placement of his grandson on the throne of Spain. It meant, rather, whether or not France would thereby come to a position of hegemony in Europe. No doubt a less headstrong and ambitious French king might have given up such a scheme, but what Louis sought was not untypical of his age. Similarly, the Napoleonic Wars involved issues more far-reaching than questions of nepotism. What was at stake was the independence and sovereignty of Europe's states (Europe's "liberties" was the expression of the time) versus the establishment of a Paris-based empire stretching from the Atlantic to the Urals. In the contemporary setting, Ayatollah Ruhollah Khomeini does not raise issues of a religious nature in order to compromise them. One can think of war avoidance in the contemporary Middle East situation, but given ideological/religious commitments, it is difficult to see where correcting misperceptions may be sufficient to alter the course of events.

The point is that these sorts of assaults on the *status quo* can rarely be settled by third party intervention. Conflict can continue short of war, but if there is to be a *resolution,* it seems to result only from conquest, successful deterrence, or exhaustion after a lengthy test of arms. There seems to be no middle ground. Victory for the ambitious is usually far more important than the loss of thousands of lives (indeed, in the case of Iran, the sacrifice of life can be easily compensated for by achieving the status of martyr). The whole intellectual edifice surrounding theories of conflict resolution seems to be inappropriate for the diagnosis and handling of these sorts of conflicts.

Perhaps even more troubling is that many causes which have received broad public sympathy have also been non-compromisable. It is not just the Louis XIVs, Napoleons, Hitlers, and Ayatollahs that have pursued goals at the expense of the core values and interests of other states and societies. War has been a fundamental, perhaps critical, source of "progressive" historical change. Virtually all the nation-states of Europe were created through war and violence. As one wit has noted, war made the state, and the state made war. The process of state formation has been organically connected to war, just as much in the sixteenth and seventeenth centuries as today. The United States, Germany, Italy, Russia, much of Eastern Europe, India, Indonesia, Algeria, Israel, Vietnam and dozens of other modern states are the offspring of war. None would have come into existence under an effective regime of conflict management or conflict resolution that precluded conquest, surrender, and withdrawals. A large portion of all the cases considered by the United Nations since its founding has had as its source questions of state creation, and the process continues as militarised secession movements plague the political life of dozens of countries, including some in Europe (K. Holsti, 1986). With only a few exceptions "national liberation" movements have not been great bargainers whose highest goal was termination of conflict through a compromise. They have sought and achieved surrenders and conquests.[2]

Of course the ideology of self-determination has rendered these conquests legitimate. But if we say that "just" conquests are legitimate whereas others must be condemned, then we put ourselves in the position of stating that conflict resolution, understood as the technique and process of locating compromises, is not an end in itself—which is another way of saying that there are values greater than those of peace. This position appears inconsistent with most of the assumptions in the conflict management and resolution literature, where avoidance or termination of armed hostilities is seen as the highest goal.

All of this leads to the conclusion that conflict resolution can be only one of several approaches to the problem of war and violence. The history of international conflict suggests that there are types of conflicts that are intractable, that cannot be settled through the technical quick fixes of mediators and conciliators, much less of international courts. The great forces of historical change, such as the creation of states and nations, are not amenable to shopkeeper diplomacy. Conflicts deriving from great ideological forces, whether secular or religious, appear compromisable only after great contests or arms have exhausted the antagonists. In some instances the only way to prevent conquest is through deterrence, and yet, as we know, deterrence also has its risks.

The historical record shows as well that even in armed contests fought over particular issues, such as control of strategic waterways and frontiers, claims to an inherited title, or the rectification of slights to national honour, there is often no realistic possibility for successful mediation or conciliation until the contestants have learned through armed conflict that conquest is not possible. Throughout the seventeenth and eighteenth century wars, for example, mediators usually succeeded only after the parties had exhausted themselves through long campaign and sieges. It took war to alter the decision calculus of the participants. Mediators who sought to fashion compromises in the early stages of armed conflict were notably unsuccessful. Vietnam, the Arab–Israel problem, and the Iran–Iraq war suggest that this pattern is by no means typical of only the seventeenth and eighteenth centuries.

This is not to say that fine-tuning of mediatory techniques, the creation of implicit guarantees for compromises, or the improvement of peacekeeping procedures cannot help. They can play critical roles in helping to ameliorate, if not resolve, certain kinds of conflicts. But the spotty record of conflict resolution in the United Nations and regional organisations should not lead us to believe that the improved knowledge or availability of third party services will make an appreciable impact on the record of war prevention and abatement. Before we proceed, we should outline briefly the main characteristics of that record.

INTERNATIONAL INSTITUTIONS AND PACIFIC SETTLEMENT OF DISPUTES

In fact, our model of international conflict between A and B is over-simplified. There are really at least six theoretical outcomes of international conflicts: (1) *conquest;* (2) *avoidance,* where A withdraws demands, claims, or actions; (3) *deterrence,* where the initiator is forced by retaliatory threats to withdraw its demands, claims, and actions; (4) *compromise;* (5) *awards,* where the adversaries agree to allow a third party to fashion a settlement through non-bargaining procedures such as court decisions, plebiscites, and arbitral awards; and (6) *passive settlement,* where there is no formal outcome negotiated by the adversaries or third parties. One party creates a new situation (alters the *status quo*) and eventually both parties learn to live with the situation to the point where no one is willing to seek modification through resort to arms. The conflict is resolved through obsolescence, although in some instances a formal settlement through treaty arrangements may legitimise that outcome. The division of Germany, the Kashmir problem, and possibly the India-China frontier may have reached that stage.

My study of 97 armed conflicts, including some where armed force was only threatened, between 1919 and 1986 reveals the following distribution of these outcomes (K. J. Holsti, 1988: 406-410):

Table 8.1: Outcomes of 97 International Conflicts, 1919–1986

Conquest	32%
Compromise	20%
Successful Deterrence	19%
Award	12%
Avoidance/Withdrawal	11%
Passive Settlement	4%

The figures do not add up to 100 percent because a further category of ongoing conflicts (Iraq–Iran, for example) constitutes the last 2 percent. They do reveal, however, a distribution of outcomes that may be disappointing to those whose expectations about war and peace converge around the United Nations. More than one-half of all the cases had outcomes fashioned by the manipulation and use of armed force: conquest and successful deterrence. Awards were fashionable in the 1920s and early 1930s, as the League of Nations used plebiscites in a number of disputes between the new states of Europe, and as several governments were willing to submit potentially lethal conflicts to settlement by the Permanent Court of International Justice (PCIJ) (Wambaugh, 1933). But for the entire period, only 32 percent of the conflicts were handled through institutionalised procedures, ranging from bilateral negotiations between the adversaries, to international conferences, mediation, and adjudication.

One would like to report significant progress in the employment of conflict resolution procedures over the years, but unfortunately the figures do not point to such a positive trend. The number of outright conquests was higher in the interwar period than in the years following World War II (42 percent compared to 25 percent). But this figure is skewed because the post-war cases exclude wars of national liberation, which are a type of conquest. The number of compromises has increased from 13 percent to 24 percent, the number of awards has declined (from 21 percent to 7 percent), avoidance has increased, and perhaps most notably, the number of passive settlements—conflicts frozen through time—has comprised 8 percent of the total. There were none in the interwar period. The amount of blatant aggression has perhaps declined, but the availability of conflict resolution facilities in international and regional organisations has not led to an increase either in their use or in their rates of success.

Indeed, a recent study by Ernst Haas (1983) indicates that in recent years the international community seems to have developed a higher tolerance for armed conflict. He has identified a universe of 282 "disputes" between 1945 and 1981 that have been referred to various international organisations. Of these, 217 involved armed conflict; 123 went immediately or eventualy to the United Nations; 80 were placed on the agendas of regional organisations; and 20 were handled at both levels. About one-quarter were not referred to any organisation. Haas' findings suggest that the United Nations has had considerable success in "managing" (which is not the same as "settling") these disputes until approximately 1965, after which the record falters. The number of cases referred to the UN remains high, but its capacity to bring about some sort of outcome, whether abatement, stopping hostilities, isolating the conflict, or helping to forge a final settlement, has declined over the years. For example, the UN wholly or partly managed 65 percent of the disputes referred to it in its first five years, but only 42 percent between 1976 and 1981. Regional organisations have fared no better.[3]

Some have argued that there are institutional reasons for this record. After all, the Charter is a backward-looking document. Understandably, it was designed to help prevent the kinds of aggressions that occurred in the 1930s. The framers of the Charter can be excused for not being able to predict the nature of conflicts that would be typical of the post-war era These have included cold war conflicts, where the UN could play only a peripheral role, wars of state creation and decolonisation—where, however, the UN was perhaps unexpectedly successful in helping to arrange many peaceful transitions—and other conflicts such as Vietnam that became linked to cold war concerns.

What of judicial and arbitral procedures? The record is not promising, for legal remedies appear relevant only for a highly circumscribed set of conflicts. Between 1921 and 1986, the PCIJ and ICJ (International Court of Justice) helped to resolve only five conflicts. The ICJ has considered 52 cases (excluding advisory opinions) since 1946. Of these, only four involved the threat or use of force, and only one involved on-going use of force (Nicaragua–US). The remainder would be classified as disputes, concerning relatively minor issues between normally friendly states, cases in which the interests of private citizens or minor territorial adjustments were at stake. The explanation of this record is not complex. Court decisions have winners and losers. Any government that believes it has less than an open-and-shut case would prefer to negotiate a compromise with an adversary than risk losing all in a court decision. (On some territorial issues compromises can be fashioned, as was the 1985 decision to delineate the boundaries of George's Bank between Canada and the United States.) The adversaries have to agree on the jurisdiction of the court and as we know, there are many loopholes here, including the claim that an issue resides essentially within the domestic jurisdiction of a state. Moreover, most problems referred to international tribunals involve disagreements over facts or the interpretation of existing laws and treaties. In most international conflicts, however, one of the parties is deliberately attempting to *change* the other's rights and jurisdictions. Since judicial decisions are more or less bound by precedent, they are conservative rather than creative. Parties that are attempting to change the *status quo,* unless they have strong legal bases for doing so, are not likely to seek that change through judicial means.

Given this record, it is difficult to conclude that institutional tinkering will help bring significant improvement. John Burton (1987) has suggested a more sociological approach to conflict resolution, whereby the parties are encouraged to discuss their mutual needs rather than to submit to a more formal mediation or conciliation process. He reports some success in several cases, but one has to remain sceptical about the possibilities of this approach in conflicts where the problem is not that the parties fail to understand each other, but that they understand each other only too well. Burton is probably right, however, in arguing that many of the mechanistic approaches to conflict resolution are inadequate, and right too in his suggestion that some types of conflicts require approaches radically different from those that international institutions have so far been able to offer.

None of this is meant to belittle significant achievements. There have been numerous successes of institutionalised mediation and conciliation, some of them of significant magnitude. They have seldom fashioned legitimised, formal settlements, but they have abated crises and helped cease armed hostilities. The underlying causes of conflict remain, but it is no mean achievement to put an end to the killing. No doubt some of the conflict management and resolution strategies have prevented escalations that could have threatened much wider wars. But given these successes, it remains that our theories and institutionalised procedures of conflict resolution are inadequate to diagnose and cope with certain kinds of conflicts.

Even for more limited confrontations, the United Nations and the regional agencies are often poorly positioned to act in a timely manner. For example, these organisations have seldom anticipated conflicts; they do not have monitoring capabilities that can identify those kinds of issues that are likely to generate crises and wars; the organisations have done little in the way of developing preventative measures. Crises usually reach the magnitude of a "threat" to the peace, a "breach" of the peace, or an "act" of aggression before there is even the assumption of appropriate jurisdiction. Given all the immediate problems on the UN agenda, few diplomats are going to demand various forms of intervention into situations that are only potentially dangerous. The UN usually acts only after the crisis stage of a conflict has been reached, indeed often only after the shooting has started. This is exactly the stage when expectations of conquest are highest, and therefore the acceptance of outside intervention the lowest. [Bueno de Mesquita (1981), has established that few governments will risk initiating hostilities if they think that the chances of winning a military confrontation are relatively slight.]

The practice of international organisations, and some of the literature on conflict resolution, has the aura of offering remedies without appropriate and early diagnosis; of intervening when intervention is least likely to bring results; and of ignoring the issues that gave rise to the conflict in the first instance. Moreover, in their focus on crisis management and violence abatement, they have generally ignored the problem of peaceful change, an issue that was popular during the 1930s but which seems to have been forgotten in the post-war years.

The theory of conflict resolution tends to be mechanistic and legalistic. It has been more concerned with the manifestations of conflict and crisis than with the birth and development of conflict-producing issues. Conflict, above all, involves change, and until we have a better grasp of the dynamics and etiology of change in the international system, we will not have come to the heart of the issue. We also need typologies of conflicts, followed by strategies of conflict resolution appropriate to their main characteristics. At present, the concept of conflict remains undifferentiated. Minor border disputes are lumped together with cold wars. An examination of the characteristics of international conflicts in previous eras, compared to the cold war, illustrates why this lack of differentiation limits the practical applicability of existing approaches to conflict resolution.

CONFLICT RESOLUTION AND THE COLD WAR

The simple model of conflict behaviour between A and B outlines the essential features of numerous crises and wars of the last three hundred years: whether the Swedish–Danish war of 1700, the War of the Bavarian Succession, the Balkan Wars of 1912–1913, the Munich crisis, the Korean War, the Cuban missile crisis, and hundreds of others. They all started when party A made demands, pressed claims, or took actions that were at the expense of B's core interests and values. In the case of those situations that resulted in wars, A usually made extensive calculations about the relative power situation of the adversaries, and struck in the belief that the probabilities of victory were reasonably high. There were, of course, numerous instances where the calculation of those probabilities was skewed by poor information, unanticipated events, wishful thinking, or just a willingness to take high risks. However, in the seventeenth to nineteenth centuries, the costs of losing wars—at least by today's standards—were not disastrous. Countries were seldom occupied by victors; peoples' lives outside the immediate campaign routes were largely unaffected; regimes were not toppled upon defeat,[4] and terms of settlement did not emcompass the notion of unconditional surrender. Provinces and territories changed hands, fortresses were razed or strengthened, losers accepted obligations not to join coalitions against the winners, and the winners never sought to eliminate their adversaries as legitimate actors in the international system. (The scandalous partition of Poland was an exception that proved the rule.) Defeated actors were reincorporated into the diplomatic system as fully legitimate partners.

War was reasonably limited through the combination of crude technical capabilities, notions of honour, international law, and the well-defined and concrete issues underlying most conflicts. Territory had a very specific value, usually some combination of strategic importance, sources of revenue for dynastic coffers, and trade opportunities. Loss of territory, while hardly pleasant for the vanquished, was not mortal. Indeed, losers often expected various forms of compensation, a rather admirable practice that allowed face-saving. And for those victors who had gained what others might have thought as disproportionate spoils, there was a willingness to offer compensations to many states. This practice had the result of lowering suspicions and maintaining rough balances of capabilities between the main actors. The international systems of those eras were therefore flexible; change occurred, but compensations and exchanges could reduce their costs. States could wax and wane but with the possible exception of Louis XIV's ambitions, none of the dynasts wanted to create a new system. They accepted the system and only tried to improve their position within it, but usually mindful of maintaining a balance.

The cold war has had very different characteristics. The issues that give rise to conflict are not concrete and circumscribed, although there have been some of these. The leading policy-makers of some states have not operated within a shared conception about the essential rules of the game in the system, about the legitimacy or illegitimacy of various actors, about the importance of limited aspirations, and of compensation, balance, and moderation. Views of the meaning of history and of its future evolution have differed fundamentally. For the Soviets, the *status quo* has no ideological or moral legitimacy. For the United States and some of its allies, regimes based on traditions and practices other than those encompassed within liberalism have only dubious legitimacy and sometimes no legitimacy at all. Concrete issues become imbued with transcendental importance, symbolic of the major actors' prestige, reputation for meeting commitments, and indicative of adherence to fundamental political values. Quemoy and Matsu, two little islands of no particular importance off the coast of China, quickly become a test of the US will and resolve to counter "communist aggression." The reforms of the Prague spring were viewed in Moscow as imperialism combined with reaction, both potentially mortal threats to the interests of the working class throughout the socialist commonwealth. In short, issues quickly escalate into mega-issues, laden with all sorts of symbolic, ideological, and status connotations.

In this sort of system, it is difficult to imagine fertile opportunities for the operation of conflict resolution mechanisms such as those embedded in the Charter of the United Nations. Indeed, the history of that organisation in dealing with cold war issues and crises has been dismal, and there is no trend in an upward direction to suggest contrary conclusions in the foreseeable future. The technical literature on conflict resolution says little about this type of intractable conflict. Its focus on the mechanics of third party intervention into conflicts which are compromisable is not sufficiently broad to encompass the etiology and dynamics of cold war syndromes.

Cold war conflicts are multi-dimensional. They have the attributes of rivalry, competition, conflict, added to concerns of leadership, status, prestige, and reputation for meeting commitments. Above all, there is the arms racing aspect that has a built-in momentum fuelled by scientific research, by the expectation of developing weapons systems that will "solve" the national security problem, by giant military–industrial–scientific complexes committed to the technological quick-fix, by ever more sophisticated (if not always more effective) weapons, and by the publicists of the myth that the adversary is just waiting for an opportunity to launch a disarming first strike. The whole national security edifice is sustained intellectually by a phalanx of academic and think-tank strategists whose analyses are noted for their bare-bones logic, construction of scenarios that are divorced from the real world of international politics, and ethnocentrism. The establishments feed upon each other, each dedicated to peace but also convinced that the adversary is committed to the opposite.

Today there are few concrete issues that divide the Soviet and American competitors. (I have used the term *cold war syndrome* to indicate sets of predispositions and attitudes, as well as institutionalised forms of conducting rivalries. The comments, though amended in each case, would apply as well to Israel–Arab relations, Iraq–Iran, India–Pakistan, and perhaps Greece–Turkey. I will discuss only the Soviet–American relationship.) The problem of Berlin, once the source of at least three post-war crises, has been resolved in a fashion that provides only low prospects for flaring up. The succession in Yugoslavia has been completed without Soviet intervention—one of the great fears of western Soviet-watchers in the 1970s. The CSCE (Conference on Security and Cooperation in Europe) process has lent legitimacy to the post-war boundary settlements, and its attendant series of confidence-building measures provides at least some margin of safety as far as the significance of military manoeuvres is concerned. The "lessons of Afghanistan" will probably act as constraints on future Soviet policy-makers in somewhat the same way as the "lessons of Vietnam" have constrained American options in Central America. There are elements of military rivalry in the Middle East and in the northwest Pacific, but these do not revolve around concrete territorial issues or even mortal threats to the great powers' allies in the regions. There are concerns about the "Finlandisation" of Western Europe, but these are based on faulty understanding of the Soviet–Finnish relationship, and on highly skewed assessments of Soviet conventional military capabilities on the continent.

Despite the lack of concrete issues as a source of Soviet–American conflict, the cold war continues in many guises. Ideological incompatibilities play a significant role, but they do not offer a sufficient explanation for persisting mutual hostilities, lack of trust, and arms competition. After all, the United States has been able to fashion a tolerable relationship with China, whose formal commitment to socialism has not eroded despite substantial experimentation both in foreign and domestic policies. Differences on human rights problems do not account for the continuities either, although from the western perspective, they do underline the fundamental incompatibilities between the two systems. Trade competition plays little or no role in the relationship. We are left, then, with historical memories, symbols such as the Berlin wall, the competition for influence in the Third World, a continuing lack of trust, different perspectives on the roots of political legitimacy, and in particular, the arms race.

The existing literature on conflict resolution offers little guidance about the means of overcoming these problems. Broader analyses, which locate the sources of the cold war in general categories encompassing domestic political institutions, economic systems, and inabilities to meet peoples' aspirations, may be correct (see Burton, 1984), but there is no way we can test them, nor do they provide practical guidelines for policy-makers. The dismantling or radical alteration of domestic political/social/economic institutions is an old nostrum for peace, but it is hardly realistic. Nor does it suggest a sound diagnosis, since numerous empirical studies show that there are no significant correlations between types of political and economic systems and nations' war-proneness. After all, it was Alexis de Tocqueville—and not Joseph Stalin or Harry Truman—who predicted the Soviet–American rivalry at a time when their domestic institutions were vastly different. More general theories of international politics argue that the status of super-powerhood makes conflict between the leading states inevitable. Power and war-proneness do correlate, but Burton takes a more attractive stance in suggesting that something can be done about it. Power determinism can only breed fatalism.

If neither technical quick-fixes, whether of the weapons or conflict resolution types, nor broad programmes requiring fundamental social, economic, and political restructuring provide practical guidelines for ameliorating the most dangerous aspects of the cold war, what alternatives remain? At least three come to mind: (1) the adversaries will "learn" their way out of the most serious dilemmas and threats; (2) structural changes in the world economy, combined with changing bases of leadership, status, and prestige, will force the protagonists to place decreasing emphasis on traditional-style power politics; and (3) arms control/disarmament agreements will have significant potential for reducing mistrust and "spilling over" into the diplomatic realm. Though I will discuss these separately, all three are probably combined. The discussion, while optimistic, does not suggest any form of determinism. Significant changes in personnel, political–strategic aspirations, or weapons systems could alter the analysis in significant ways. I am discussing possibilities, not certainties.

Learning Curve

There is evidence that the cold war protagonists have learned a great deal through their post-war experiences with conflicts and crises. Christer Jonsson's study of the behaviour of the superpowers (1984) suggests that there are significant differences between the ways in which the Soviet Union and the United States handled their crises in the late 1940s and 1950s, and their subsequent record in the 1960s and 1970s. The parties have learned increasingly sophisticated means of bargaining and managing crises so as to reduce the risks of escalation. There is, for example, an increasing appreciation of the costs of poor communication, the risks involved in attempts to humiliate the adversary, the importance of signalling commitments in such a way that policy options are not reduced to war or surrender, and the necessity of employing decision-making procedures that check for misperceptions, incomplete information, and many other faults that can give rise to poor decisions. Compared to military advice that in the eighteenth and nineteenth centuries usually underlined the necessity for taking quick military action, the record in the post-war period, at least for the United States, shows that military advice has usually been on the side of prudence, caution, and the use of armed force only as a last resort and in a measured manner (Betts, 1977). One does not know the secrets of the

Kremlin, but there is little evidence that, despite highly augmented capabilities, the Soviets have become greater risk-takers (Adomeit, 1979). However, the Soviets have become adept at "signalling" with military forces. This is in the tradition of all great powers. The United States leads in the incidence of non-violent uses of military force, including various forms of gunboat diplomacy. (See Blechman, 1978; Cable, 1981; and Kaplan, 1981.) It may be premature to speculate on the long term, but surely there is some significance to the lack of a Soviet–American military crisis since 1973, whereas in the late 1940s, the 1950s, and the early 1960s war scares occurred every two or three years.

More recent trends and events in Moscow and Washington also give rise to limited optimism. Despite the early Reagan administration's cold war rhetoric, vigorous arms buildup, development of provocative military strategies for the north Atlantic and northwest Pacific, and a seemingly limited interest on arms control questions, the realities of cold war politics have come to bear upon decision-making in Washington. The Reagan administration has been pushed and shoved into summit meetings, arms negotiations, re-establishment of cultural relations, and many other measures that were anathema to the unreconstructed cold warriors of the early 1980s. The external and domestic constraints on American policies have been extensive and effective. Although in other areas of policy (law of the sea, for example), Washington has taken the stance of unilateralism, pursuing its interests with scant regard for the larger community, there seems to have developed a respect for the risks involved in brinkmanship and a certain caution in committing American military resources to conflict situations abroad. Even the former Secretary of Defense Caspar Weinberger—who otherwise displayed most of the attitudes connected with the cold war syndrome—urged the President to commit American troops only in highly circumscribed situations, including strong support for such actions by the American people and Congress.

The learning curve appears to apply no less in the case of the Soviet Union. Perhaps the most significant fact of the 1980s was a non-event: the non-intervention (military) of the Soviet Union in the Polish situation. The ideological implications of the Solidarity movement were enormous; indeed, it can be argued that they constituted a challenge, to socialist orthodoxy and the position of the workers' parties throughout the socialist commonwealth, that was far more serious than the threats represented by the forces of Alexander Dubcek in Czechoslovakia in 1968. The takeover by the Polish military did put an end to militant *political* action by Solidarity, but that was probably the result of a fundamental strategic error on the part of Solidarity. Until it sought to dismantle the political leadership of the Communist Party (PWP), there is evidence that the Polish regime *and* the Soviet Union would have accepted a free, independent trade union movement whose objectives were limited to concerns of the workplace. By initially acknowledging the status of Solidarity as a legitimate working class movement, the authorities implied that the Communist Party was not the sole representative of working class interests—a heresy of monumental proportions. The reasons for Soviet restraint in Poland were no doubt numerous (including concern about the inevitable western economic boycott of both Poland and the Soviet Union), but whatever the reasons, we see a distinct break from the pattern of Soviet intervention in East Germany in 1953, Hungary in 1956, and Czechoslovakia in 1968.

Mikhail Gorbachev's domestic and foreign policies have also provided grounds for guarded optimism. With the exception of the Soviet position on the Strategic Defence Initiative (SDI), the Russians for all practical purposes have accepted all the major American positions on arms control and disarmament—thus putting some NATO allies in the embarrassing position of having to put up or shut up. Soviet acceptance of intrusive inspection procedures—once totally anathema to the Kremlin—is also a notable step forward, not just because it represents a major concession, but also because it signals the Soviet acceptance of a major requirement for *any* effective arms control and disarmament measures: the generation of trust. If one compares contemporary Soviet attitudes and diplomacy on arms questions with positions put forward in the 1950s and 1960s, then the changes have been monumental.

While at the rhetorical level the Soviet commitment to the revolutionary cause abroad has not diminished—peaceful coexistence does not terminate historical processes and traditional revolutionary roles—at the level of action and policy the Russians have come to accept the main contours of the international system, they have incorporated its "rules of the game" in their foreign policy thinking, and in many respects they have become supporters of those norms rather than detractors and destroyers. The Soviet Union's priorities, despite the rhetoric, have become more self-centred. Revolution abroad and the search for more client states—always an expensive process with dubious rewards—seem to have taken a lower priority compared to the necessity for reform at home.

Structural Changes in World Economy

The second approach focuses on the diplomatic consequences of fundamental transformations taking place in the world economy. We have seen numerous analyses of the reforms attempted and instituted under Gorbachev's leadership. Explanations emphasise the fossilised structure of the command economy. Projections for the future suggest a strong need for change. But perhaps the reforms sought in the Soviet Union and China are symptomatic of a broader change occurring in the international system, one that may have profound consequences on the nature of international relations and particularly on the etiology and character of international conflict. For centuries the prime concern of states has been to provide security. Even regimes with blatantly expansionist programmes often justified them as means of coping with external threats. Welfare and commercial opportunities, while always prominent in the calculations of diplomacy, for the most part were matters of lower priority. When there was an incompatibility between security and welfare broadly conceived—the old guns versus butter dilemma—security predominated. There is unfortunately little systematic evidence that for most states the priorities have been reversed, but one could make the case that the provision of welfare and the pursuit of commercial opportunities have assumed such central importance to the legitimacy and continuity of regimes that the relative emphasis on the two values has shifted in favour of the latter. In the West, there is pronounced opposition to increased defence spending, particularly among those that do not share official American perspectives on the Soviet "threat." Those who are attempting to commit more than one percent of Japan's GNP to defence are having a difficult time breaching the symbolic barrier. In Europe, justification for maintaining intermediate range (INF) missiles has been as much economic as strategic; the costs of mounting conventional defences are seen as prohibitive compared to nuclear deterrence which is much cheaper.

Since the 1970s, international relations have been increasingly defined in economic and technological terms. Rivalry and competition among the industrial countries no longer focus on territory, claims to inherited titles, control over strategic terrain, and the like. Technological leadership is what counts, and not just because such leadership can be translated into military hardware. Technological leadership means jobs, social welfare programmes, prestige, status, and all the other paraphernalia that are associated with economic modernisation and the transformations of the information revolution. Put in other terms, a great power today can no longer sustain that title by virtue of a massive military machine alone.

The reforms in the Soviet Union may reflect a realisation that parity of nuclear and other military capabilities is not enough. The Russians must have great concern for their status as a superpower when Japan's economy threatens to out-produce that of the Soviet Union; when Nikita Khrushchev's boasts about the Soviet economy "burying" American capitalism have long been buried themselves; when the European Community is trying to find ways to eliminate scandalous agricultural surpluses while the Soviet Union cannot even feed itself; and when the Soviet Union has a trade structure more reminiscent of the so-called "dependent" Third World countries—importing technology and exporting raw materials and semi-finished goods. To put it bluntly, the Soviet Union, looking ahead, must see itself fading fast in a race where technological and scientific achievements increasingly define who will be the diplomatic leaders of the age.

The United States faces similar dilemmas but in less pronounced ways. The Reagan administration's extensive military buildup has been partly at the expense of numerous social programmes, a balanced budget, a strong dollar, and a favourable balance of trade. The choice of funding defence expenditures by compromising welfare goals and commercial research and development can be sustained where there is an immediate threat to national security. But how long will Americans opt for guns instead of technical–industrial–trade leadership when the major adversary is conducting a reasonably successful peace campaign, and when all the inflated and mendacious figures about the growing Soviet military "threat" are held up to empirical inquiry (Schloming, 1987)? One has the feeling that the balance between welfare, commercial, research, and investment priorities on the one hand, and defence priorities on the other, will shift soon after the end of the Reagan administration. The alternative, to reassert American industrial leadership through protectionism, is likely to backfire as economic warfare and rivalry could spill over into the defence domain. Alliances whose members are at each others' economic throats are not likely to be very effective military coalitions.

Susan Strange has summed up well in a recent critical review the fundamental transformation that is taking place, of which recent reforms in China and the Soviet Union are only manifestations: ". . . Hinsley's shrewd observation that change in the international system is such that leading states may come to abstain from war with each other . . . might be not only because of technology (nuclear weapons) but also because the globalisation of markets is in the process of transforming the competition between states from one for control over territory to one for scientific and technical pre-eminence." (Strange, 1987: 400). Proxy wars, military rivalry and occasional crises may occur—no structural change happens overnight—but the combination of the acknowledged risks involved in nuclear confrontations, and the changing bases of international leadership, status, and prestige, may render direct war less likely, if not impossible.[5]

Arms Control and Disarmament

The third avenue for ameliorating the multi-dimensional conflict we call the cold war is through arms control and disarmament. Here the prospects are brighter than they have been for a long time, although it requires very astute mental gymnastics to make the case that nuclear disarmament is consistent with a unilateral SDI programme. (The opponents of SDI do not have their act together either: if they are convinced that SDI is technically impossible, then it can hardly be termed a threat to mutual deterrence.) Since the literature on disarmament and arms control is so extensive and well-known, there is no need to summarise it here. There is also a burgeoning literature on technology and the problem of accidental nuclear war. This is a highly technical literature which I am unable to evaluate.

Our broader concern is with the consequences of arms control and disarmament on cold war patterns of behaviour. We can only speculate on these, of course. But just as the technical literature on conflict resolution cannot offer comprehensive guidelines for handling all sorts of international conflicts, neither can we assume that disarmament measures by themselves will be sufficient to erode the habits of thought and action associated with the cold war syndrome. Moreover, if our expectations about the consequences of disarmament are too high, we sow the seeds of rearmament. We should be concerned that "quick-fix" solutions—which do not bring about all the anticipated and totalistic results—are not therefore used as a justification for starting a new nuclear arms race. No sound diagnosis of the cold war can be based on the assumption that the arms race by itself causes the syndrome. Therefore, it is unlikely that termination of the arms race will provide a total solution. What, exactly, can we expect from disarmament programmes such as those advanced by Gorbachev and Reagan?

The first consequence would be a reduction of the probabilities of accidental nuclear war. While I do not share the fatalistic view of a statistical certainty that nuclear weapons will someday be used, even less sanguine projections provide cause for immense concern. Technical and human malfunctions, combined with incredibly short decision-making times available in a crisis, are recipes for disaster. Short missile flight times force policy-makers to veer towards "launch-on-warning" strategies. Decapitation targeting policies make a mockery of all the assumptions underlying strategies of nuclear war-fighting; they are likely to assure escalation rather than to inhibitit. Removal of INF weapons addresses some of these problems, and presumably "deep cuts" in strategic launchers and/or warheads will somehow reduce the probabilities of technical malfunction. But targeting options and strategies for actually fighting nuclear wars are not solely a function of the numbers and types of weapons. Arms cuts may have little impact in these areas, which remain mired in unsolvable contradictions and pre-1945 concepts of war.

Second, nuclear disarmament would render obsolete that favourite nightmare of theoretical strategists, the disarming first strike. This should have immediate and important consequences regarding perceptions of threat, and thereby, levels of trust. While the apocalyptic first strike scenario has never been convincing when we look at the real world, it has developed a reality of its own so that presidents and general secretaries have to respond to it, usually in the form of augmenting the numbers of strategic weapons, some of which, while declared to be retaliatory only, have their own first strike implications. The biggest debate, however, is what to do about retaliatory forces. In a regime of total disarmament, they go as well, which means that the load of deterrence will be shifted entirely to conventional forces.

A third consequence, then, is that zero options could make the world safer for conventional war. Whatever the dangers of nuclear weapons, they have undoubtedly increased the risks associated with aggressive foreign policy behaviour. Prudence takes on a new meaning in the nuclear age. Nuclear disarmament is not likely to lead to a security *nirvana*. It will involve, rather, a very difficult trade off: lower risks associated with aggressive behaviour, and therefore higher probabilities of the direct use of force between the Soviet Union and the United States, in exchange for a vastly lower probability of a nuclear exchange. Nuclear disarmament by itself may well bring into sharper focus real or imagined imbalances at the conventional level. Politicians and military leaders will not be less concerned with issues of national security just because the spectre of nuclear armageddon has receded. International politics will not end with the elimination of nuclear weapons. Insecurity, humiliation in a crisis, "blackmail" accomplished with conventional arms and/or massive conventional interventions abroad could force the abrogation or abandonment of nuclear disarmament treaties, thus starting a new race. The early stages of such a competition would be particularly harrowing since a lead of, let us say, 10 missiles to 2 or 3 could provide strong incentives for pre-emptive first strikes. A margin of several hundred missiles or warheads on a base of thousands creates no such dangers.

A fourth consequence, which follows from the above, is that levels of spending on arms could increase rather than decrease. If power becomes measured solely on the basis of conventional capabilities, then pressures for parity and possibly superiority would be similar to those that have been based on counts of missiles and warheads. But conventional weapons and their attending manpower requirements are generally more expensive than nuclear weapons, so the final bill may well be higher. Disarmament should have the broad objective of contributing to the diminution of all aspects of Soviet–American conflict, competition, and rivalry. It is likely, therefore, that steps will have to be taken to curb the growth of conventional capabilities as well. Nuclear disarmament could well have important "spill-over" effects into some aspects of the relationship, but saving money and terminating all forms of military racing are probably not among them.

A fifth consequence of nuclear disarmament would be to hinder the spread of nuclear weapons. The major exchange in the Non-Proliferation Treaty (NPT) is the promise of the non-nuclear signatories to forego developing nuclear arsenals in exchange for nuclear disarmament by those who already possess them. So far, the nuclear states have not kept their side of the bargain. Their failure to do so erodes the legitimacy of the NPT and provides ready excuses for the Pakistans of the world to move ahead, at least in the domain of research. Nuclear disarmament, or perhaps even significant arms control measures between the present club members, could provide important incentives for collaborating to suffocate horizontal proliferation.

CONCLUSION

Let me now summarise the argument. The technical literature on conflict resolution is based on assumptions, rooted in classical liberal views of international relations, that do not seem germane to certain kinds of conflicts. Where there are concrete issues at stake (as in the case of territorial disputes), where the protagonists maintain limited objectives whose fulfilment is not at the expense of the core interests and values of other parties, and where the chances of military victory are remote or extremely costly, there third party intervention can be very helpful. Creative mediation can fashion settlements that bring relative if not equal benefits to both sides. But such intervention is not always necessary nor even desirable, particularly where fundamental change rather than compromise is justified. Some conflicts can be "settled" only by force and time, where the protagonists learn to live with a situation which in many instances has been created by coercion and violence. The emphasis on war avoidance at all costs may be incompatible with a commitment to conflict resolution, if by that term we mean a final settlement. One is not necessarily presenting an apologia for killing in pointing out that war may be a necessary prelude to successful conflict resolution. And we must also face the dilemma that some wars are truly just, particularly if negotiations, mediation, and other techniques consistent with the Charter of the United Nations have been tried, but failed. The broader question is how we arrange or manage change so that it can take place *without* recourse to arms. This part of the task has generally been ignored in the literature.

The literature is also deficient, as are the constitutions of international organisations, when it comes to multidimensional conflicts of the cold war type. These conflicts are not rooted solely in incompatible positions on concrete issues. Distorted images, excessive fears and distrust, fundamental divergences on political, economic and/or religious values, and vast bureaucratic–scientific–intellectual establishments committed as much to perpetuating conflict as to peace are in play. There is the obduracy of "true believers," and their grandiose plans of regional or universal conquest. For these types of conflicts, we need broad, sociological analyses and better understanding of the great contests between civilisations.

The United Nations can play a crucial role in conflicts and disputes between many states. But it, like its predecessor, has not been up to the task of coping with those bent on the destruction of the system nor with states imbued with cold war syndromes. The League of Nations assumed a community of nations dedicated to peaceful changes. The dictators believed in fundamentally different values, for which appeasement was an inappropriate response.

Deterrence has more or less worked in the post-war world, but unfortunately it carries with it great risks. The challenge of the future is to find means to reduce significantly those risks without inviting a proliferation of conventional wars; of changing attitudes and institutions characterised by cold war syndromes; and of developing means short of war and coercion that can help to bring about changes in the international system that are required by justice and equity.

132

NOTES

1. Another study lists 157 inter-state wars and 209 civil wars between 1740 and 1974. The data are not so carefully defined as in the Small–Singer study, but they do include wars in China prior to the twentieth century (Bouthoul and Carrere, 1976).

2. Perhaps a distinction can be made between conquest and secession; most national liberation movements are the latter. In our model, however, party A's secession constitutes a fundamental alteration of the *status quo*. Most central authorities have viewed secession as no less of a threat than foreign invasion.

3. The record of the League of Nations is considerably better than that of the United Nations. Its organs considered 66 cases ranging from technical-legal disputes to major cases of aggression. Twenty were referred to other agencies. Eleven cases involved settlement by dictation or conquest contrary to League procedures. The League was successful in the remaining 35 cases (76 percent). Although the League has often been called a failure, in fact it was a highly successful organisation in all conflicts and disputes except those where the dictators were resolved on conquest. The UN has been significantly less effective. Data in Wright (1942, vol. II, Appendix XXXIV: 1429–1431).

4. In the Great Northern War between Sweden and the Russian-led coalition of Tsar Peter, Charles XII developed the radical idea of unseating the elected King of Poland, Augustus of Saxony, in the event of military victory. Charles' advisers were concerned at this seeming deviation from custom, but acquiesced when Charles noted that removal of an elected king through military means was permissible, whereas it would not be allowed in the case of a hereditary monarch.

5. Another observer of international politics has made the same point, but without the implication that there is in fact a structural change occurring in the system: "Whenever economy was made the sole content of our people's life, thus suffocating the ideal virtues, the State collapsed. . . . that [the virtues of sacrifice for the community] have really nothing whatsoever to do with economics is shown by the simple realisation that man never sacrifices himself for them; that means: one does not die for business, but for ideals." (Hitler, 1939: 199-200). Hitler was of course wrong. Whether Strange is right remains to be seen.

9

Controlling International Crises in the 1980s

Victor A. Kremenyuk

The first half of the 1980s saw deepening tensions in international relations which threatened to develop into a crisis. There appeared certain grounds for optimism in the second half of the decade. The Soviet–US summits in Geneva and in Reykjavik, meetings at the ministerial and experts levels, the attempts to ease progress to a settlement of disputes, gave rise to the hope that the international atmosphere would change for the better before the decade ends.

The problem of international crises should be again considered in this context. The fact that there were no serious upheavals in the first half of the 1980s although tensions continued to escalate, does not mean that the world will be immune from them in the future. Crises are not always produced by a purposeful policy of states. They may also break out spontaneously, as a result of an accidental combination of factors or the escalation of regional conflicts. If world tensions are high, they are bound to have global repercussions and to engender a global threat.

SOURCES OF CRISES

Much has been written about international crises. Researchers have studied their mechanism, driving forces, their escalation and de-escalation, the questions of control and decision-making. The sources of crises were not broadly discussed. Usually, the researchers and practitioners were following the line of thinking described by Thomas Schelling in the late 1950s: "We are all, in fact, participants in international conflict, and we want to 'win' it in a proper sense" (1960: 3).

Even at that time those who knew more about the potential results of a nuclear conflict, called into doubt the feasibility of winning it. Now the majority of researchers believe that there will be neither winners nor losers in a nuclear conflict if it happens. The governments of the nuclear powers share this view. So, it is even more important to establish the sources of a potential conflict. Since such a conflict is inadmissible, it is essential to look for ways of preventing it, and this cannot be done without finding out its sources.

The easiest way would be to write that a crisis or conflict is engendered by a policy which is based on the use or threat of force as the main means of settling international disputes. This is true, of course. Such a definition would be correct in all times, and remains adequate now. And to rule out conflicts, it is crucial to renounce the policy which creates a conflict or threat of such. However, this is a long-term task, considering today's realities and the scale of the difficulties blocking the road to its solution. Meanwhile, the issue of preventing or settling crises is immediate. It may emerge before the leaders of the nations in the near future and they will have to settle it without delay, regardless of the numerous difficulties and contradictions which divide the countries of the world.

Hence, the very topicality of this problem suggests a need to single out those causes of crises, which could be removed in the near future, and the removal of which will help prevent world war. Therefore, one should concentrate on those sources of potential crisis which may prompt political leaders to adopt decisions that can lead to such a crisis or aggravate it.

Summing up everything which has been written on the subject in the last few years and even decades, one can single out several direct causes of a potential crisis: misinterpretation (deliberate or not) of the actions or intentions of the other side which leads to an incorrect assessment of the situation, and to the advancement of goals that can only worsen the situation; deliberately false or erroneous assessment of the alignment of forces which can also lead to fallacious decisions; exaggeration of the threat to national interests, prompting the people in charge to over-react, which may eventually result in a crisis; and, finally, a combination of unforeseen factors, something gaining increasing importance as such factors can put the great powers up against a crisis which has broken out and developed without their involvement.

Probably, the rapidly changing world situation will produce more causes of crises. But even those already mentioned are enough to make us realise that the threat of a crisis in relations between the two world systems persists. These causes are linked with the lack of confidence in relations between the great powers and major military–political alliances, and the clear inadequacy of cooperation which could restore such confidence and turn it into a norm for today and tomorrow.

The seeming simplicity of the causes which engender international crises with all the ensuing grievous consequences should not mislead anyone. In his 1986 New Year address to the American people, General Secretary of the CPSU Central Committee Mikhail Gorbachev attached much importance to confidence. Speaking about the duty of our powers to guarantee to the whole world an opportunity to enter the third millennium without fear, he stressed: "We shall hardly manage such a goal if we do not begin to accumulate by bits the vaulable capital—confidence between states and nations. And it is essential to start eliminating the existing deficit of confidence in Soviet–US relations" (*Pravda,* 1 January 1986).

The question of confidence, or at least of mutual understanding, is of key importance for avoiding a crisis. The ideological contradictions between the two systems can never be settled either diplomatically or militarily, or in any other way, because they stem from a different view of history and a different understanding of its perspective.

Military confrontation between the two world systems is inadmissible because it threatens to escalate into an all-out suicidal nuclear conflict. Marshal of the Soviet Union N. Ogarkov has noted: "It would be practically impossible to keep a nuclear war within any limits. No matter how limited the use of nuclear weapons might be, it will inevitably prompt the sides to bring into play immediately their entire nuclear arsenals" (1985).

Consequently, both sides are "doomed" by the current situation to long-term coexistence and peaceful competition which rules out military solutions to their disputes. In such conditions the lack of proper confidence is turning into a major cause of persisting tensions and continued arms race, which create the atmosphere in which crises are most likely to occur. This is a kind of a system which is reproducing an aggravation of the situation, and keeping the entire world community on the brink of a crisis.

THE MECHANISM OF POSSIBLE CRISES

An international crisis is a situation which has grown in the soil of real contradictions and has resulted from the impossibility to reconcile them and which, therefore, quickly leads the confronting sides to military conflict.

The two world wars which took place in our century were preceded by international crises. The diplomats managed to settle some of them and to prevent their development into wars. But in 1914 and 1939 there occurred crises which were not prevented from developing into large-scale military clashes. Thus, the politicians of our century have learnt a first lesson, namely that it is possible to prevent quite a number of crises from developing into wars but, if proper measures are not taken in time, there can finally occur a crisis which will be followed inevitably by war. The politicians drew from this lesson the conclusion that during a crisis the level of responsibility for the decisions adopted sharply increases. And researchers paid attention to the fact that a crisis is an extremely unstable situation requiring an unavoidable decision: either a settlement, or war.

The second lesson drawn from the study of the international crises of the twentieth century was that such crises can develop into military clashes in different ways. The simplest case is the deliberately inspired crisis followed by aggression by the side which has declared its reliance on military force as the basis of its national policy. But there may arise more complex situations in which, as a result of the interference by the powers and coalitions struggling in the international arena, a local incident in an atmosphere of general tension and lack of confidence gives rise to new contradictions and becomes the epicentre of a general crisis. This type of crisis is known as a "Sarajevo scenario" and is a reminder, to politicians inclined to attain their aims by all means, of the dangers of ignoring the consequences of their actions on a larger scale.

The sober-minded politicians concluded from this crisis first of all that aggression must be prevented and the persons responsible for it punished. This conclusion formed the basis of the charges against the leaders of the Nazi Reich by the Nuremberg International Tribunal. It also formed the basis of the work of the UN mechanism created in 1945 for maintaining international peace and security. As for researchers, they used the results of the lesson for preparing scenarios of possible international crises and for shaping corresponding recommendations on their prevention.

The history of the international crises in our century has taught a third lesson. Its essence is that in the development of any crisis there may emerge a stage at which it gets beyond the control of the decision-makers, and further develops according to its own laws. As the crisis aggravates, the number of accompanying factors that begin to operate becomes so great that the crisis situation becomes a super-complex system with a control mechanism, the resolving capacity of which is several times lower than that of the crisis.

The conclusions drawn by politicians from this lesson found expression in the attempts to build up a control system, both national and international, which could at least give a hope of controlling the crisis. The researchers offered the politicians a whole package of decisions which were considered capable of ensuring effective control over a crisis.

But, despite all this, an international political crisis has not ceased to be a most dangerous situation causing well-grounded concern in government departments, in the academic community and, naturally, among the public at large. The complexity of each specific crisis situation keeps increasing parallel with the growth in the influence of such factors as the technological standards of the weapons systems which can be used if the efforts to settle a crisis fail; the increasing complexity of the mechanism of international relations; above all, the growth in the number of participants in them, as well as the number of pressing international problems. And there exists a high degree of risk that the system of settlement would fail in a crisis.

NUCLEAR RISK ADDED

The factor of nuclear missile weapons which defy mankind in the management of its own problems relating to the danger of a military conflict plays a special, even unique role in this respect.

First of all, the nuclear weapons factor itself has caused a dangerous and protracted crisis in the system of international relations. This crisis began after the bombings of Hiroshima and Nagasaki in August 1945 and has lasted for more than forty years. Its essence is that international relations, as a sphere in which nuclear weapons can be used, are under constant strain resulting from the pressure of this factor, which aggravates knots of contradictions complex enough as it is.

Ordinary, "traditional" international crises take place against the background of this crisis. They are outbursts of tension, protuberances of the invisible activity in the depth of world politics. But, since they are inseparable from the essence of the contradictions which have engendered them, the nuclear weapons factor has made its imprint on these crises too.

Thus the 'cost' of the danger bred by a crisis has increased immeasurably. The development of an international crisis into a war now threatens not tens or even hundreds of millions of people but, in effect, all civilisation.

Second, the delivery vehicles of nuclear weapons, which have emerged as a result of the development of these weapons, have maximally tightened the time of a crisis, the time for its settlement and for adoption of appropriate decisions. With computers and management science, the political and military leaders have somewhat enhanced the effectiveness of the utilisation of this time but, despite this, its intensiveness is already coming close to the limits of human ability to take reasonable and well-grounded decisions.

Third, the load on the peoples' psyche, both those who make decisions in a crisis and those who show well-warranted concern over its development, has dramatically increased. Nuclear crisis or, to put it in other words, an international crisis in the nuclear era, has surpassed all the previous types of crises by far in all its characteristics—the danger, the short duration and the difficulty of control—and has set new problems for decision makers.

To begin with, it has demonstrated the very limited character of the national or unilateral means of settling crises. Logically, one of the lessons of the Caribbean crisis of 1962 was the Soviet–US accord on the establishment of a direct communication link ("hot line") in 1963. Furthermore, the nuclear crisis has shown the total invalidity of "crisis diplomacy"—it is senseless to try to deter the other side by a nuclear strike threat because such a threat is reciprocal. The nuclear crisis has shown the need for an even more responsible attitude to the decisions made—it can go out of control at much earlier stages of development than before because of its short duration and very dangerous character.

SDI—Destabilising Factor

In this context, it is quite understandable why the prospect of President Ronald Reagan's "Strategic Defence Initiative" (SDI) causes well-grounded criticism in the USSR. Without analysing the details of this initiative, it is necessary to note that the two countries' approaches to the SDI issue are diametrically opposed. The logic of the American side's reasoning of a need for SDI is engendered by the logic of the theory of "mutual guaranteed destruction." Despite all the camouflage of the arguments in its favour, it is clear that its aim is to build up the US strategic potential and, hence, according to this logic, to boost "strategic stability."

From the Soviet viewpoint, translation of SDI into reality would contradict the logic underlying the ABM Treaty of 1972, logic aimed at stabilising relations on the basis of equal security and stronger confidence; and would also dramatically increase instability in a possible crisis because it would make the American side feel (whether correctly or incorrectly is a question of a different order) that it is secure compared with the USSR. The above-said sources of possible crisis make it perfectly clear that such a feeling would only promote decisions to aggravate the crisis. The US administration either cannot or does not want to understand this, being under exaggerated expectations from SDI.

Besides that, introduction of SDI would raise two other major obstacles to avoiding crises. First, the time for decisions would be further reduced. Intensive elaboration of ready scenarios of possible actions and enhancement of the role of computers in the process of decision-making, which makes those who take decisions lagely dependent on pre-computed scenarios, is considered to be a way out of this situation. Second, the increasing complexity of the technological components of strategic systems increases by several orders the danger of an error in these systems, an error which could cause a crisis reaction on the political level.

The Soviet Scientists for Peace Committee prepared a report entitled "Strike Space Weapons and International Security" which gives an all-round analysis of the possibilities of SDI and of its influence on the strategic situation. The Soviet experts hold the view that in the event of development and deployment of the "Star Wars" weapons, the risk of an outbreak of nuclear war "will increase, specifically because of fortuitous errors in the evaluation of the strategic situation as a result of the newly-emerged self-activation of the space echelons of the large-scale anti-missile system."

STRATEGIC STABILITY

There are SDI advocates in the United States who claim that its implementation would have a "stabilising effect" on Soviet–US relations. But I think that it would lead to even greater mistrust in bilateral relations, making crises more likely.

Strategic stability is a complex macrosystem of different parameters of the alignment of forces which testify to the rough parity of the sides in opportunities and positions. It thereby ensures relative stability of the international situation. It includes obvious material parameters (the strength and characteristics of armed forces, their capabilities, groupings, reserves, etc.) and not so obvious factors like the interests and intentions of the sides, their cooperation, opportunities for verification, and the level of confidence. Put together, they testify to military stability based on rough parity and to political stability resting on the principles of equal security and equal consideration of the interests of the sides.

Thus it is transparently clear that the problems arising in Soviet–US relations should be settled politically on the basis of documents signed by both sides. The Soviet government fully understands the importance of such settlement and by its political initiatives tries to suggest an acceptable basis of relationships to the American administration. It also considers necessary, as was spelled out clearly in General Secretary Gorbachev's article (1987), to include in this process as much of the nations of the world as possible. This could turn the issue of resolution of conflicts into a major international effort.

The US permitted itself not to observe this principle way back in the seventies when it walked out of the talks with the USSR on a number of problems (the Indian Ocean, the conventional arms transfers) or buried in oblivion some of the signed documents (such as the joint statement on the Middle East). By its rhetoric, diplomatic moves, and its decision to test and deploy new components of strategic arms, the Reagan administration has reduced the potential for trust in bilateral relations. The initiative of a group of US senators, who began in 1982 to probe the problems of reducing the risk of nuclear war, was a timely response to some excesses in the policy of the administration which in some cases toughened the dialogue with the USSR beyond any reasonable limits.

The declared goal of the US administration is to ensure strategic stability. But an analysis of more detailed programmes of the administration, especially the SDI, suggests the conclusion that by "stability" it means a certain advantage for the US at both the strategic and regional levels. The administration claimed that it will be ready for a dialogue with the USSR, and, possibly, for agreements only after it achieves such an advantage. In other words, the US government considered it possible to upset the military balance in order to "stabilise" the existing system of relations and thus make it immune to crisis.

Through a set of bold political initiatives at the Reykjavik summit and later [the proposal to single out Intermediate Range Nuclear Forces (INF) and to include into the agreement nuclear weapons with shorter range] the Soviet government moved the US administration to a more serious regard of the problem of stability. It is now understood by both parties that this stability could be enhanced through a lower level of armaments, eliminating a whole class of them and significantly reducing the others. This common understanding has greatly contributed to an increase in mutual trust and to the crisis stabilisation component of the relationship.

The US also justified its bid to upset the military balance by saying that its superiority will produce regional "stability," thus making it possible to "balance out" our relations on a broader plane. But it is clear that in this case the US makes stability in bilateral relations dependent on unexpected turns in world political developments, which makes its sincerity very dubious.

If strategic stability is viewed as absolutely essential for at least the minimum of confidence in Soviet–US relations, then it is obvious that any attempt to change it in one's favour is bound to reduce such confidence and automatically enhance the likelihood of a crisis.

First, the Soviet leaders have stated more than once that they will not allow the existing balance to be upset. The USSR is not seeking any superiority, but will not accept US superiority either. Hence, the arms race will continue and the danger of a crisis will grow accordingly. Second, the spread of military confrontation in the world (which is exactly the result of "horizontal proliferation") will make the situation in Soviet–US relations even more dependent on political developments in other regions.

The experience of the seventies and the findings of the eighties suggest only one conclusion: it is necessary not only to preserve the stability of the military balance, but also to lower its level to the minimum possible for reasonable sufficiency. And it is necessary to hold talks and consultations on a whole range of controversial issues to achieve such mutual understanding as would allow special mechanisms for controlling crises to operate quite effectively.

CRISIS PREVENTION AND SETTLEMENT

One of the main problems which countries now face as a result of the danger of crises in the nuclear/space age is to develop a special regime for the prevention and settlement of crises. This is a demanding task and its fulfilment implies effective solution of military, economic, judicial, social, cultural and technical problems.

The said mechanism already has its foundation—the UN Security Council. The universally recognised United Nations Charter gives it adequate power to ensure the maintenance of peace and security. But the post-war period has shown the need for additional agreements between the great powers, above all the USSR and the USA, which would make it possible to achieve the necessary level of trust and to harmonise procedures for stabilising the situation in a crisis.

In this respect the formation of the Soviet–US hotline in 1963 was just a first step. It was taken further in 1971 in the Soviet–US agreement on measures to modernise it and in subsequent accords. In 1971 the USSR and the USA drew up the Agreement on Measures to Reduce the Risk of Outbreak of Nuclear War, and in 1972 the Agreement on the Prevention of Incidents On and Over the Sea. In 1973 the USSR and the USA signed an Agreement on the Prevention of Nuclear War.

Owing to the efforts of the Soviet government, this system of measures to limit to the utmost the possibility of an accidental or unsanctioned use of nuclear weapons (first and foremost, in a crisis) was extended to cover relations with other nuclear powers. In 1976 an exchange of letters between the foreign ministers of the USSR and France produced the Agreement on the Prevention of Accidental or Unsanctioned Use of Nuclear Weapons. In 1977 the USSR and Britain signed an Agreement on the Prevention of Accidental Nuclear War.

The said measures helped to stabilise international relations and safeguard them against crises involving nuclear powers. The latest crisis in which the threat of the use of nuclear weapons emerged was the crisis triggered off by the 1973 October War in the Middle East.

To reduce the risk of a crisis during the deterioration of the international situation in the first half of the eighties, the Soviet Union unilaterally made a number of commitments. In the summer of 1982, at the UN General Assembly special session on disarmament, the USSR pledged not to use nuclear weapons first. This measure could have reduced the risk of nuclear war if the US administration had reciprocated.

But since it did not, there emerged a dangerous assymetry which, even in the opinion of US specialists, sharply enhanced the "crisis instability" or inability to predict how crises will develop. Apparently, this fact was one of the considerations that evoked concern among the American senators, who in 1982 proposed first studying the readiness of the US crisis-control mechanism, and then the ways in which a crisis might develop.

A realistic assessment of opportunities for settling and preventing international crises in our time implies consideration of at least the following fundamental issues of bilateral relations:

— observance of the principle of equality and mutual security in strategic relations;
— maintenance of strategic equilibrium at the lowest possible level;
— reciprocal respect for each other's legitimate interests, especially in the field of security;
— peaceful settlement of disputes through talks and consultations.

Unilateral gestures of goodwill can only be welcomed, but one should not count on them too much, because the importance of such gestures diminishes if the other side does not reciprocate. One example is the moratorium on nuclear explosions which the USSR announced on 6 August 1985. The US did not follow suit and continued staging underground nuclear tests. The Soviet Union freed itself of this commitment by ending its 18-month unilateral moratorium on nuclear testing on 26 February 1987.

The Soviet–US talks in Geneva, and then the summit meeting in November 1985 showed that both sides agreed in principle to develop relations on the basis of parity and equal security. This is why the text of the joint statement on the results of the meeting between Mikhail Gorbachev and Ronald Reagan on 19–21 November 1985, said that the sides agreed "to study at the expert level the question of centres for nuclear risk reduction, taking into account the issues and developments at the Geneva negotiations...." It read further that they "took satisfaction in such recent steps in this direction as the modernisation of the Soviet–US hotline." This agreement in principle laid the foundation for further talks which finally ended in September 1987 with the signing of a Soviet–US agreement on establishing national nuclear risk reduction centres.

It is obvious that to reduce the risk of nuclear war, and, hence, to create a mechanism for preventing and settling crises, it is not enough to work out certain procedures which facilitate the attainment of this goal. Speaking at the hearings in the Senate Foreign Relations Committee devoted to Resolution 329 (on centres for nuclear risk reduction), its former Chairman Charles H. Percy mentioned two major ways of reducing the risk of nuclear war: talks on reaching agreement on deep and verifiable cuts in nuclear weapons, and talks on elaborating procedures to guard against accidental nuclear conflict.

Prevention and settlement of crises in Soviet–US relations is a difficult political and technical task. Any technical proposals which ignore the political aspect are bound to run into political obstacles, particularly suspicion as regards the intentions of the other side and lack of confidence. Likewise, political agreements, which are not backed by technical measures, may remain paper treaties. So both aspects should be taken into account in order to fulfil this task.

A whole range of common interests of the nations of the world necessitate its solution. We recognise that the task is expedient and solvable and that the necessary technical and diplomatic means are available.

10

In Pursuit of Disarmament

Inga Thorsson

The world finds itself today at a crossroads and must choose its direction. It can continue to pursue the arms race, or it can move with deliberate speed towards a more sustainable international economic and political order. It cannot do both.

That was said by the United Nations Governmental Expert Group on the Disarmament–Development Relationship which in 1981 submitted its report to the UN General Assembly, a report which the Assembly approved at its 32nd session in 1982, with its conclusions and recommendations. Thinking has not advanced very much, if at all, among political leaders since then. It remains to be seen what influence the UN International Conference on the Relationship between Disarmament and Development, held in New York in early autumn 1987, will have on possible advancement, not only in thinking and words, but also in action by governments. I intend to return to this issue.

There were three main conclusions accepted unanimously by the UN Governmental Expert Group. The first I have quoted already. The second reads:

Irrrespective of economic systems and level of economic development all countries would benefit economically from an effective disarmament process. They would thus have a mutual enlightened self-interest in disarmament.

And the third:

In a disarmament situation governments would face certain conversion problems. If solutions to these problems were well planned and prepared, they would cause no serious technical and economic difficulties.

I should like, once again, to state and to emphasise that effective disarmament would bring benefits to *all*. The reason is of course that the militarisation process brings about underdevelopment and/or maldevelopment everywhere, including the richest and most powerful countries.

What comes first and foremost to mind is, however, the effects, in two respects, of the ongoig process of militarisation on too many Third World countries. They are doubly affected: first in proportion to the expenditures they incur themselves, and second due to the disturbing effect of military expenditures on the industralised countries, since their economic interaction with those countries is crucial.

So too is their military interaction. Not least is this reflected in the flow of arms from the industrialised to the developing world, which entails the rapid growth of a military culture. Admittedly, as a direct consequence of the worldwide economic crisis and the closely related debt problems faced by so many countries in the Third World, this trade in arms has declined in recent years. While in the late 1970s the developing countries accounted for 75 percent of arms imports, their share has now declined to 60 percent.

A few more words are necessary on the debt burden of the developing countries, which has now increased to represent 160 percent of their Gross National Product. In a study which I undertook for the Swedish Government a few years ago, it was found that arms imports are responsible for around 25 percent of this debt burden. Another estimate, reported in the 1985 UN Report on the World Social Situation, indicates that in at least four of the twenty countries with the largest foreign debt in 1983, the value of arms imports amounted to 40 percent or more of the rise in debt between 1976 and 1980.

And the effects of the militarisation process on the economic and social development in countries in the South are indeed still there. A number of research reports submitted to the UN Governmental Expert Group show that increased military spending tends to be related to lower investment, to greater tax burdens, to cuts in consumption, to social welfare spending, and to inflation.

The negative effects in social and human terms are also considerable. In one of the reports to the UN Group two American economists estimated, through an econometric model, various social opportunity costs of arms purchases, examining their potential relationship to health and literacy. They found that for an average developing country, with a population of 8.5 million and a GNP per capita of around $350 (in 1970 dollars), the first $200 million of arms imports would add approximately 20 additional infant deaths per 1,000 live births, decrease average life expectancy by 3–4 years, and result in 13–14 fewer literate adults out of every 100.

It can reasonably be assumed that such a deterioration in conditions of human life would also result in increased social tensions and political unrest. And in the unfortunately numerous developing countries ruled by military or authoritarian regimes, this could well be another reason for the use of military force to keep internal tensions and unrest under control.

In its September 1985 issue the *Bulletin of the Atomic Scientists* published a table called Africa Profile, which in a very illuminating way provided evidence for what I have just said. The African country with the highest military budget as a percentage of the state budget also had the lowest life expectancy of all African countries. On the other hand the African country with the lowest military expenditures, in fact 0.0 percent, also had the highest life expectancy figures.

The arms race and world military expenditures are derived from a way of priority-setting which seems to be extremely hazardous. This is particularly so when we lok at the alarming political instability resulting from the neglect of economic, social and human development. Let me just quote a few concrete examples from Ruth Leger Sivard's well known reports on World Military and Social Expenditures:

— there is one soldier per 43 people in the world, one physician per 1,030 people;
— every minute 30 children die from hunger, starvation and disease; every minute the world spends $2.5 million for military purposes;
— the US and the USSR, first in military power, rank 14 and 51 respectively among all nations in their infant mortality rates.

This last example brings me to consider militarisation and maldevelopment as a crucial issue, not only for developing countries in the South, but for the rich industrialised countries in the North—in fact the richest of them—as well.

There is rather clear evidence that the new leadership in the Soviet Union is undertaking a reappraisal of the defence policies that have been pursued so far in that country, although unfortunately we do not have clear facts and figures.

But the same should be the situation in the US, where we have clear facts and figures. Whatever is said by spokesmen for the Reagan administration, the US economy is in serious difficulties. The problems apparent in US civilian industry will remain, and the competitiveness of American products will continue to decline, unless US military expenditures are brought to a standstill, and then reduced. An economy, whose GNP growth has mainly depended on an absurd military build-up, and which devotes around 40 percent of its total Research and Development (R & D)—more than 70 percent of federal R & D funds—to military purposes, thereby denying civil industries the resources badly needed for innovation, modernisation and increased productivity, cannot be rescued by, e.g., a trade war with Japan or Western Europe. Record military expenditures, together with a stubborn refusal to raise taxes, are the main reasons for a budget deficit of around $200 billion. At the same time the trade deficit has increased during the Reagan years from $40 billion to $166 billion. And President Ronald Reagan will in 1989 leave behind a time bomb in the form of federal debts which will have increased at a greater rate than during the years of all his 39 predecessors. All this means that the richest economy in the world has turned into the highest net debtor to the outside world, in the magnitude of $200 billion. And, between 1982–1986, the country's total debt leaped to 200 percent of the rise in GNP.

It is generally acknowledged that the only really safe basis for national security is a strong and sound economy. The US economy is at present not strong and sound. True, it has a strong base, favoured as it has been by a series of fortunate circumstances. But it has misused these circumstances to such an extent, that the time will come, perhaps in the early 1990s, when the degree of maldevelopment brought about by militarisation will compel the administration then in power to change the present course, to reduce military spending and to convert their available and productive resources to civilian production. Before I return to the now highly topical issue called the disarmament–development relationship—particularly so following the recently held UN International Conference on the issue—I should like to follow up on what I just said about conversion by making a brief remark of a more principal character on the importance of conversion planning.

I should like to point to the psychological importance of advance government preparations for conversion, as spelled out already in 1967 by the American psychologist Jerome D. Frank in his book *Sanity and Survival.* He says, *inter alia,* that "If, for instance, a country of significance published detailed plans for a conversion of its weapon industry to civilian production in the event of a future disarmament agreement, this would increase the confidence of other countries in the credibility to disarm."

During many years of work on the disarmament–development issue, I have been convinced of the truth of this statement by Professor Frank. There will undoubtedly be economic, social and human problems connected with a disarmament and conversion process. If governments present at the international disarmament negotiation table were prepared to plan for the solution of these problems through planning the conversion process, it would indeed add considerably to the credibility of their desire to achieve results in the negotiations. As a matter of fact an American economist specialising for many years in this field said some time ago: "If you want to disarm, first plan for conversion." Such unilateral steps would be a major confidence-building measure, improving the international atmosphere without incurring any risk at all. Against this background, it is a pity that governments have not adhered to the General Assembly resolution in 1982, under which governments were urged to undertake national follow-up studies to look into preparations for conversion.

That sentence leads me back to activities within the UN aimed at stimulating governments, at the national level, to promote thinking and action on the disarmament–development relationship, including planning for conversion. What did the UN General Assembly do in this respect at its 37th session in 1982?

In approving the Governmental Group report, including its recommendations, the Assembly urged governments of Member States:

— to reconsider their present policies of secrecy concerning the real costs, economic, social and human, inherent in military resource use;
— to start to plan and prepare for a conversion process which could be implemented in a disarmament situation.

It also decided to place the relationship issue on its agenda for renewed consideration at regular intervals. And already in 1984 it decided to convene the special relationship conference which I referred to a short while ago.

The General Assembly's urging that governments should undertake conversion studies at the national level went unheeded for several years. In autumn 1987 there is still only one government of a UN Member State which has completed such a study: the government of my own country, Sweden. I was commissioned to make that study which was completed in late 1985, by the publication of a report of about 700 pages called *In Pursuit of Disarmament: Conversion from Military to Civil Production in Sweden.* As this is, so far, the only national study made, I can only base my conclusions on the possibilities for conversion on my own findings.

The main tasks entrusted to me by the government were the following:

— to describe the nature and magnitude of Sweden's present defence efforts in economic and social terms;

— to give examples of defence resources which, in the event of varying degrees of disarmament in our part of the world, can be converted to other purposes;

— to state the feasibility of defence-sector conversion and its problems in different peace perspectives;

— to state how a conversion of resources from defence to civilian use might also make a contribution to Sweden's international development cooperation with the developing countries.

In my reports which—as I said earlier—were completed at the end of 1985, I have clarified by means of an exhaustive compilation of facts relating to the defence forces and the defence industries, of studies on the spot of all main defence industries and of thorough discussions with management and unions of these industries, the use of resources for military purposes in Sweden, which are over and above budgetary allocations. The reports further provide examples of how, in the event of future international disarmament, these resources could be reallocated for other purposes, within Sweden as well as in development cooperation with developing countries. Also they explain why preparations for such a conversion must start well in advance of a disarmament process. Finally, the reports recommend that Sweden—as a second stage of its implementation of the UN resolution—should decide on some appropriate measures in order to plan and prepare for the transfer of resources from military to civilian purposes.

Sweden has a comparatively large defence–industrial sector. Its breadth corresponds to that of the defence industries of the largest West European countries. Most of the equipment procured by the Swedish armed forces is produced by the domestic defence industry. There is a widespread political acceptance of the fact that Sweden's policy of neutrality would be less credible were Sweden to become too dependent on foreign defence equipment.

According to the study it would be possible to reduce Sweden's defence expenditures if the military blocs started to reduce troops and weapons in Europe, with particular emphasis on offensive weapon systems. Such a disarmament scenario would enable the conversion of resources within the military sector. This would not cause any significant macroeconomic problems. But it would create difficulties on the microeconomic level, i.e. locally and in human terms. These problems would have to be looked into carefully, and plans would have to be worked out in advance in order to prevent their occurrence.

Another important consideration emphasised in the report is that society has a specific responsibility to promote defence–industry conversion, since these human and technical resources used in the defence industry have been built up for national defence purposes. A conclusion reached is that the Swedish defence industry needs financial incentives to expand its production into new civilian areas. A number of other measures ought to be taken in order to plan for and facilitate a conversion from military to civilian production.

In some respects I should like now to go into more detail.

My collaborators and I reviewed thoroughly the characteristics of the defence industry, including the R & D intensity, the differences between military and civil technology, the specialisation of production resources, the degree of excess capacity maintained, the financing of development costs and the profitability of the defence–industrial sector.

The collected information shows that R & D intensity, measured as total R & D costs as a percent of value-added, is higher among companies which manufacture military equipment than among comparable firms where production is entirely oriented towards the civilian market. In 1981, the R & D intensity of Swedish defence producers was 18.4 percent against 15.7 for civil-sector producers. However, those defence–industry facilities where military equipment accounted for more than half of total output, had an R & D intensity of 29.3 percent in 1981, while those facilities in the same companies which were dominated by civil production registered an R & D intensity of 11.8 percent.

In many cases military and civil technology are closely related. But there are also a number of technologies used in the defence–industrial sector which do not have any significant civil applications. Researchers, engineers, technicians and skilled workers who work with such specialised military technology cannot easily transfer their knowledge to the civil sector. There are, for example, no civil-sector anti-tank missiles or anti-aircraft guns. But both of these weapon systems consist of several sub-systems, and each of these requires the knowledge of one or more technical disciplines. A close analysis of the technologies required to design and manufacture missiles or guns indicates that most have civil-sector applications.

Where there is a strong link between military and civil technologies, the former is the leading technology because of the strong forces behind military development. The purchasers of military equipment tend to push technological development into new areas more than their civil-sector counterparts and are also better able to pay for such development. New technologies often penetrate the military sector faster than the civil sector. One recent example would be graphite composites.

As far as defence–industry specialisation is concerned, only a small portion of the machinery and facilities used by the Swedish defence industry is military-specific and cannot be used in the civil sector. Moreover, current trend in the development of new materials and new production methods within industry are contributing to increased standardisation.

It is likely that the defence-industry workers are more specialised than the defence industry's production facilities. Where work is largely done manually, for example the assembling and soldering of a small number of circuit boards or the welding of sheet metal on submarines, it is often carried out somewhat differently than in comparable civil production. It is rare that the same degree of precision is required for circuit boards used in civil prdoucts or for the welding carried out on civil ships.

The defence industry frequently maintains considerable excess production and R & D capacity. Firms are dependent on the procurement schedules of the armed forces and slack periods often arise between orders. In some cases companies can make use of their excess capacity during such periods to produce for export or to manufacture other goods for the civil market.

The defence industry can also be differentiated from other industries by the methods of financing and procurement. The development and production of defence material by Swedish companies normally occurs only after a contract has been signed with the Defence Material Administration (in Swedish: Försvarets Materielverk, FMV). For systems which are developed at the request of the Swedish armed forces, FMV usually pays all development costs.

Some of the military-related R & D carried out within the defence–industrial sector is company-financed. In 1981—the most recent year for which information was available at the time of the study—a group of companies which produced primarily military equipment financed 32 percent of the costs of their military research and development themselves.

In the slack periods between different projects, FMV frequently provides companies with financial support to enable them to maintain their development capacity while waiting for new orders from the armed forces. The same result can be obtained by ordering various studies which involve industry's R & D personnel from the very first stages of a civil project.

Profitability is generally not higher for defence-sector companies than it is for civil-sector firms, but it is considerably more even over time.

Evaluations of defence-industry profitability depend to a large degree on which measure of profitability is employed.

One problem with such comparisons is that FMV provides the defence industry with considerable interest-free advance payments when equipment is ordered. The provision of such payments generally means that the contract price is somewhat lower than it would have been in their absence. The advance payments improve the company's financial profits but, to the extent that they induce lower prices, they reduce its value-added and its operating profits, both of which are calculated on the basis of invoiced sales. At the end of fiscal year 1983, outstanding advance payments to the Swedish defence industry were valued at approximately 4.2 billion SEK. It is estimated that advance payments improved the financial profits of the companies by at least 500 million SEK during 1983. Interest-free advance payments enable companies to produce goods with relatively little equity capital. This is one factor which makes it difficult for these companies to adapt to civil-sector production.

All in all, a reduction in the size of the Swedish defence effort along the lines discussed in the report would result in 34,000 fewer jobs within the armed forces and the defence–industrial sector over the course of a 25–year period. If new recruitment and retirement were taken into account, some 1,430 people would have to leave their jobs in the defence sector each year as a result of disarmament. This would involve less than 1 percent of Sweden's labour force. I have pointed out already that from a macroeconomic point of view conversion would scarcely present any serious problem. But other factors play a decisive role. Disarmament is a political process which, if it is to succeed, must be strongly supported by the entire population and backed up by a firm political will. Disarmament must not be prevented or slowed down due to fears that it will produce unemployment or other economic difficulties. In addition, the armed forces and the defence–industrial sector employ many well-educated individuals with considerable technical capabilities who, in the event of disarmament, could use their skills in the civil sector.

The reports have identified a number of criteria which are considered more important than others in determining the prospects that Swedish defence producers would have of converting successfully from military to civil production:

- an orientation towards high-technology products;
- a close relation to civil products and technology;
- relatively little dependence on specialised personnel and equipment;

- existence of a marketing organisation oriented towards the civil sector;
- low level of dependence on military-related exports;
- low level of dependence on the production of defence material at both the corporate and the plant level.

When companies fail to establish themselves in the civil market, it is primarily due to their lack of experience in civil marketing. Many companies lack the organisation and knowledge necessary to market civil-sector products commercially. Various means of solving this problem have been reviewed.

In the reports I also drew attention to a factor which has considerable importance for the success of conversion attempts but which is difficult to measure objectively: the involvement, interest and capabilities of management. To deliberately promote reduced dependence on military orders and to dare to take the risks associated with that course of action are prerequisites for the successful transformation of production. Even a company in which the internal and external conditions favour conversion cannot expect the process to occur by itself.

I have concluded that a disarmament process, as envisaged in the reports, implying a halving of the Swedish defence sector over a 25–year period, would not necessarily create any insurmountable conversion problem. It is, however, I repeat, of particular political importance that such disarmament does not lead to increased unemployment. Defence-sector employees should not experience disarmament as a threat to their future. The promotion of *détente,* peace and a reduction in defence expenditure must not be allowed to be retarded either in Sweden or in any other country because of concern for increased unemployment. This is particularly relevant for the companies and the local communities that are more highly dependent on defence orders than others. The problems emerging from a disarmament and conversion process at that level must be met by effective preparation and planning.

Irrespective of when global disarmament might begin, it is important to start planning defence-industry conversion as soon as possible. The defence industry's experience of conversion to date shows that it normally takes a long time to develop competitive products for the civil market. Diversificiation of production, in order to reduce dependence on defence contracts, cannot therefore begin only once orders from the armed forces have actually begun to decline. This process must be initiated much earlier if a firm's employment and profitability are not to be harmed by the loss of defence orders. All Swedish defence producers ought to have a sufficiently large civil sector and built-in flexibility so that the decline in defence orders could be dealt with internally.

Against this background I have proposed that the Swedish Government should:

— establish a Council for Disarmament and Conversion;
— set up a central conversion fund, linked to this Council;
— promote the creation of local conversion funds within each defence company.

What kind of momentum will be maintained? Which governments will undertake the same kind of action as the Swedish government? Will it be possible to ensure, at the international level, some kind of follow-up machinery; a continuing process, the future of which will have to be ensured? Because, again, it is my firm conviction that disarmament will take place. And then, resources released and badly needed for sound development purposes must not be wasted.

For the time being, I have one practical proposal: in the future, estimates must be made of the savings to be accrued by specific disarmament agreements, and these are to be included in every such agreement.

Let me now return to the international scene. It has often been said, not least by myself, that the efforts undertaken by the United Nations to promote thinking and action on the Disarmament–Development relationship must not be allowed to be an isolated project but must be recognised as part of a dynamic process, facilitating the understanding of the importance of basic economic, social and human needs, and thereby contributing to stability and security, both at the national and the international level, and promoting disarmament.

The peoples of the earth are waiting for the realisation of common sense among politicians and decision-makers, particularly in the militarily significant countries. And what is more, they will not only be waiting, they will be demanding.

I have already referred to the important event which took place at UN Headquarters in New York from 24 August to 11 September this year, the International Conference on the Disarmament–Development Relationship.

The Conference, described by the many government members present as a landmark historic conference, was preceded by a thorough preparatory process, in which more than 90 member states participated and which was attended by 150 member states; unfortunately, the most important military power and the one which would have been, more than any other member state, in need of attending in order to listen and learn, namely the United States of America, was not among them.

Excellent preparations for the Conference were made by the UN Secretariat and channelled through the Preparatory Committee to the Conference itself. The documents represent a complete updating of facts and data from the 1981 Expert report. One part of the preparatory process was the convening for three days in April 1986 of a Panel of Eminent Personalities, with the purpose of having issued a Declaration on Disarmament–Development, to serve as a reference point for the conference.

NON-MILITARY SECURITY THREATS

As I was very much a part of that exercise, having been elected its moderator, I feel a certain need to elaborate to some extent on the result of the three days of endeavours, that is: a unanimously adopted declaration. In doing so, I enter a new phase of my discourse, which might be called an effort to discuss the dynamic triangular relationship between disarmament, development and security from a politico–psychological more than a military and technical point of view. It is my belief that this approach has a rather direct bearing on the theme of this symposium.

Anyone from outer space, for example, would look at the present state of this world of ours, an overarmed and undernourished world, and would, I presume, be right in asking if this was the result of acts of serious political madness. There is no need to quote detailed figures on world military expenditures, the number of nuclear warheads, the costs of one submarine or one modern tank, not to speak of the R & D costs of the Strategic Defence Initiative (SDI), compared with the number of starving, sick, uneducated people out of the 5 billion inhabitants of this earth; we all know them. Suffice it to say that we also know that it is well within our collective capacities and within the carrying capacity of this earth, to provide for the basic needs of the world's entire population, and to make progress towards a more equitable world economic order. But it is also well understood that the arms race is incompatible with the objectives of such an equitable economic order. On the other hand, we also know that what the UN Governmental Expert Group called "a global management of interdependence" would be in the economic and security interests of all states.

This leads me to a few remarks on the concepts of interdependencies and security, both national and international.

One main idea, which in my view, is both self-evident and urgent, is the following:

— while, as a matter of course, disarmament negotiations must continue to be pursued, with energetic vigour, there is a growing sense of the need for new directions in our search for peace and security.

This theme could be elaborated in two points:

— the concept of security has so far been defined in too narrow terms;
— disarmament has been discussed, and negotiated too much in isolation and too much based on narrow and outdated concepts of security.

As a matter of fact, we cannot manage the problematic and complex issues of our times, if we do not learn how to:

— apply a holistic view of the world and its peoples;
— apply a holistic approach to problem-solving;
— draw the political, practical and human conclusions to be derived from what we know theoretically about the ever-increasing inter-dependencies between nations and peoples, and also among issues.

We speak often about these inter-relationships these days. But we still do not know enough about the way in which they function. They comprise many of the problems that we have to discuss in the context of security.

People traditionally associate the term security, and particularly national security, with military security, i.e. security against military aggression or threats of military aggression. This remains the interpretation made by most nations. But not so the superpowers. As is so often the case concrete examples of this fact will have to be taken from the open and frank political debate in the US, although I am certain that the attitudes of the Soviet Union are the same.

Let me just quote two former American presidents:

— President Gerald Ford: "Dependence on others for our supply of energy is unacceptable for our national security";
— President Jimmy Carter: "The establishment of a Rapid Deployment Force is a symbol of our desire to defend our interests throughout the world."

The superpowers do indeed recognise the existence of so-called non-military threats to security, as the serious international problems that they are. But they regard them through the eyes of narrowly conceived national interests, masked as legitimately founded requests for national security. And they feel themselves entitled to undertake the solution to these problems, as far as they themselves are concerned, in their old way of dominance, in their own short-sighted and narrow-minded self-interest and—if necessary—also by military means.

In other words, and to quote a Dutch professor of international law, the late Bert Röling, as far as the superpowers are concerned and, for that matter, also some other great powers, the concept of security has shifted from being applied solely to "military security" to what Professor Röling called "all-out security," related to a wider definition of "interests" anywhere in the world which must be defended, if necessary also by military means. In a world of ever-increasing mutual dependence, a world of limited resources and growing gaps between rich and poor, this obviously constitutes a significantly increased element of risk.

An enumeration of what is now increasingly referred to as non-military threats to security will show this quite clearly. It will, furthermore, show clearly the interdependencies of countries and peoples, as well as the commonality of issues. These are:

— the world economic crisis, affecting the developing countries much more than the industrialised countries, characterised by such phenomena as unemployment, inflation, debt burdens, imbalances in international trade and international monetary instability;
— the threatening shortages of resources, particularly those of energy and non-renewable resources;
— the short-term and long-term deterioration of the human environment;
— the continuing world population increase;
— the morally unacceptable and politically hazardous polarisation of riches and poverty;
— the arms race itself and its negative economic and social effects.

One of the implications of the commonality of these global issues is that if, or as long as, they remain unsolved, they will mutually reinforce their negative effects on our future.

It should be considered a truism that a constructive solution of these problems can never be achieved by any state at the expense of others. There are no national solutions to international problems. They cannot be solved by confrontation and conflict, only by cooperation and compromise.

This leads up to the needs: to recognise our common interests, in the language of the Brandt Commission; to impart credence to the concept of common security, in the language of the Palme Commission; to visualise a common future for all of us, in the language of the Brundtland Commission.

Such a process can never be implemented within the old and outdated concept of national security. It will require new value systems, new attitudes, new priorities, new patterns of political behaviour, and a new kind of international relations.

The Panel Declaration, in its concluding paragraph, expressed our present dilemma in the following words:

> Our small planet is getting endangered: by the arsenals of weapons which could blow it up; by the burden of military expenditure which could sink it under; and by the unmet basic needs of two–thirds of its population which subsists on less than one–third of its resources. We belong to a near universal constituency which believes that we are borrowing this Earth from our children as much as we have inherited it from our forefathers. The carrying capacity of Earth is not infinite, nor are its resources. The needs of national security are legitimate and must be met. But must we stand by, as helpless witnesses of a drift towards greater insecurity at higher costs?

The implications of this statement—and the whole content of the Declaration as well—is, in my view, that the all-important priority for world political leaders should be to put *people* first. Why have efforts in this direction been unsuccessful so far?

Before I try to answer that question, a few words on the United Nations Conference itself.

It had not aroused great advance expectations, even if peace movements and a number of other organisations of concerned citizens had prepared themselves thoroughly for their participation and their contributions.

The main reason for doubts about the final outcome of three weeks of deliberations was the declared absence of the United States, the reason of which was explained to be refusal to recognise any link whatsoever between a process of genuine disarmament and possibilities for a more effective process of economic and social development.

The necessity and the usefulness of the preparatory process, mentioned earlier, was obvious. Through the years since 1982, governments of UN member states had shown themselves singularly and regrettably indifferent to the urging of the General Assembly to undertake studies, preparations and planning at the national level on the possibilities for conversion of resources used for military purposes to constructive civilian use in an international disarmament situation.

The fact that the relationship issue was the only item on the Conference agenda had forced the governments of the 150 participating member states to think about, not disarmament or development *per se,* but the relationship between them. The result was that, in the general debate as well as in the Final Document, there is a beginning of a new thinking, a new language and a new vocabulary.

In other words and to repeat, it was for obvious reasons that so many delegates, including foreign ministers, spoke about a historic conference, a landmark conference.

A few words on the content of the Final Document. First: it cannot be said to contain very much of concrete substance, in terms of action-oriented proposals. Neither could that have been expected. The task that the conference had been given was to examine and negotiate the principles based on the texts of the drafts submitted to it by the preparatory committee, including the Declaration of the Panel of Eminent Personalities, discussed above.

On the other hand, the Final Document was intended to serve as a guideline for the next steps to follow on the conclusion of the conference. As such, it contains much more substance than I had believed possible. It provides quite a lot of guidance for the follow-up process.

Second: many delegations expressed regret that the Final Document did not explicitly endorse the proposal to establish an International Disarmament Fund for Development. I do not share this feeling. Very briefly these are my reasons. In my view the fund is not a magic formula for implementing, in concrete terms, the relationship concept. One has to compare the possible impact of additional financial transfers from the industrialised and weapon-producing countries in the North in a disarmament situation—possibly rather small—with the necessary and fundamental change in the structural relationship between countries in world economy, including world trade. This is, after all, the aim, purpose and content of the New International Economic Order (NIEO). And this can only be brought about, in a disarmament situation, through the conversion and the transfer of human talents and skills as well as material resources from military to constructive developmental purposes, thus taking a step towards the NIEO. In this context, the establishment of a fund can only be marginal. And after all, it was the basic thinking behind the UN General Assembly mandate to the Governmental Expert Group for its three–year study 1978–1981 on the relationship issue, to have its conclusions and recommendations placed in the framework of the NIEO.

Third: this is why the follow-up mechanisms to be established are, in real terms, the most important result of the conference. As to the format of these mechanisms I hope for something that will function at both the inter-governmental and the secretariat levels, keeping watch on progress to be made at national levels. And, of course, with some kind of a Non-Governmental Organisation (NGO) presence.

Next: what about the absence of the United States? Many were worried, I was not. Contrary to some optimists who believed that a United States present at the conference would have adopted the consensus Final Document, I think that the US presence would have reinforced the doubts and the resistance of some West European NATO countries to such an extent that the developing countries would have felt it impossible to accept the emerging draft.

And with the adoption of the consensus Final Document we have now a situation of a world community versus the United States. That missing superpower will learn that the world community can do without it. The US will sooner or later—hopefully sooner—have to start doing its homework and to adjust to the realities of our age.

But great care should be taken not to allow governments of UN member states to forget what they have said and agreed to at the conference. Their work is indeed not completed; the important part of it still remains to be done. In this process, the NGOs have an indispensable part to play in keeping watch on the accountability of governments.

Let me go back to the statement made a while ago and the question put. The all-important priority for world policial leaders should be to put *people* first. Why have efforts in this direction been unsuccessful so far?

In trying to give my own answer—or part of the answer—to that question, I should have to look for indications of a much needed capacity of world political leaders to involve themselves in efforts to redefine the old concepts of interests and security that I criticised a while ago, to start "new thinking," to use that favourite catchword of General Secretary Mikhail Gorbachev. Unfortunately, it is still not possible to find such indications. And I remember the book by the well-known American historian Barbara Tuchman *The March of Folly,* in the introductory chapter of which she gives some historic examples of this march of folly—something she defines as policies having been pursued which are contrary to self-interest. I earlier called it "political madness." Let me quote:

Wooden-headedness, the source of self-deception, is a factor that plays a remarkably large role in government. It consists of assessing a situation in terms of preconceived fixed notions while ignoring or rejecting any contrary signs. It is acting according to wish, while not allowing oneself to be deflected by the facts. It is epitomised in a historian's statement about Philip II of Spain, the surpassing wooden-head of all sovereigns: "No experience of the failure of his policy could shake his belief in its essential excellence."

There is not one dominant political leader today to whom this is not applicable.

Speaking of King Louis XIV of France she states: "Never had so self-centred a ruler so effectively despoiled self-interest." It could easily be said of today's leaders.

After the publication of the Brundtland report *Our Common Future,* at the end of April this year, the Swedish government organised, in early May, a Nordic conference on Environment and Development, with broad international participation, particularly from developing countries. One of the many committees of the conference discussed what I have tried to elaborate here, i.e. the inter-relationships between the various global issues. One of the paragraphs of the committee's report underscores very much what I have tried to say:

> The committee viewed the deteriorating environmental situation as not merely a threat to development but as one of the non-military challenges to the security of individuals, nations and the planet itself. Governments have a responsibility and an opportunity to consider these challenges alongside their traditional concerns with a military arms race which wastes and distorts much needed resources. Until all people feel secure in their everyday lives, there will be security for none. The urge for security thus becomes a global issue.

And the committee's main conclusion was: "It is against this background that the committee calls for radical reversals of traditional thinking about development priorities, policies and strategies."

The most decisive prerequisites for such radical reversals of traditional thinking among governments are of course: knowledge, imagination and the mobilisation of the so much talked about but still mainly invisible political will. I happen to believe that elements of a new way of thinking are developing, promoted *inter alia* through pressures on governments by non-governmental sources, i.e. what the Secretary-General of the United Nations has called "the basic constituency of the United Nations."

And this is how it should be. Because, in my view, people have increasingly the qualifications to be wiser than their governments believe them to be. I can make this statement even more pointed: people might even be wiser than their governments.

Sometimes, people's projects for peace and security are judged to be naive by those who believe themselves to be more knowledgeable, and more experienced, and more rational. That judgment should be taken gladly. Naivety can be—and often is in matters of a peaceful future—an utter expression of realism.

We should never forget the opening words of the United Nations Charter:

— WE THE PEOPLES OF THE UNITED NATIONS, DETERMINED
— to save succeeding generations from the scourge of war,
— to unite our strength to maintain international peace and security....

The Charter does not speak of member states of the UN. It does not speak of the governments of UN member states. It speaks in the name of the *peoples* of the United Nations. Therefore we the peoples have an obligation and a responsibility.

And when governments act in the UN, they act on behalf of their people. Thus, the people have the right to question their governments about their international policies, they have the right to demand answers to their questions. The governments have the duty to give the answers. They are accountable to the people.

In this way the people will be able to enter a political dialogue with governments, to influence the political process.

This is the philosophy of one of many Non-Governmental Organisation (NGO) projects, the Great Peace Journey, a project which originated in Sweden and which is now a worldwide undertaking.

In the present world situation it is the right and the duty of enlightened and concerned citizens to intervene in the political process, with knowledge and responsibility.

I have already quoted the final paragraph of the declaration of the Panel of Eminent Personalities. It ends with a question mark. The answer to its rhetorical question is of course a firm no.

But the negative answer carries with it a great responsibility. The British author C. P. Snow said in one of his many books on the nuclear world of today, a world faced by many people with a feeling of despair and hopelessness: "It is only when men think that events are too big for them, that there is no hope."

Events will never be too big. It will never be beyond man's capacity to overcome events and build a better and more humane future.

If governments fail to change values, attitudes, priority-setting and directions, then public opinion, the public will, must speak.

My last sentence will contain, not rhetorical assertions, but a firm belief. When mobilised, when having found its expression and its form, "the power of the powerless" will represent the great opportunity for peace and security.

11

Mediation as a Technique of Dispute Settlement:
Appraisal and Prospects

Alain Brouillet

This chapter will deal with mediation as a conflict resolution technique. The topic will be surveyed broadly, looking at the reasons why and the circumstances in which mediation has been successful, and those where it has been a failure. This outline will use a number of case studies, from a pragmatic standpoint, with the aim being to draw a number of general conclusions, suggesting when and how mediation might be used to solve future conflicts.

Three recent examples of successful mediation will be given, i.e. in a chronological order: the Holy See mediation between Argentina and Chile on the Austral area (1979–1984); the Algerian government mediation between the Islamic Republic of Iran and the United States for the release of US hostages in Tehran, (1980); and the Habib plan leading to the evacuation of Palestinian fighters from Beirut (1982). We shall also consider three mediations which have failed: the Galo Plaza mediation over Cyprus; the Gunnar Jarring mission between Israel and Arab States; and the Alexander Haig mediation between Argentina and United Kingdom over the Falkland issue. These examples will be examined in succession. Specific conclusions will be drawn in each case. Then we shall come to general conclusions.

SUCCESSFUL MEDIATIONS

Austral Dispute

The Holy See mediation on the Austral area followed the rejection by Argentina in 1977 of the Queen's award on the Beagle Channel case. To settle the dispute Argentina and Chile resumed diplomatic talks in 1978. But here again the outcome of the negotiations was a failure. In December 1978, the two countries were on the verge of warfare. This is the time when Pope Jean-Paul II proposed his mediation, which was accepted by both states. Two treaties, initialled in Montevideo, set up the mediation process, on the initiative of the Pope's representative, Cardinal Antonio Samoré.

What were the specific features of this mediation?

On Cardinal Samoré's request both states undertook to abide by specific commitments, which can be analysed as interim measures, i.e. to refrain from taking any action which might aggravate the tension between the two countries or render the existing dispute more difficult to solve. For this reason, the Pope's mediation was original since, as a rule, a mediator cannot be empowered to prescribe interim measures. In this specific instance the provisional measures were only binding upon the two states, because they had initially accepted them. But the mediation could only be enforced, if Argentina and Chile agreed on this prerequisite.

The second original feature of this mediation was that it did not proceed informally, contrary to most mediations, but rather it developed on the basis of an organised procedure. The approach was based on the combination of two types of meetings between states and the mediator: separate meetings of each state with the mediator, and joint meetings of both states with the mediator. The "shuttle system" from separate to joint meetings and *vice versa* was left to Cardinal Samoré's discretion, with joint meetings being used to endorse the concessions granted in the course of separate meetings.

The final original feature of this case was that although the mediation was carried out in secrecy—which is the case for most mediations—it was given some degree of publicity. At regular intervals *joint communiqués* were issued, that stated the progress made and acted as a kind of incentive for the parties.

During the whole process the mediator gathered information from the parties alone. He never attempted to use other sources. He never acted as an investigator. Because information came exclusively from states, the mediator's proposals were strengthened, since parties could not entertain any doubt on their authenticity.

Besides the mediator proceeded step by step, taking into account the parties' readiness to go along with his proposals. The Pope's solution was presented in 1980. But it was not accepted immediately by one party. And the mediation process came to an end only in 1984.

Tehran Hostages

Algeria's intervention for the release of the American hostages in Tehran provides our second example of successful mediation.

This mediation was a short one: it took place between 10 November 1980 and 19 January 1981, the deadline being the inauguration of Ronald Reagan as President.

Its first characteristic feature was that an Algerian served as an active intermediary, working around the clock, resorting to all means of communications, and even shuttle diplomacy.

Second, Algeria was keen to assess all points of agreement and disagreement, so as to clarify the scope of the negotiations: i.e. the release of hostages demanded by the US government and the unfreezing of Iranian assets, which was the prerequisite set by Iranian authorities.

Third, Algeria insisted that each party discard factors and arguments that could not be accepted by the other party, the Iranian government no longer asking for the Shah's extradition, nor for the restitution of the imperial properties. As a trade-off the US government agreed to have the Shah's properties assessed and confiscated.

Lastly, the final treaty between Iran and the US provided for the setting up of a mechanism for the settlement of future disputes that might arise from the implementation of the agreement. This offered a guarantee for the Iranians, after the release of the hostages. An arbitral tribunal has been established in the Hague: it is the US–Iran claims tribunal, still on duty at the present time.

Beirut Evacuation

Our third example of successful mediation is the Habib plan of 1982 on the evacuation of Palestinian fighters from Beirut. The mediation by Philip Habib, President Reagan's representative for the Middle East, started during the siege of Beirut. Its outcome was the arrival of a Multinational Force to supervise the withdrawal of the *fedayeen* from Beirut. What were the specific features of this mediation?

There never was a confrontation of all parties with Habib, which was not possible, due to the absence of diplomatic relations between Israel, Lebanon and Syria. Besides, by virtue of the Kissinger doctrine, the US never had any relation with the Palestine Liberation Organisation (PLO). This is why Lebanon, Egypt, and Saudi Arabia spoke for PLO. The whole process was based on a succession of bilateral talks: between Israel and the

US; the US and Lebanon; the US and Egypt; the US and Saudi Arabia; and between each of the last three states and the PLO.

Habib resorted to shuttle diplomacy in order to get his plan accepted, going back and forth from one capital to another.

A second specific feature was that Habib dealt exclusively with the withdrawal of Palestinian fighters from Beirut. He always refused to link the evacuation to the general settlement of the Palestinian issue.

Third, Habib readjusted his proposals continually to the progress made in the parties' positions. Thus Israel was in favour of an unconditional surrender of the *fedayeen*. Eventually the latter were able to leave Beirut with light armament.

UNSUCCESSFUL MEDIATIONS

I now come to three examples of mediations that failed. What are the causes of these failures? Do they lie in the way the mediator carried out his mediation? Or is it that the parties were not willing to settle the dispute, in spite of the mediator's efforts, and in this case the latter's responsibility was somehow limited?

As to the deep-rooted reasons of the failure, we know very little. And this is why the conclusions that we have reached can only be sketchy.

Cyprus

For instance, one of the reasons of the failure of Galo Plaza's mediation over the Cyprus conflict was that his mediation resorted to publicity. As soon as his report was released, the Turkish government requested his dismissal, because they were of the opinion that publicity was a means of exerting unacceptable pressure, and that it distorted the mediation process.

Middle East

By contrast, Gunnar Jarring's mission, on behalf of the UN Secretary-General, just like the Galo Plaza mediation, was carried out with the utmost discretion. But here again the outcome was a failure. Several factors must be underlined in the post-mortem of the Jarring mission.

First of all, at the outset of the Jarring mission, neither Egypt nor Israel was ready to enter into direct talks, with or without a mediator's assistance. The issue of Israel's right to existence remained unsolved for many Arab countries. And there was no official communication channel between the two states.

Second, Jarring did not have the monopoly of the conduct of talks. Concurrently with his action, bilateral talks took place between the USA and the USSR, and there were even talks between four of the five permanent members of the UN Security Council. The failure of such negotiations led the US into the path of unilateral diplomacy with the Rogers Plan, proposed by the Secretary of State William Rogers on 9 December 1969.

Third, Jarring had enlarged the scope of his terms of reference excessively. On 8 February 1971, he submitted to Egypt and Israel a plan for settlement that included the essential element of a future peace treaty between each state. This was too ambitious, and Jarring was accused by Israel of acting *ultra vires*.

Lastly, Jarring never got the support of the two superpowers, the USA and the USSR. The backing of the other major powers was essential in this case. Indeed Jarring was seen as inadequately equipped to impose his own views. And this empty persuasion could not be convincing enough.

Falkland Islands/Islas Malvinas

Secretary of State Alexander Haig's mediation in the Falkland conflict was also a case of failure. From the outset the parties' positions could not be reconciled.

Their opposite standpoints, at the time when hostilities started, implied that the mediator's mission was doomed to failure. The Argentinian objective was to rule the islands. And the United Kingdom refused to negotiate its sovereignty over the archipelago under constraint.

Besides, the US government, which was the mediating power, took the side of one of the two belligerents, during the mediation itself. The US informed Argentina that should Haig's mission fail they would stand by the British government. In doing so they jeopardised the mediator's effort, who was blamed by Argentinian authorities for being partial.

These two factors explain why Haig's mission failed, in spite of an intensive shuttle diplomacy, which is not very likely to succeed anyway in the case of remote states in terms of geography, and with such different views as to the merits of the case.

LESSONS

I now come to some final points concerning the major features specific to mediation, as a means of dispute settlement.

The advantages offered by mediation are self-evident. States favour diplomatic means of settlement, because they can exercise some control over them. Mediation, like good offices and conciliation, does not threaten the state sovereignty with its result. Just like mediation is optional, its outcome is not binding.

The advantage of mediation is that it can apply to any kind of conflict, be it a purely legal dispute or a combination of legal, political, ideological or economic factors. Moreover, mediation can not only settle disputes between states, but also conflicts between states and entities that are not entitled to go before a judge, such as a national liberation movement or insurgents in a civil war.

Who can best serve as a mediator? It can be either a state or an international organisation or a private citizen. This is left to the parties' decision. According to the nature of the dispute one solution will be preferred to another.

Suffice it to underline two prerequisites to the fruitful outcome of a mediation. The mediator must be able to fulfil his mission in complete independence. Four conditions must be met. There must be no pressure exercised on him in the course of his mission. Moreover he must stand to lose nothing in the event of a failure. He must be given wide terms of reference, so as not to run the risk of acting *ultra vires*. Lastly he should not be partial.

We now come to the question of whether the mediator should be an individual·or a collective entity; if a government acts as mediator, there must be a leader, who is ultimately responsible.

What should be the qualities of a mediator? Much has been written on the subject by Oran Young, Marvin C. Ott, P. Wehr. For Oran Young (1967), the capabilities of a successful mediator are the following:

1. Impartiality regarding the issues in dispute;
2. Independence from all parties;
3. Acceptability to all protagonists;
4. The respect of all parties;
5. The knowledge and the skill to deal with the issues;
6. The required physical resources.

According to Marvin C. Ott (1972), a mediator's ambition must be:

1. To change for the better the behaviour of the disputants;
2. To facilitate communication;
3. To clarify the facts;
4. To provide a break in hostilities;
5. To suggest specific solutions;
6. To permit the parties to save face;
7. To provide "service activities," such as supervision of a cease-fire.

For P. Wehr (1979), the required attributes of a mediator are:

1. Knowledge about conflict situations;
2. Ability to understand the positions of the antagonists;
3. Active listening;
4. Sense of timing;
5. Communication skills;
6. Procedural skills;
7. Crisis management.

I should like to add two other conditions. First, the mediator must be widely recognised as an eminent personality. Secondly, the gist of his mission should be an endeavour to achieve a *rapprochement*. He should emphasise the points of agreement that gradually emerge during the reconciliation process.

The issue of facts is an important point. Without information the mediator will not be able to fulfil his mission. Therefore he must have all the elements of the dispute available. Must he investigate? I do not think so, because it would distort the nature of his task. Fact-finding must always be carried out in close conjunction with the parties involved.

Usually a mediation is an informal procedure; it is more likely to succeed if it follows an organised and scheduled procedure, if it is based on a sophisticated machinery. This is because the existence of institutional bodies in the mediation process will support the mediator's efforts. The parties' will can then be structured within a framework that gradually will become familiar.

This organised procedure will trigger off a dynamic process, that will serve as a guideline for the parties and help them come to terms. That is what happened during the Holy See mediation between Argentina and Chile.

The mediator must have control over the unfolding of procedure, so that at the first stage contacts between the parties do not become a direct round, in order to avoid the risk of a mutual cross-examination. This would be tantamount to a conventional type of negotiation that failed before.

The problem of time is most relevant too but everything must be seen on a case by case basis. A mediator may be successful within a very short time-limit—this was the case with the Habib mediation; or it can go on and on for several years—this was the case with the Holy See mediation between Argentina and Chile.

If the mediator is not short of time, it is desirable to go step by step, so that he structures the process on the basis of existing institutions, establishing a clear-cut distinction between the fact-finding stage and the proposal stage.

It is desirable for the mediator to have both parties observe interim measures, since the future of his mission will depend on the implementation of these provisions. In this respect the mediator can exert pressure over the parties: if they do not abide by the provisional measures, then the mediator may put his terms of reference at stake.

The mediator must make sure that the parties fulfil their duty to negotiate. The parties must act with the genuine intention to settle the dispute, which implies: first, the readiness to understand the other party's viewpoint; second, to agree to discuss all aspects of the dispute.

And one could define as follows the scope of action of the parties: between their initial positions on the one hand and on the other hand the mediator's proposals. They are under no obligation to accept as such the mediator's proposals, but they should not reject them altogether.

A mediation can be carried out in secrecy but this must be compatible with the need to keep public opinion informed of the progress of the mediation. This is why publicity is desirable, at least under the form of *joint communiqués*.

A mediation plan can only be accepted by the parties, if it provides for a dispute settlement mechanism, after the mediator's mission has been fulfilled. This will eliminate the potential difficulties arising from the mediation.

To this end the mediator may offer his services once his mission is over, which is a kind of continuous mediation, or he may suggest the use of other means of dispute settlement, jurisdictional or non-jurisdictional.

Mediations between Argentina and Chile, and between the USA and Iran were successful because in both cases the settlement included mechanisms of conflict resolution.

Lastly, I shall propose four concrete measures to strengthen recourse to mediation.

The mediation as a means of dispute settlement remains unknown to some extent. This points to the need for more research into the field of mediation on a case by case basis. We still need a general theory of mediation, of its mechanisms, of its functions. More symposia should be organised on the subject in the future. And the mediators' direct testimonies would be very helpful and valuable in this respect, provided that they are able to speak.

One could envisage a Staff College of Mediators for scholars and practitioners interested in the process of mediation and/or who have responsibilities in this field.[1] This Staff College would organise courses on the subject of mediation and its techniques, in collaboration with former mediators.

One could also envisage the creation of a Permanent Assembly of Mediators, on the same pattern as the Permanent Court of Arbitration. Each state would appoint four persons who could be selected to act as mediators in an international dispute.

Lastly, compulsory mediation clauses could be included in treaties. And before they come to other means of settlement, states should first attempt to resort to mediation, and should this attempt fail, only then would resort to other kinds of dispute settlement be permitted.

NOTES

1. Arthur Goldberg, in the same perspective, suggested, years ago, the establishment of a Staff College for UN conciliators.

12

International Peacekeeping

Ramesh Thakur

In 1987, peacekeeping forces were proposed for the Gulf and for Fiji, contemplated for Afghanistan, and mounted in Sri Lanka. The last was a one-nation peacekeeping force of the regional hegemon India. Another country for which an international force has long been mooted is Namibia. China's attitude towards launching and financing UN peacekeeping forces underwent a favourable change in the early 1980s, and there are indications that Soviet attitudes may be in the process of a similar transformation under Gorbachev's influence in the mid-1980s (Hawkes, 1987). It is timely, therefore, to reflect upon the origins, meaning and experiences of international peacekeeping forces as a technique, not of conflict resolution, but of conflict regulation.[1]

PACIFIC SETTLEMENT AND COLLECTIVE SECURITY

One of the most enduring if least endearing features of human history is systematic violence between members of the human family. In the modern era of the nation-state, this has taken the form of organised warfare between states. International organisation is an important means for arranging the functioning of the state-based international system more satisfactorily than had proved to be the case in conditions of international anarchy. But international organisation in turn is characterised by a certain tension. On the one hand, international organisation can be regarded as a step towards the establishment of a world government which would transcend the state system. On the other hand, international organisations are set up and managed by nation-states; the sovereign state remains the basic entity of international relations; and states have shown themselves singularly reluctant to accept significant encroachments upon their sovereignties. Thus international organisation, in addition to serving as a possible pointer to a future world government, can also be viewed as merely an agreement by, for and of states to engage in regular consultation and establish joint machinery for the formulation and implementation of collective decisions.

The two major international organisations of the twentieth century have been the League of Nations after the First World War, and the United Nations Organisation after the Second World War. Their chronological linkage to the two world wars is not just a coincidence. In both instances, peoples horrified by the destructiveness of modern wars decided to create institutions for avoiding a repetition of such catastrophes in the future. The problem of peace and order is not new. The Napoleonic Empire imposed temporary order and unity on Europe by means of conquest. The other European powers set up an alternative Concert system in reaction to Napoleonic ambitions. They did this by transforming the original impulse of a military alliance for the single purpose of defeating Napoleon into the longer-term political goal of preventing a similar domination of Europe by any one power in the future. The Concert of Europe was the most comprehensive attempt until then to construct new machinery for keeping the peace among and by the great powers.

The Hague Conferences of 1899 and 1907 signalled the broadening of international relations in participation and agenda. They pointed to an emergent extra-European international system, in the management of which the lesser powers would demand a say; and, with their emphasis upon mediation, conciliation and inquiry, they demonstrated a rationalistic and legalistic approach to the problem of international disputes.

The League of Nations was the first permanent, general-purpose international organisation to embrace the full international community. Yet even the League was built around Europe as the core of the international political system. It also accepted the sovereign state as the central unit of international affairs, with the great powers as the predominant participants; and it did not challenge any of the fundamental principles of the traditional multistate system. The League began as the embodiment of humanity's aspirations for a better world. The Italian invasion of Ethiopia presented the League with its moment of greatest triumph: for the first time, the international community, acting through institutionalised channels, had condemned aggression, identified the aggressor, and imposed sanctions. But Ethiopia also stands as the symbol of failure to realise the high hopes held of the League at its creation, for the aggressor nation secured its ends through the means of its choice, namely conquest.

The interwar years were not entirely free of conflicts between the lesser powers. Efforts by the League to involve itself in these contained interesting pointers to future UN experience as well. In the Vilna dispute between Poland and Lithuania in 1920, the League Council proposed to resolve the status of Vilna by means of an international plebiscite, and began to form an international armed force to supervise them. The plan was dropped, however, in the face of hostile reaction from the Soviet Union, as well as because of Lithuanian reluctance to submit the dispute to plebiscite. In the Greco–Bulgarian conflict of 1925, by contrast, Aristide Briand of France, in his capacity as President of the Council of the League of Nations, successfully cabled both parties to cease hostilities immediately. Briand's order proved effective, the Greek offensive was called off, a League commission consisting of British, French and Italian observers supervised the ceasefire, and the dispute was settled by peaceful negotiations. In the Chaco War between Bolivia and Paraguay (1932–1935), Paraguay was able to defy the League and achieve most of its aims by force of arms.

Thus the Chaco case was a complete failure of the League; the Vilna case demonstrated a degree of loyalty to League principles, but not to the extent of military engagement; the Greco–Bulgarian case was successfully settled by decisive League intervention. In the last instance, Britain and France were interested in maintaining the *status quo,* and were able to give effect to their will. It is open to question as to whether Briand's directive proved effective because he had the authority of the League or of France behind him. The Chaco and Vilna, by contrast, were far removed from the centres of the League powers (the USSR was not a member of the League in 1920), the vital interests of the League powers were not threatened, and forceful intervention could have been treated as encroachments upon the spheres of interest of the USA or the USSR. Thus even successful collective action under the League did not suspend balance of power considerations, since League involvement in the Greco–Bulgarian case could be construed as coincidental rather than contingent. Conversely, nevertheless, in the Vilna dispute, the League did perform the useful function of enabling the weaker state, Lithuania, to concede defeat without loss of *amour propre* by doing so ostensibly to the League rather than to Poland (Carr, 1977: 107).

The League was killed by the Second World War; its legacy of international organisation lives on in the United Nations. The most important part of the legacy was the concept, by now firmly entrenched, yet revolutionary in 1919, that the community of nations has both the moral right and the legal competence to discuss and judge the international conduct of its memebrs. In particular, both the League and the UN embodied the idea that aggressive war is a crime against humanity, with every state having the interest, right and duty to collaborate in preventing it. An important step in the development of the idea was the Pact of Paris of 1928, wherein signatories condemned "recourse to war for the solution of international controversies and renounce[d] it as an instrument of national policy in relations with one another." The practical significance of the Pact was eroded by its non-enforceability and by the several qualifications attached by various signatories, e.g. the extension of self-defence to embrace colonies. Yet the declaration of principle, even if it fell well short of being a contractual obligation, was of great symbolic significance in underwriting the conception that war was henceforth to be treated as an illegitimate method of dispute settlement.

In a sense the interwar years were witness to an increasing infusion of idealism as manifested in the League of Nations. The organisation was prepared to condemn Japanese aggression in Manchuria, despite there being no prospect of any collective action being undertaken. In the case of Italian aggression against Ethiopia, the League took the additional step of imposing economic sanctions. Their eventual failure does not negate the advancement of the ideal that the international community can take collective enforcement measures against outlaws. Some of the other innovative ideas that were carried over from the League experiment to the United Nations included respect for the rights of small nations, economic and social cooperation, the habit of public debate on international crises, the formation of an international civil service, and the establishment of a world court.

The closeness with which the UN was modelled upon the League was testimony also to the fact that while the League had failed, people still had faith in the idea of an umbrella international organisation to oversee world peace and cooperation. While many of the Charter provisions were borrowed directly from the Covenant, others represented substantial codifications of League procedures or logical developments of nascent League ideas. Seemingly the most significant advance from the League to the UN lay in the area of enforcement machinery. The UN incorporated the League proscription on the use of force for national objectives, but inserted the additional prescription to use force in support of international, that is UN, authority. As proof of the added potency of the new organisation, the UN Security Council was given the power to decide whether international peace was threatened, whether sanctions were to be imposed, and, if so, then the nature of the sanctions, including military force. Most importantly, such decisions by the Security Council would be binding upon all the members of the United Nations.

The appearance of enhanced effectiveness by the UN was a major argument advanced in its favour in 1945 in comparison with the discredited and discarded League. Force, it was argued, would henceforth be put to the service of law, for the Security Council was being established as the equivalent of a supreme war-making organisation of the international community. Article 1.1 of the Charter declares the primary purpose of the UN as being to maintain international peace and security. The Charter specifies two chief means to this end, namely pacific settlement of disputes and collective enforcement against threats to or breaches of the peace. The trend towards narrowing the permissible range of unilateral resort to force by nation-states has been matched by the historical movement to broaden the range of instruments available to states to settle their disputes by means short of war. The UN Charter devotes the entire Chapter VI (Articles 33–38) to the subject of the pacific settlement of disputes. The techniques of peaceful settlement range from bilateral negotiations between the disputants to formal adjudication by third parties. Pacific settlement thus assumes that war is an outdated technique for settling international disputes, that prevention of war is both possible and desirable, that the way to achieve this goal is by providing a functional equivalent to war, and that the task of international organisations therefore is to provide a variety of peaceful substitutes to war and encourage disputants to use them. The Security Council cannot however compel member states to implement resolutions adopted under Chapter VI. The efficacy of UN action for the peaceful resolution of disputes is circumscribed by this retention of the principle of voluntarism. Nevertheless, the proposition that the international community has a stake in war-avoidance justifying its involvement in bilateral disputes between member-states is no longer questioned. Similarly, states wishing to resort to armed force beyond their borders must today act under the pressure of demonstrating that prior attempts at pacific settlement were tried, exhausted and proved fruitless. That is, the normative principle of the primacy of peaceful over forceful means has become firmly entrenched.

The resolution of international disputes by peaceful means, facilitated if need be by the United Nations, is a desirable goal. The prevention of a major war among the family of nations is the essential and minimum test of the UN. At its core, therefore, the UN represents the world's second major attempt at establishing a collective security system, which rejects the pursuit of security by policies of isolation, self-help, alliances or world government. After the First World War, collective security under the

League was a conscious substitute for systems of alliances and balance of power policies that were 'forever discredited'.

Unlike pacific settlement, collective security is not concerned with the causes and conditions of war. Only one assumption is necessary, that wars are probable; only one normative premise is required, that wars must be prevented or stopped. The variety of causes and types of war are irrelevant to the theory of collective security. Because collective security is concerned just to restrain military action, it leaves aside the pacific settlement techniques of "negotiation, enquiry, mediation, conciliation, arbitration, judicial settlement ... or other peaceful means of their own choice" by disputants (Article 33 of the UN Charter). Predicated upon the proposition that war can be prevented by the deterrent effect of overwhelming power being brought to bear against any state contemplating the use of force, collective security entails the imposition of diplomatic, economic and military sanctions against international outlaws. Thus where pacific settlement seeks to persuade disputing states to resolve differences peacefully from a world-order perspective, collective security seeks to dissuade them from resorting to violence for the larger good of preserving world peace or, failing that, from the narrower consideration of avoiding certain defeat. In specific instances, collective security elevates peace over justice, although a continuing lack of congruence between peace and justice will lead to the eventual atrophy of any collective security system.

Enforcement measures available to the UN are contained in Chapter VII of the Charter (Articles 39–51). Articles 42 and 43 in particular authorise the Security Council to "take such action by air, sea or land forces as may be necessary to maintain or restore international peace and security," and require member-states to make available to the UN such "armed forces, assistance, and facilities" as may be necessary for the purpose. Thus while the United Nations as a settler of disputes can only recommend desirable courses of action to disputing members, as a policeman it can impose decisions upon violently erring states. That is, while the nations of the world have been adequately aroused to the dangers of war to make it an offence, they still lack sufficient commonality of interest to accept compulsory third-party jurisdiction in disputes short of war.

Efforts to devise an operational collective security system in the League and the UN have been thwarted by a fundamental tension in the concept. Almost by definition, only major powers can threaten international peace and security. War between lesser states may be deplorable and unhealthy for their nationals; but it cannot of itself endanger *world* peace. Only the prospect of war between powerful states directly, or their involvement on rival sides in a quarrel between minor powers, can pose a challenge to the international order. Collective security understood as the maintenance of international peace and security is therefore superfluous in respect of small states. Equally, however, collective security is impossible to enforce against major powers. For, and again by definition, any attempt to launch military measures against a great power would bring about the very calamity that the system is designed to avoid, namely a world war. This was true even in pre-nuclear times; it is a truism in the nuclear age.

The United Nations has sought to avoid the latter eventuality by conferring permanent membership of the Security Council upon the great powers, and by providing permanent members with the power to veto any UN action launched by the Security Council (Article 27.3). The practical effect of the clause is that the extensive decision-making competence of the Security Council, necessary for the successful operation of a collective security system, is severely curtailed by the extensive decision-blocking competence of the permanent members.

The veto clause thus effectively negates the collective security aspect of the UN. Yet its insertion was necessary for sound political reasons which remain as valid today as they were in 1945. In reality, peace depends less on the virtues of international organisation and more upon agreement among the great powers. The Congress system of Europe of the last century acknowledged that the power of the major states both enabled and obliged them to accept a special responsibility for the management of international order. The Council of the League of Nations in conferring a privileged position upon the permanent members was an embodiment of the Congress concept; the Security Council of the UN gives it similar structural continuity. That is, permanent membership of the Security Council allows the great powers to act jointly to keep peace among the rest of the world community. The veto clause is the symbol of their special status as much as the chief constitutional instrument by which to defend their exclusive position. The requirement of great-power unanimity for decisive Security Council action can also be viewed as an assurance of cooperation rather than conflict between the great powers, with fatal consequences for the organisation in the latter event. It is worth remembering too that by comparison with the League with its unanimity requirement for the entire Council, the UN in fact took the power of veto away from non-great powers rather than conferred it upon great powers. The point is that, in the final analysis, the veto registers the power realities of the international political world. In most cases where UN efforts to deal with outbreaks of international violence are frustrated by a veto, it is in reality the fact of great-power opposition, and not its expression in the form of a Security Council veto, which is the obstacle to peace.

The mistrust between the great powers also put paid to the idea of a Military Staff Committee (MSC) which would function as the Security Council's strategic adviser. Articles 45–47 of the UN Charter called for the establishment of an MSC, consisting of the Chiefs of Staff of the five permanent members, to tackle the organisation and deployment of military forces which would be placed at the Security Council's disposal by UN members. The MSC was to be responsible for making plans for the application of armed force before they were needed, and for the strategic direction of armed forces when they were used. There is no expectation today of the MSC functioning in the foreseeable future as was intended in 1945. The failure to conclude special arrangements governing the allocation of armed forces by member states to the UN has freed the members of legal obligations to supply the Security Council with armed forces other than on a voluntary basis.

The closest that the UN has come to engaging in collective enforcement action was in Korea in 1950. Yet the collective security character of the UN action in Korea was heavily qualified. In essence, the US responded to communist North Korean invasion, and the UN responded to the immediate US reaction. The initiative was American, taken in the context of the cold war, and invoking the moral support of the UN for a resort to force that would have occurred anyway. That is, the UN action in Korea was made possible by a temporary marriage of convenience between collective security and collective defence. Action in Korea did not signify American acceptance of fresh obligations to replace national power politics by community policing that would protect all victims of aggression everywhere. Rather, the US identified American interests with those of the non-communist world and demonstrated its determination to resist direct or proxy Soviet aggression anywhere (Wolfers, 1962).

Furthermore, even the UN response to the US initiative for military action was made possible by a rather fortuitous combination of circumstances. The Soviet Union was absent from the Security Council in protest at an unrelated issue. Subsequent Soviet protestations that the UN action was illegal because the resolution did not meet the unambiguous criterion of Article 27.3 requiring the concurring votes of the permanent members was of limited academic interest only. The United Nations was helped by the fact that it had its own commission 'on the ground' when the invasion occurred. A UN commission was able to confirm immediately that aggression had occurred, and identify the aggressor. The ready availability of American troops in nearby Japan allowed the UN to overcome the problems posed by the non-implementation of Article 43. An important background factor was that in this early test of the UN so soon after the Second World War, member-states and Trygve Lie, the first Secretary-General of the UN, were more readily inclined to adopt a firm policy towards a clear case of unprovoked aggression. Yet even in Korea, action was formally taken in response to a "breach of the peace" rather than an act of aggression.

The record of the UN in the field of pacific settlement of disputes is a similarly qualified one. On balance, the organisation has helped states to behave less conflictually, to form habits of cooperation, to develop shared norms and perceptions. A number of different studies show that a substantial number of international disputes has been referred to the UN, and that this tendency has increased in comparison to the League record in the interwar period (Butterworth, 1978; K. J. Holsti, 1977; Jacobsen, 1979). A majority of disputes that do not find their way to the UN involves the major powers: "experience has paralleled the understanding implicit in the veto provision in the United Nations charter, that international organisations do not have the capacity to deal with all disputes involving the most powerful states" (Jacobsen, 1979: 211). In other words, while the United Nations cannot honestly be said to have maintained international peace and security, the Security Council has nevertheless played a *peace-influencing* role, and the General Assembly too has undertaken a *peace-shaping* role, in their engagements in crisis decision-making and management.

PEACEKEEPING

International peacekeeping as a conflict management technique is of relatively recent development. The United Nations, as we have seen, was entrusted with the maintenance of world peace in two ways: the search for peaceful settlement where disputes arose, and the enforcement of collective security where states involved in disputes abandoned negotiation to resort to force. The principles of the UN Charter are clearly acceptable to the overwhelming bulk of countries today, as signified by their formal signature of the Charter. Unfortunately, acceptance of the practical application of UN principles is a larger task, made more difficult by encroachments upon the sacred concept of national sovereignty.

With the attainment of a reliable system of collective security being deferred to a distant date, states moved to guarantee national security by means of collective defence, and the international community groped towards damage-limitation techniques to avoid and contain conflicts. Peacekeeping as an institution evolved in the grey zone between pacific settlement and military enforcement. It grew side by side with preventive diplomacy. The last was practised and articulated—in that order—by Dag Hammarskjöld. The United Nations was to aim at keeping new conflicts outside the sphere of bloc differences. The technique of preventive diplomacy was to be used to forestall the competitive intrusion of the rival power blocs into conflict situations that were either the result or potential cause of a power vacuum in the cold war.

Preventive diplomacy differs from peaceful settlement of disputes, then, in that while the latter consists of facilitating the reestablishment and maintenance of peaceful relations, the former aims chiefly to confine the conflict within local limits. It is a policy designed to contain a peripheral war, to achieve a kind of 'disengagement before the fact'. And preventive diplomacy was given concrete expression by inserting the thin blue wedge between combatants.

The linkages between preventive diplomacy and international peacekeeping, established in UNEF, were articulated by U Thant (1963). Both resulted from the impracticality of collective security, which necessitates three elements that are in opposition to peacekeeping requirements: a definition and determination of aggression; identification of the guilty party; and a contribution of forces by the major powers. It was not until 14 December 1974 that the United Nations adopted, without vote, a definition of aggression as "the use of armed force by a State against the sovereignty, territorial integrity or political independence of another State, or in any other manner inconsistent with the Charter of the United Nations" [General Assembly Resolution 3314 (XXIX)]. The United Nations has never determined an act of aggression to have taken place.

The Hammarskjöld approach thus focused on noncoercive and facilitative activities rather than on repelling aggression through armed combat. Specific United Nations activities have been varied, ranging from observation and supervision to trying to prevent contacts between opponents, resolving socioeconomic problems, and mediating and conciliating. The theme common to all is to promote international stability and support peaceful change outside the axis of great power rivalry. The primary purpose of peacekeeping remains to bring about and preserve a cessation of hostilities.

A general matter that has received some attention is the parallels between municipal and international peacekeeping functions. Swift has argued that peacekeeping operations are more akin to armed police work than to standard combat. They have no military objectives, they are barred from active combat, they are located between rather than in opposition to hostile elements, and they negotiate rather than fight. Nevertheless, few states acknowledge that United Nations peacekeeping requires special training and preparation, and fewer still provide it. Peacekeeping operations are not quite analogous to municipal police forces either: the two operate under entirely different assumptions and conditions, and derive legitimacy from different authorities.

Examples

In sum, international peacekeeping forces can never enforce world peace, for they lack both mandated authority and operational capability to do so. Yet even while failing to bring about world peace, UN forces have nonetheless succeeded in stabilising several potentially dangerous situations. UN peacekeeping has been used essentially as a mechanism for dealing on an *ad hoc* basis with crises in which third party involvement is viewed as desirable or necessary.

In actual practice, therefore, peacekeeping operations have been diverse in function and size, ranging from a few observers (around 40) on the India–Pakistan border,[2] to a 20,000-man force in the Congo.[3] The diversity in functions results from the need to confront different types of situations. The tension on a volatile international frontier or ceasefire line can be dampened somewhat by placing a UN patrol as a physical buffer or intermediary, for example the two Emergency Forces between Egypt and Israel.[4] Or the UN can help to keep intra-national tensions from becoming international powder kegs, as in Cyprus.[5] Indeed, in the Congo a UN force was used to reestablish the authority of the central government in order to dam the tide of political disintegration that threatened to wash away the newly proclaimed republic. Finally, international units have also proven useful in easing the process of transition from a colonial administration to an indigenous one, as in the case of Irian Jaya [West New Guinea].[6]

The first steps towards a pragmatic contribution to peacekeeping had already been foreshadowed by the League. In the Vilna dispute referred to earlier, the League contemplated the establishment of a nine-state "supervisory force" to monitor the proposed plebiscite. Its role was characterised by the League Council as being a peace force, not a fighting force, simply there to perform police duties. The idea was actually implemented in 1935 in the case of the plebiscite to determine the disposition of the Saar. The international force under British command was structured on a similar basis to the Vilna force concept, and was "entrusted with the maintenance of law and order before, during and after the plebiscite" (Rikhye *et al.*, 1974: 120).

The earliest UN peacekeeping missions of the supervisory-observer variety had already been undertaken by the end of the 1940s in the Balkans, Greece, Kashmir, Korea, Indonesia and Palestine. Their experience shows that observer groups are needed, and they work: not as a panacea, but as long-lived expedients. The Korean operation cannot be said to represent an instance of UN peacekeeping proper. Instead, it was UNEF (1956–1967) in the Middle East which first fully described the new institution of part-time soldiering for the UN, and which threw up difficult custodial problems in the wake of the divorce between security requirements and political issues. UNEF established that the cardinal distinction between collective security and peacekeeping lay in their reliance upon force and consent respectively. The immediate goal of the Force was to provide a fig-leaf of respectability for the withdrawal of the aggressors. Britain and France were able to argue that their actions had been undertaken in discharge of great power responsibility for the management of world order. Once their actions had galvanised the UN into decisive intervention, they could gracefully withdraw. Whether or not the Anglo–French rationalisations carried any international conviction is beside the point. What is important is that the arguments facilitated their withdrawal. Once the aggressors had withdrawn, UNEF's mission was transformed into the larger role of separating the erstwhile Egyptian–Israeli combatants. It did so not by means of the Charter formula of collective security involving the might of the major powers, but by means of a peaceful interpository force made up of contingents from the minor powers. UNEF was neither expected nor equipped to engage in hostilities; its deterrent effect was to be produced by its very presence as a symbol of the international community.

In fact the Egyptian–Israeli border experienced more than a decade of peace and calm unlike any preceding period since the creation of Israel in 1948. The Force kept Egyptian and Israeli troops physically apart. It produced a marked reduction in cross-border commando raids by Arab *fedayeen* units. It shielded Egypt from a possible Israeli invasion: Israeli willingness and ability to use large-scale force is a fact of Middle East life. Conversely, its very presence signified Egyptian desire not to heighten tensions with Israel.

By the same token, once Egypt ordered UNEF out in 1967, President Gamel Abdul Nasser signalled a change of course from low-tension policy to brinksmanship, or even belligerency towards Israel. From a peacekeeping point of view, the most important lesson of 1967 was the demonstration of UNEF's real significance. "What it did during its 10 years in the Middle East was not to keep the peace. Rather it helped Israel and Egypt to implement their temporary disposition to live in peace" (James, 1969: 205).

The manner of UNEF's demise in 1967 was as dramatic as had been its creation in 1956. In the gathering storm of the Six Day War, UNEF was asked to withdraw by the Egyptian chief of staff on 16 May 1967. The commander of UNEF referred the request to the UN Secretary-General. On 17 May, Arab forces were on the international frontier and in occupation of all UNEF posts. U Thant met his Advisory Committee, composed of the representatives of Brazil, Canada, Ceylon, Colombia, India, Norway and Pakistan, in New York. The committee failed to find a consensus solution. Inexplicably, neither the Secretary-General nor any member of the Advisory Committee referred the matter to the General Assembly, UNEF's mandating organ, which could have been called into special emergency session. Nor did any member of the Security Council seize the initiative. Thant ordered UNEF's withdrawal on 18 May; the straits of Tiran were blockaded by Nasser on 22 May, despite earlier Israeli warnings that this would be regarded as a *casus belli* as well as Anglo–American–French promises of March 1957 to assure free passage through the straits; the Canadian contingent with UNEF was withdrawn by 29 May; Israel launched its preemptive strikes on 5 June; the last UNEF units were evacuated on 17 June, but not before 15 UN troops had been killed.

Thant's decision to withdraw UNEF provoked immediate political and a lingering academic controversy. The "good faith" agreement of November 1956 between Egypt and Hammarskjöld had required the presence of UNEF until its task was completed. Whether UNEF in 1967 was engaged in the task referred to in the 1956 agreement is debatable (Comay, 1983; Elaraby, 1983). Thant argued that legally, UNEF's presence was conditional upon Egyptian consent; once the latter was withdrawn, the former had to follow. Politically, the Force would have quickly disintegrated with the announcement by India and Yugoslavia on 18 May that they would withdraw their contingents from UNEF, whatever the decision of the Secretary-General. Practically, the Force was made redundant in its interpository role once Egyptian troops were on the international frontier and had renewed visual and physical contact with Israeli forces.

U Thant's decision has since been supported by a troika of peacekeeping practitioners, including the UNEF commander of the time, General I. J. Rikhye (Rikhye *et al.*, 1974: 59–63). An academic analyst of peacekeeping summed it up thus:

... if the U.N. had tried to maintain UNEF in its place contrary to Egypt's express will, it would not have been making an effective contribution towards pacification, would thereby have damaged its own reputation, and might also have reduced the likelihood of it being asked to engage in peace-keeping operations in respect of other disputes (James, 1969: 312).

The political reality of 1967 was that any attempt to maintain UNEF against the express wishes of Egypt would have encountered a Soviet veto in the Security Council. It is difficult to imagine that a majority of the small-state membership of the General Assembly would have countenanced the forcible occupation of Egyptian territory by UN troops against Egyptian will. Politically, an interpretation contrary to Thant's would in effect have penalised the victim of the original aggression requiring the emplacement of UNEF in the first place. As the Egyptian foreign minister said in 1956:

Our clear understanding—and I am sure it is the clear understanding of the Assembly—is that the Force is in Egypt only in relation to the present attack against Egypt by the United Kingdom, France and Israel, and for the purposes directly connected with the incursion of the invading forces into Egyptian territory. The United Nations Emergency Force is in Egypt, not as an occupation force, not as a replacement for the invaders, not to clear the Canal of obstructions, not to resolve any question or settle any problem, be it in relation to the Suez Canal, to Palestine or to any other matter; it is not there to infringe upon Egyptian sovereignty in any fashion or to any extent, but, on the contrary, to give expression to the determination of the United Nations to put an end to the aggression committed against Egypt and to the presence of the invading forces in Egyptian territory (Elaraby, 1983: 71).

Between the establishment of UNEF in 1956 and its ignominious withdrawal in 1967, ONUC highlighted custodial problems in the Congo arising from the sudden departure of an irresponsible colonial power, with the United Nations dealing with the resulting authority vacuum only through floundering efforts. The force in Cyprus is a good example of time being a more likely solvent of a historical conflict than the UN—but the latter is the most likely means of gaining time. The 1970s saw a return of UN forces to the Middle East in the form of UNEF-II (1973–1979), UNDOF,[7] and UNIFIL.[8]

MULTINATIONAL PEACEKEEPING IN THE MIDDLE EAST

The Middle East was also the setting in the 1980s for a steady displacement of UN peacekeeping by great power multilateral peacekeeping in the Sinai MFO[9] and the Beirut MNF.[10] I have analysed elsewhere the tension between the pursuit of limited peacekeeping through United Nations authority on the one hand, and a markedly more coercive effort by a group of powers to keep the peace in Beirut through a Multinational Force (Thakur, 1987).

One of the originators of UNEF, Canadian foreign minister Lester Pearson, aptly characterised a UN peacekeeping force as "an intermediate technique between merely passing resolutions and actually fighting" (Pearson, 1957: 401). The constraining effect of many of the core principles of UN peacekeeping—non-use of force because of military neutrality between the belligerents, non-intervention in domestic quarrels because of political neutrality with respect to the conflict, non-participation by great powers because of their mutual suspicions—has occasionally produced controversy and frustration in the organisation. The United Nations has refused to abandon them, however, because they represent a middle way between abdication of responsibility for management of the international order, and turmoil if the organisation attempts to shake off the Charter shackles on collective military action. Experience, including that of the MNF, has reinforced the soundness of the principle of non-use of force by peacekeeping operations. Impartiality becomes progressively harder to sustain with increasing use of force, for then the UN becomes a stake in the power struggle concerned. Perceptions of partial use of force erode the UN's authority and diminish the organisation's capacity to play a distinctive role in world affairs. The use of force at the behest of a UN majority is risky because majorities re-form as interests shift, and the number of minorities whose support has been lost could add up to constitute a majority.

The incapacity to take decisive executive action has heightened the role of declaratory action by the UN and strengthened its legitimising function. Or, to put it another way, the role of the UN as authoritative expositor has increased in proportion to its ineffectiveness as authoritative allocator of international values. The fact that the MNF was organised outside the UN framework demonstrated a reduced role for the UN in the foreign policy ideologies of the four MNF countries.

This is not to deny the special role of the great powers in international peacekeeping. Indeed permanent membership of the Security Council consecrated their special position in the UN scheme of helping to shape international peace. The veto clause conferred the further competence upon the great powers to protect international encroachments upon their own vital interests. In return, as part of their obligations towards a responsible management of international order, the great powers agreed to eschew unilateral interventions in favour of concerted action through the UN system. Consequently, even great power concert today needs the legitimising approbation of the UN for optimum effectiveness in regulating international behaviour.

In this context, if the 'international villain' in the case of the MFO in Sinai was the Soviet superpower, in the Beirut MNF it was the Americans. One of the chief original impulses to UN peacekeeping as a distinctive technique of conflict control was to preserve peace by avoiding unilateral superpower intervention. A militarily and politically neutral international peacekeeping presence, underpinned by the authority of the UN, can help both superpowers to steer clear of confused local conflicts which lie beyond their power to solve but could drain their prestige. The tragedy of the MNF was that four important countries had to relearn this painful lesson at considerable human and political cost.

Moreover, the use of national power rather than UN authority as an instrument of behaviour control also entails certain 'opportunity costs', including a reduced ability to make the peace. The goal of peacekeeping units is not the creation of peace, but rather the containment of war, so that others can search for peace in stable conditions. Unlike the United Nations, however, the United States as a superpower cannot be impartial towards the issues themselves. It has adversaries and allies, and is ever mindful of national interests. These inescapable realities sucked US marines into the morass of Lebanese politics. There was a contradiction between the reality of sectarian war and peacekeeping's principle of non-intervention. In the end the US failed to reconcile the logical and practical incompatibility between the role of firefighter and chief supplier of incendiaries to one of a group of arsonists. The role of American marines was reduced to that of a superpower militia by 1984, and their task had contracted to defending their own presence. As Washington grew more firmly committed to the Gemayel government, so opposing factions identified the marines increasingly as part of enemy forces. Once this happened, the presence of marines was no longer impartial third party peacekeeping, but an obstacle to Lebanese reconciliation and peace. Such a transformation is inconceivable with UN forces. At worst they can become ineffectual peacekeepers, but never hurdles to peace.

The United Nations system has since inception encouraged non-UN action designed to assist in restoring peace in a troubled world. Nevertheless there are at least three further adverse consequences that may follow from the non-UN peacekeeping forces set up in the Middle East in 1982.

Firstly, we still need an authority such as the United Nations as the main instrumentality for maintaining international peace. No one denies that the UN has worked less than satisfactorily, and that it has failed to satisfy expectations lowered even to much more modest levels than the original hopes at its creation. Yet it is also true that only an organisation such as the UN can offer any prospects of a functioning international system of collective peace. The UN Security Council possesses ultimate and predominant authority in the sphere of international peace and security. Establishing peacekeeping forces outside the UN framework can only weaken its status and authority. (Critics of the UN would probably argue that the MFO and MNF did not so much dilute as register the fact of prior erosion of the organisation's authority.)

Secondly, the development harms the basic concept that responsibility for maintaining international peace and security belongs to the world community as a whole, acting in a politically impartial manner. For all its faults, the United Nations remains the one organisation that houses the divided fragments of humanity. The advantages of UN peacekeeping stand out more sharply in the longer perspective—a united international command set up by the Security Council and enjoying the support of the entire membership of the UN. Institutions such as the UN cannot be built instantly, but require constant constructive work and loyalty to its founding principles. A properly functioning United Nations is still the most likely pathway towards the indispensable objective of a civilised world order. The short-term advantages of politically expedient measures can cut across the need to nurture the UN as the centre for harmonising national actions in the attainment of common goals as expressed in Article 1.4 of the Charter.

Thirdly, UN peacekeeping is still useful as a means of insulating a regional crisis from extra-regional conflicts. The establishment of the MFO in the Sinai and its smooth functioning was important to US interests in the Middle East. The MFO was the final step in implementing the Egyptian–Israeli peace treaty, which in turn was the curtain raiser to the preferred American approach to a peaceful resolution of the Arab–Israeli conflict. The MNF in Beirut was made up entirely of NATO countries. Understandably, this did nothing to diminish Soviet and radical Arab suspicions. Unlike the United Nations as an organisation, the United States—or any other major power—cannot be impartial towards the issues themselves; hence the transition from "peacekeeping" to "peace–cum–containment" in Lebanon.

The peace of the world may well depend upon the political wisdom, moral resoluteness and military power of the United States. The experience of the MNF vindicates the soundness of the principles of UN peacekeeping, and suggests that the US would be better advised to channel its efforts through the authoritative framework of the United Nations.[11] Soviet Foreign Minister Eduard Shevardnadze recognised this principle recently, when in his address to the UN General Assembly in September 1987 he suggested that keeping the Gulf open for navigation by the world's merchant fleet should be a job for the entire world community, "on whose behalf the UN will be acting" (Hawkes, 1987).

The UN cannot use force without first becoming an international enforcement machinery, capable of exerting military power against aggression and in anticipation of aggression. This could not be done without overcoming the problem of divided views and divided interests. But in order to overcome this obstacle, the UN would have to abandon the consensual approach in the plural assembly for the centralisation of authority in its executive organ. It is precisely because the UN would have to develop along these lines in order to function as a successful collective security system that it has failed to do so. The lesson is not that the UN can be made to function more satisfactorily in its enforcement role with enhanced political will, but that political realities rule out any substantial improvement in the UN collective security machinery. Brian Urquhart argues that "It is precisely because the [Security] Council cannot agree on enforcement operations that the peacekeeping technique has been devised, and it is precisely because an operation is a peacekeeping operation that governments are prepared to make troops available to serve on it" (1983: 165). There is another very important implication which follows from this regarding judgments of the value and utility of peacekeeping operations. Since peacekeeping evolved as a second-best substitute for a non-obtainable collective security system, it is neither fair nor logical to assess its worth on the criterion of collective enforcement.

Fortunately, in the course of the development of the UN, this reality received early recognition. Peacekeeping as a substitute for collective enforcement resulted from such recognition. The MNF was defeated in the end because it tried to blur the important conceptual distinctions between peacekeeping, collective enforcement, and collective defence. It was unable to escape the same fundamental constraints that had hampered the UNIFIL operation, and proved itself to be even more ill-equipped to overcome those obstacles. The gradual drive towards realism at the United Nations has seen the displacement of the system of collective security by "a general doctrine of collective peace-keeping" (Cassese, 1978: 237). The important point about this transformation is that it marks a partial reversion to the Charter system. Specifically, it is based on the premise that appropriate collective actions in the sphere of international peace and security can best be authorised by the UN Security Council. Such authorisation is not possible without the consent of the permanent members. The Soviet Union and the United States risk little in authorising a politically neutral UN peacekeeping force if requested or consented to by the parties. Indeed, by stamping it with the authority of the Security Council, the major powers ensure that they retain control over the policy directions and destiny of the force without incurring the stigma of intervention themselves. United Nations peacekeeping enables both superpowers to pursue a policy of area denial to the adversary without asserting a direct military presence.

At the same time, the Sinai Field Mission demonstrated a role that great powers alone can play in underwriting UN peacekeeping operations. While national military forces use the most modern military technology available, UN missions are typically hampered by access to equipment of world war vintage. The Sinai Field Mission, manned by US "civilian personnel and equipped with moden surveillance and communications equipment ... provided strong evidence of the utility of technology in peacekeeping and in the enhancement of the confidence of invaded parties ... in their reliance on the disengagement of forces" (Stokes, 1983: 218). The Sinai Field Mission operated independently of but in close coordination with UNEF-II to buttress Egyptian and Israeli confidence in the UN peacekeeping force.

Finally, superpower support for UN peacekeeping forces has also been described aptly as "a policy of limited liability" (Pelcovits, 1984: 84), in that a superpower can extricate itself from a UN venture at minimal political cost and much more easily than from a peacekeeping force of its own choosing. Direct participation in the MNF meant that American presence in the Middle East became as politically exposed as the marines were militarily exposed at Beirut airport. Ready availability as a convenient scapegoat may be a valuable if unappreciated contribution to international peace and security by the United Nations. There will be occasions when political leaders will welcome the United Nations' ability to provide a 'golden bridge' across which national governments can retire to safety, as well as a 'lightning rod' for deflecting and burying the more violent political reactions at home to international events.[12]

The question that should be asked, therefore, is not how effective UN peacekeeping is, but whether international peacekeeping represents value for money for an annual investment of 6 cents per capita.

CONCLUSION

The history of United Nations peacekeeping is a mirror to the record of the organisation's own evolution: the initial high hopes, the many frustrations on the ground, and the sometimes bitter disappointments in the end. Another thread that is common to both the United Nations and its peacekeeping ventures is the failure of states to make full use of the international machinery available to them for the avoidance of war and the peaceful resolution of conflicts. The cold war, the era of decolonisation, the years of *détente,* the fear of a nuclear war: these have all had their microcosmic reflections in the United Nations.

Since the establishment of the United Nations in 1945, the nature of crises requiring peacekeeping rescue missions has undergone important transformations, and the mandates of the peacekeeping forces have become correspondingly more complex and variegated. In the process, peacekeeping has not just survived as an institution; it has in fact acquired enhanced legitimacy in certain circumstances. The Middle East region, and the Arab–Israeli conflict, are particularly instructive in examining the potential and limitations of the effectiveness of the United Nations in contemporary conflicts where local dynamics intersect with superpower rivalry. Tensions in the area, punctuated by outbursts of hostility, have spanned the entire period of UN existence. The frontier between Israel and Lebanon remained relatively quiet for more than twenty years after the armistice agreements of 1949. By contrast, the Lebanon crisis has presented one of the gravest and most complex challenges to international order in the 1970s and 1980s. The country itself, an unfortunate but largely innocent bystander in the main Arab–Israeli dispute, has been in complete disarray. The status of one of the chief belligerents, the PLO, continues to be in contention. The events of Lebanon have seriously strained relations between Israel and the United Nations, and between Syria and the United States. The UNIFIL and MNF peacekeeping forces, never clear of danger, suffered more casualties between them than any other peacekeeping operation.

The contribution of the two non-UN peacekeeping forces, the MFO in the Sinai and the MNF in Beirut, towards an overall Middle East peace settlement cannot be regarded as significantly greater than that of the various UN forces in the region over the years. But international peacekeeping clearly goes on. It has shown itself remarkably resilient. When the circumstances are right, if a military solution proves illusory and a peaceful setllement remains elusive, then international peacekeeping forces are both needed and desired.

International forces do, therefore, have a modest role to play as a useful multilateral instrument of de-escalation and conflict control. In the final analysis, the olive branch brigades are valuable stabilising elements in volatile environments. They cannot enforce the peace; but they can buy time. Given the intensity of conflicts and depths of distrust between local belligerents, peace would be even more tenuous in the absence of international forces. Moreover, they can help to contain sporadic incidents that are not meant to initiate a large-scale war. In other words, an important justification for peacekeeping is contemplating the alternatives—chaos or nuclear conflict. The deficiencies in the machinery of peacekeeping merely highlight the fact that such forces cannot be self-sustaining. It is perhaps more accurate, therefore, to speak of war-dampening rather than peace-keeping forces. Peacekeeping is useful because it is a substitute for a universal system of collective security which to date has proven unattainable. The danger is that peacekeeping may be mistaken as an adequate substitute for conflict resolution.

NOTES

1. This chapter draws substantially upon different parts of my *International Peacekeeping in Lebanon: United Nations Authority and Multinational Force* (Boulder: Westview, 1987).

2. United Nations Military Observer Group in India and Pakistan (UNMOGIP), 24 January 1949–present.

3. United Nations Operations in the Congo (ONUC), 15 July 1960–30 June 1964.

4. United Nations Emergency Force (UNEF), I: 12 November 1956–June 1967; II: 25 October 1973–24 July 1979.

5. United Nations Peacekeeping Force in Cyprus (UNFICYP), 27 March 1964–present.

6. United Nations Security Force in West New Guinea, 3 October 1962–30 April 1963.

7. United Nations Disengagement Observer Force, 3 June 1974–present.

8. United Natons Interim Force in Lebanon, 19 March 1978–present.

9. The Multinational Force and Observers in the Sinai, 25 April 1982–present.

10. The Multinational Force in Beirut, 21 August 1982–13 September 1982, and 24 September 1982–31 March 1984.

11. Somewhat paradoxically, the experience of the largely successful MFO may also be said to vindicate UN peacekeeping: "The MFO so closely resembles the UN model as to constitute an advertisement for UN peacekeeping" (Nelson, 1984–1985: 89); "the UN

can take pride in the fact that the Sinai force has been entirely organised on the basis of the UN experience in peacekeeping, that its commander is an old UN hand, and that the force was prepared, assembled and deployed with the advice of a former senior UN administrator" (Rikhye, 1984: 73).

12. A good illustration of both these advantages is provided by the dispute between New Zealand and France over the sinking of the Greenpeace boat *Rainbow Warrior* in Auckland in July 1985. Two French secret service agents involved in the bombing were sentenced to ten years' imprisonment, but France exerted economic pressure on New Zealand to secure their release. Having decided to give way, New Zealand looked for a face-saving formula, and submitted the dispute for binding arbitration to Javier Pérez de Cuéllar. Asked why, having agreed on the broad options, New Zealand and France could not settle the issue by themselves, Prime Minister David Lange replied: "Because ... it is a matter of having ... a political and sustainable verdict without the appearance of either side having capitulated"; "Prime Minister's Press Conference," 16 June 1986. That is, it would be easier politically to sell a deference to a ruling by the UN Secretary-General than a rank capitulation to France. Besides drawing upon the legitimacy of the UN and the authority of its chief executive, New Zealand could also claim some credit for resolving its international disputes through the approved channels of a civilised community. Similarly, the UN provided a convenient lightning rod along which to deflect most of the violent New Zealand reactions so as to render them harmless. Whether or not New Zealand agreed with the Secretary-General's ruling in its entirety, it had to uphold international law by accepting his binding decision to release the two agents: so argued the government, and who in New Zealand could openly say otherwise?

13

The Moral Paradigms of the Superpowers:
A Third World Perspective

Ali Mazrui

From an ethical point of view, one of the most disturbing things about the superpowers is that there are only two of them for the time being. Their physical duality has fed on the theme of ethical dualism.

After all, two lends itself to the notion of opposites and to the condition of dichotomy in political affairs. It lends itself to the obstinacy of believers against unbelievers, Jews against Gentiles, slave against freeman and friend against foe. Out of dualism has emerged the whole moral paradigm of evil at war with good. The two superpowers of the contemporary world are caught up in that history of dualism.

It is in the face of this dualism that the Third World has had to deal with the superpowers. Ideological preferences are of course part and parcel of superpower ethics. Socialism is supposed to be a redistribution of economic power in favour of the dispossessed. Liberalism is a redistribution of political power in favour of the marginalised.

The United States is a liberal polity domestically. But at the global level does American policy favour the redistribution of political power in favour of marginalised nations? The Soviet Union is a socialist system. But at the global level does Soviet policy favour the redistribution of economic power in favour of the dispossessed nations?

Although doctrinally an economic determinist, the Soviet Union's impact on economic change in the Third World is negligible. Although doctrinally liberal, the United States' impact on the liberation of the Third World is worse than negligible—it is negative. There are solid reasons for these doctrinal contradictions. Let us examine them more closely.[1]

THE SUPERPOWERS AND ECONOMIC REDISTRIBUTION

Even in the post-colonial era the Soviet Union and its allies have played a much smaller role in the economic development of, say, Africa than the West has done. There are a number of reasons as to why the capitalist world has been more economically relevant for Africa and other developing areas than the Soviet bloc.

In the first place the world's economic system is dominated by international capitalism in any case. The rules of international exchange are capitalist-derived—including a strong international leaning towards the principle of supply and demand as well as autonomy of market forces. The international conventions of economic behaviour are part of the western lexicon—including the rules of the General Agreement on Tariff and Trade (GATT).

The major international currencies of exchange are western currencies—the pivot of which is the American dollar itself. The major commercial banks of the world are—almost by definition—capitalist, casting out chains of indebtedness to one Third World country after another. Also western dominated are the major developmental banks of the world—with a pinnacle consisting of the World Bank under an eternal American presidency and the International Monetary Fund (IMF) under a continuing Western European director-generalship. In confrontations with the IMF, Third World countries have sometimes defied the Fund's conditionality. But in the end, most have recognised the mirage of "butter" on the wrong side of the bread—and capitulated to the tempting illusion.

As for the markets of Third World products, these are again primarily in the western world. The colonial structure of African economies especially has ignored the opportunities of trade with immediate neighbours—and sharpened the North–South and South–North flows of trade instead.

Then there is the whole dialectic of global production. While the genius of socialism may indeed be distribution, it is capitalism which has demonstrated a genius for production. No system in human history has shown a greater capacity for economic expansion than capitalism.

One result is that the West produces far more of what the Third World "needs" than does the Soviet bloc. And the quality of western products is usually superior to comparably priced products from the communist world. Western civilian technology tends to be more sophisticated—and western mass production and unit-cost efficiency ensures more competitive prices in commercial sales to the Third World.

Also relevant as part of the explanation for the western impact on Third World development is the role of foreign aid and international charity. Charity has often been capitalism's classical answer to problems of maldistribution. In the history of capitalism within the western world itself, charity has sometimes been capitalism's gesture of penance to the Christian conscience. In more pragmatic terms, charity has sought to diffuse not only the suffering of the poor but also their anger. Within the class structure of a capitalist society charity has also been a strategy of cooptation and of consolidating allegiance. The poor are made more loyal—and their leaders could respond to the lure of upward social mobility.

Of the four major reasons for extending foreign aid (charity, solidarity, cooptation and self-interest), the West operates on all four, depending upon the particular case. The Scandinavian countries and the Netherlands score high on aid for reasons of pure charity. So do the many private humanitarian groups from the Christian world generally. The Soviet bloc has no comparable private effort in aid and humanitarianism. For one thing, Soviet official atheism has eliminated missionary church organisations which might otherwise have operated in the Third World. Nor must it be forgotten that the focus of western missionary work has shifted from saving souls for the Hereafter to saving lives in the here–and–now. There has been a shift from a focus on salvation to an emphasis on service.

The Soviet system also lacks such private secular charities as the Ford and Rockefeller foundations and such crisis-oriented organisations as OXFAM and other famine relief bodies. Nor is the Soviet tax system geared towards providing tax incentives for those who want to be charitable. The system does not even acknowledge that it has millionaires of its own.

Then there is the Soviet Union's policy posture that underdevelopment in the Third World was caused by western imperialism—and has to be corrected by western compensation. It is indeed true that most of the flaws in African economies especially are directly due to the whole legacy of western imperialism. These flaws include such economic distortions as undue emphasis on cash crops, a leaning towards monoculturalism, the North–South orientation, the urban bias in development, and the elite bias in priorities. African problems of balance of payments, balance of trade, unstable export earnings and the accumulation of debts are substantially derived from those underlying colonial causes. The Soviet Union feels that it is not up to the socialist countries to bail out the West in the face of these post-colonial responsibilities. Nor do the socialist countries have the capacity—even if they had the will—to amend the international system in favour of the dispossessed. The West is in charge of the global economy.

Nor does the Soviet Union have the equivalent of the western world's private investment in developing countries. By definition the Soviet system has no multinational corporations to balance out the activities of western entrepreneurs. This whole area of western private initiative in the Third World has no mirror-image in Soviet experience.

Finally, there is the persistent Soviet belief that conditions of underdevelopment are fertile ground for a social revolution. Karl Marx himself argued that it was development—rather than underdevelopment—which created a revolutionary situation. It was because of this thesis that Marx expected the first socialist revolutions to occur in such advanced capitalist countries of his era as England and France. But Soviet policy-makers today know better—partly from the experience of their own revolution of 1917 but also from the history of Third World recruits to the ranks of the socialist community. Contrary to Marx, it is the weakest links of the capitalist chain which have been prone to breaking after all.

In the light of these ideological calculations, the Soviet Union can be forgiven for regarding underdevelopment in the Third World as at worst a mixed curse. If underdevelopment is a potential breeding ground for revolution, Soviet intervention in favour of development may turn out to be a thrust against revolution.

Which comes first—development or revolution? Karl Marx thought development came first in each epoch. Soviet policy-makers in the twentieth century have been tempted to reverse the order—to regard revolution as the mother of development rather than its offspring.

It is against this background that although socialism is ultimately an ethic of distribution, the Union of Soviet Socialist Republics is not a major practitioner of that ethic in its relations with the Third World.

THE SUPERPOWERS AND LIBERATION

On the other hand, the United States is doctrinally liberal—and liberalism is an ethic of the redistribution of political power in favour of the marginalised.

And yet the United States—though a child of revolution late in the eighteenth century—has become father of imperialism late in the twentieth. Why? In a sense, America was once revolutionary and has now become imperialist for the same reason. And the reason is that the American founding fathers were right in their distrust of concentrated power. Because those founding fathers distrusted such political concentration within the body politic, they ensured decentralisation at home. They worked out a system of checks and balances, a doctrine of separation of powers, a principle of separating church from state, an economic ideology insulating the economy from government and a whole constitutional apparatus of a federal division of authority between the local and the national levels.

But the same America which distrusted concentrated power domestically acquired it internationally. The concentration of economic power made America overly sensitive to strategic calculations—sometimes at the expense of the independence and territory of small countries elsewhere.

The most disastrous strategic miscalculation was the American military involvement in Vietnam. The miscalculation cost the United States fifty thousand lives and Vietnam more than a million and a half. But American administrations—unlike the American Congress—have refused to learn the full lessons of the catastrophe of Vietnam. The latest strategic experiment is Ronald Reagan's policy in Central America—another case of abuse of military might. Fortunately, the constitutional checks and balances of the founding fathers domestically have helped to restrain even the international intervention of Uncle Sam in Central America—at least for the time being.

Behind the latest exercises in Central America is a whole history of the growth of the United States into an imperialist power. It did indeed begin with the expansion of the domestic base itself. To that extent the growth of the Soviet Union into a superpower has a lot in common with the growth of the United States into the same rank. Both countries needed to extend their territorial size earlier in their histories before they could acquire superpower credentials by the second half of the twentieth century.

The Czars did most of the territorial expansion before the October Revolution of 1917. Russia conquered one principality after another—across two continents. By the time that the October Revolution occurred Russian sovereignty extended across territory larger than anything experienced in the Old World since the Roman Empire.

Soviet Communism's own expansionist thrust has since added to that territorial vastness—as the Baltic states and World War II acquisitions have been absorbed into the body politic of the Soviet Union itself.

The United States' own territorial expansion reveals a similar sense of 'Manifest Destiny'. Sometimes it took the form of 'buying' territory—including of course its inhabitants without their consent. The purchase of Louisiana from France and Alaska from Russia were not simply transactions in real estate; they were also purchases of people without regard for their preference.

Then there was the United States' war with Mexico—one of the earliest confrontations with post-colonial Latin America. Again American territorial appetite and imperial self-aggrandisement sought new levels of satisfaction. Areas like California and New Mexico were forever absorbed into the body politic of the United States.

Texas was of course also a large chunk of territory. A Trojan horse strategy of annexation served the United States well. In time the Lone Star became part of the American union—destined to become over time among the richest of the member-states, as well as the largest territory after Alaska within the union.

The beginning of superpower ethics is sheer size—for without a basic massive size, there can be no superpower status. Both the Soviet Union and the United States were served well by the older territorial ambitions in their own respective histories.

The United States had also a relatively modest intermediate role as a colonialist power—in the sense of ruling other societies without incorporating them into the metropolitan body politic. American rule in the Philippines was, in a sense, the most important of the United States' colonialist experiments. Residual roles of that kind include Puerto Rico, the American Virgin Islands and a number of other oceanic "territories" and "possessions" currently under the American flag.

It was not until after World War II that the United States entered the stage of global imperialism—America as a global sheriff. Yes, America—the incarnation of liberal decentralisation of power at the domestic level—became the incarnation of the most concentrated international power in history. The United States embodied power by far greater than the strength of Rome at its most glorious; greater than the leverage of England at its most imperial.

There must have been occasions when the American founding fathers turned in their graves—as they witnessed their child grow into dangerous might. If they were in communication with Lord Acton, all of them together might have jointly reaffirmed: "Yes, power does corrupt. Absolute power is in danger of corrupting absolutely." The United States had lost its credentials of revolution—and acquired the fangs of imperialism.

But if power has corrupted the United States, has it also corrupted the Soviet Union? If the United States is a bad influence on Third World liberation, why is not the Soviet Union a similarly adverse influence on developing countries?

Needless to say, the Soviet Union has also been corrupted by power. But in the case of the USSR it is not the Third World which is primarily paying the price. Somebody else is doing so.

What has happened is that the Soviet Union is an imperialist power in Europe, a liberating force in Africa and Latin America, and a power with a mixed record in Asia. In Europe the USSR has been heir to both the Czarist and the Nazi empires. What the Czars incorporated into the Russian Empire, the communists retained. What the Nazis had subjugated in World War II, the Russian liberators retained under a new communist rule. It is in this sense that the Soviet Union has inherited the mantle from both the Czars and the Nazis. It is in this sense that the Soviet Union is an imperial power within Europe.

On the other hand, the Soviet Union has been a liberating force in Africa and Latin America. Southern Africa especially has been a major beneficiary of the military help of communist countries. Without that help the liberation of Southern Africa—from the Portuguese Empire to Rhodesia—would have been delayed by at least a generation. The communist world's hardware for Southern African liberation fighters has ranged from the sten gun to surface–to–air missile. There seems little doubt that the emancipation of Namibia and the Republic of South Africa will itself also have to rely disproportionately on the military favours of the communist world. This already includes the unique role of Cuban troops in consolidating such liberated areas as Angola.

As for the Soviet role in the liberation of Latin America, the Cuban model is of course a special case. Ideally Cuba should have been the western hemisphere's Yugoslavia—a nation which has successfully escaped from the regional superpower but without having to sell too much of its sovereignty to the opposite camp. When all is said and done, perhaps Cuba is indeed another Yugoslavia—but forced by the United States to be more dependent on the Soviet Union than Fidel Castro would have preferred.

In recompense, Cuba is more of a revolutionary catalyst in the western hemisphere than Yugoslavia has proved to be a catalyst of dissent in the Soviet bloc. Cuba is more activist in the West than Yugoslavia has been in the Russian empire. To that extent, Cuba has been more a force for Latin American liberation from the United States than Yugoslavia has been for Eastern European liberation from the Soviet Union.

The latest confrontations with American imperialism are of course in Central America—especially in Nicaragua where pro-Cuban forces are in power, and in El Salvador where pro-Castro forces are in rebellion against a pro-American regime. Grenada in the Caribbean under Maurice Bishop was a case of pro-Cuban forces in power, and so was Michael Manley's Jamaica. Behind all the elements is the basic superpower rivalry. On balance the Soviet Union has been as liberating a force in Latin America as it has been in Africa.

It is in Asia that the Soviet role is at its most ambiguous—neither decidedly imperialist as it is in Europe, nor convincingly liberating as it has been in Africa and Latin America. Soviet hardware support for Vietnam helped Hanoi defeat the United States and its allies in the struggle for controlling South Vietnam. The Soviet factor has continued to be a major pillar for the independence of a unified Vietnam in the face of a basically hostile international environment.

On the other hand, Soviet support for Hanoi has indirectly subsidised Vietnam's occupation of Kampuchea—a negation of the latter's independence. But the most imperialist Soviet action in Asia in the last quarter of the twentieth century has been the Soviet invasion of Afghanistan in 1979 and its aftermath. A superpower violated the sovereignty and territorial integrity of one of its small neighbours.

But when all is said and done, the Soviet Union has, on the whole, been an ally of decolonisation in the Third World—in spite of the glaring exception of Afghanistan. The Soviet role as a champion of decolonisation has been aided by the following factors in recent world history.

First, imperialism in much of Asia and Africa in the nineteenth and twentieth centuries arrived with western capitalism. In reality capitalist imperialism is only one form of foreign domination—but for most people of Asia and Africa the most pervasive form of alien exploitation that they have experienced arrived with western capitalism. Third World resentment of imperialism generally has therefore often spilled over into a resentment of capitalism.

Because of this link between western private enterprise and western colonisation, there has evolved a link between nationalism and socialism in the Third World. Since socialism is the enemy of capitalism, and nationalism the adversary of imperialism, and given that capitalism and imperialism were linked in the first instance, it stands to reason that nationalism and socialism should in turn also enter into an alliance.

Soviet policy towards the Third World has also gained from V. I. Lenin's impact on ideologies and political theorising in the developing regions—ranging from Kwame Nkrumah's book *Neo-Colonialism: The Last Stage of Imperialism*, to Latin American theories of *dependencia*. In other words, the Third World's favourable ideological predisposition towards the Soviet Union was greatly aided by the prior popularity of aspects of Leninist thought.

Soviet motivation for supporting Third World liberation has been strengthened by the apparent Soviet grand design to make significant inroads into the lives and politics of post-colonial societies. Supporting decolonisation in western–dominated areas is one way of winning friends and influencing people in the post-colonial era.

Soviet need for foreign exchange is another powerful motive for Soviet sales of armaments to Third World liberation movements and to post-colonial leftist governments. Pure military aid from the Soviet Union is, from all appearances, more the exception than the rule. Southern African liberation movements have often had to raise funds from elsewhere (often from western private sympathisers) in order to be able to buy military hardware from the Soviet Union and other socialist countries. Some arms have been supplied on credit by the Soviets. But on balance ideological solidarity has not had to clash with commercial self-interest from a Soviet perspective.

But that need not mean that the Soviet Union is hypocritical. Even among hardened Soviet policy-makers there may remain a sincere conviction that human destiny is ultimately in the hands of the dispossessed—and the masses of Asia, Africa and Latin America are the majority of the dispossessed of the world. Soviet support for Third World causes cannot but be affected by that wider ethical concern.

Yet the contradiction persists. The socialist superpower is the champion of the liberal cause of freedom and self-determination—with minimum participation in the more socialist mission of global economic redistribution. In global politics the United States has been more of an economic determinist than the USSR—while the Soviet Union has been more of a liberator than the USA.

We have so far focused on political liberation and economic redistribution as two ethical themes between the Third World and the superpowers. But what about the ethics of military security? It is to this third area of moral concern that we must now turn.

THE SUPERPOWERS AND THE ETHICS OF VIOLENCE

Both superpowers regard Third World states as fair markets for the sale of conventional armaments—subject to wider political allegiances. US sales are more subject to domestic restraints within the United States than the Soviet sales are within the USSR. For example, the pro-Israeli lobby in Washington has considerable say as to which arms are sold to which Middle Eastern governments.

But while American arms are more subject to private political lobbies at home, Soviet arms are more available to private political movements abroad. Certainly the liberation of Southern Africa would have been delayed by at least a generation if Soviet arms were not available for sale to such movements as ZANLA in colonial Rhodesia and MPLA in colonial Angola.

Yet both superpowers are particularly hypocritical in the field of militarism and the ethics of political violence. And within this military domain two areas are particularly subject to double moral standards—terrorism and nuclear weapons. Let us take these themes of terrorism and nuclear weapons in turn.

The first factor to note about terrorism is that it is just another form of warfare—no worse than conventional or nuclear war, and considerably less destructive in scale. Some may argue that terrorism leaves civilians particularly vulnerable. But that is a peculiarity of virtually all forms of warfare in the twentieth century. No one on the side of the Allies worried about how many German civilians were killed in Dresden or Berlin as the two cities were pulverised in the closing stages of World War II. As Thomas C. Schelling once put it, "... in the Second World War noncombatants were deliberately chosen as targets by both Axis and Allied Forces" (1976: 26–27). Harry Truman did not lose much sleep about Japanese civilians when he ordered that atomic bombs be dropped on Hiroshima and Nagasaki. And what sane person genuinely worries about civilian casualties and at the same time arms himself for a nuclear confrontation—as the United States and the Soviet Union are constantly doing? Civilian casualties ceased to be a major worry of twentieth century warfare decades ago. It is an anachronism to proclaim the concern only in the case of terrorism—which kills far fewer civilians than conventional warfare of this era. As compared with plans for a nuclear catastrophe, terrorist casualties are less than a drop in an ocean of blood.

Non-governmental terrorism is normally the warfare of the weak. The other side of Lord Acton's coin is that *powerlessness, too, corrupts: absolute powerlessness can corrupt absolutely.* After all, who took the Palestinians seriously before they became a terrorist nuisance? Not even their fellow Arabs treated them much better than refugees. The world was prepared to continue treating them as just another refugee problem. It took their own call to arms to make them a constant item on the world's agenda. "Lest we forget; lest we forget!"

More protected from moral scrutiny is *state terrorism.* Israeli reprisal raids are often a case of counter-terrorism—as insensitive to the lives of innocent civilians and often far more destructive. The anti-personnel cluster bombs that Israel used in its 1982 invasion of Lebanon was a particularly brutal response to Palestinian pinpricks.[2]

The United States also reportedly used cluster bombs in the attack of Benghazi, Libya, in April 1986. President Ronald Reagan had previously asserted that he would have no truck with killers of children. Yet American bombs dropped from the air do kill children as readily as terrorist bombs left at an airport. Similar state-terrorism has been committed by the Soviet Union in Afghanistan. Whole villages have sometimes been wiped out as retaliation against the Afghan *mujahiddeen*. Bombardment of so-called "terrorist infested" areas has often been as indifferent to innocent casualties as was Menachem Begin's adventure into Lebanon in 1982.

Apart from direct state terrorism, there is *state-supported terrorism* by private movements. Both Libya and the United States subsidise movements of violence which often resort to terrorist methods. The US Congress has voted funds in support of the Contras in Nicaragua and Jonas Savimbi's United Front for the Liberation of Angola (UNITA). Neither the Contras nor UNITA are morally fastidious about their methods of struggle. Contras place bombs in civilian buses and UNITA places mines near villages—decimating life and limb indiscriminately.

Libya has also subsidised movements of violence—ranging from the Irish Republican Army (IRA) to radical Palestinians, from Basque separatists in Spain to dissident movements in some Black African countries. In supporting "rebel" movements within the western world itself (like the IRA and the Basques), Libya has helped to teach the West a version of the Christian Golden Rule:*"Do not do unto others what you would not that they do unto you "*!

The fourth category of terrorism (after non-governmental terrorism, state terrorism and state-supported) is *state-tolerated terrorism*. The United States has been quite lenient to members of the Irish Republican Army on the run from British justice, on charges of terrorist murder and other "atrocities." Until 1986 it was extremely difficult for Britain to get the suspects extradited from the United States. Both the judges and the Irish lobby on Capitol Hill continue to favour this particular class of "terrorists" as candidates for asylum.

France has also been a haven of Basque separatists for a long time. From time to time Paris makes an isolated gesture to Madrid by extraditing a terrorist suspect. But this is rare. And yet there is far less disapproval in Washington of French "protection" of European "terrorists" than of her refuge for Middle Eastern ones.

As for the Republic of Ireland (Eire), it has had a major dilemma about what to do with the Irish Republican Army (Provisionals). Most of the time Dublin is a case of tolerating terrorists than of hunting them down—though Dublin has genuinely agonised over the dilemma.

It is against this background that the politics of international terrorism reveal such a profound moral duplicity. Double standards are at work—and the superpowers and their allies are often at the heart of that duplicity.

Even more fundamental is the duplicity of *nuclear ethics*. The whole ethos of the nuclear weapons Non-Proliferation Treaty (NPT) was based on a principle of nuclear monopoly. Those who had the weapons were insufficiently motivated to give them up; those who did not have them were to be decidedly discouraged from acquiring them. A nuclear caste system was sanctified—a division of the world between nuclear Brahmins and non-nuclear untouchables. A kind of technological imperialism was in the making. Military nuclear technology is still regarded as something not for Africans, Asians and children under sixteen.

More sophisticated defenders of the doctrine of the nuclear deterrent have argued that we as human societies have a right to take risks—even nuclear risks. But risks on whose behalf? Does country X have a right to risk the survival of countries A, B, C, and D? Does either the United States or the Soviet Union have a right to risk the lives of Indians, Nigerians, the Swiss and the Mexicans? Does anybody short of a worldwide referendum have a right to risk the survival of the human species itself?

In the absence of a global human referendum on nuclear weapons, there may be a case for extending the nuclear franchise itself—for breaking the nuclear monopoly. The extension of the nuclear franchise will require deliberate nuclear proliferation—upward nuclear mobility for the global untouchables. This would be an expansion of the ranks of nuclear Brahmins. One purpose of nuclear proliferation horizontally is simply to alarm the superpowers into recognising that the nuclear world is getting too dangerous—and speedy action needs to be taken towards universal nuclear disarmament.

Of course horizontal nuclear proliferation has its risks—but are those risks really more dangerous than the risks of vertical proliferation in the arsenals of the superpowers themselves?

Moreover, the underlying ethical priorities are different. The Soviet Union and the United States are risking human survival for the sake of national freedom. But would it not make better moral sense to risk national freedom for the sake of the survival of the human race?

We are beginning to be alarmed by accidents in civilian uses of nuclear energy—like Chernobyl in the Soviet Union and the Three Mile Island mishap in the United States. Perhaps we need also to be alarmed into constructive action by the spectre of horizontal nuclear proliferation in the Third World. Perhaps until now the major powers have worried only about "the wrong weapons in the right hands": deadly devices under the control of stable hands. This has not been alarming enough to force the major power into genuine disarmament.

When nuclear devices pass into Arab or Black African hands, a new nightmare will have arrived—"the wrong weapons in the wrong hands"—deadly weapons held by unstable hands. Perhaps that culture shock, that consternation, will at last create the necessary political will among the great powers to move towards genuine universal nuclear disarmament.

CONCLUSION

The one thing that the Third World truly remembers very distinctly is that empires do not last forever. The lifespan of my own country's founding father in Kenya, Jomo Kenyatta, testifies to that. When he was born, Kenya was not yet a British crown colony. Supposing when the British first arrived, we East Africans had the nuclear bomb. Supposing we said: "Rather than be colonised, we shall destroy the population of Kenya—and of our neighbours at the same time."

Fortunately we did not have a nuclear arsenal with which to defend our freedom. It just so happened that Jomo Kenyatta himself lived right through the colonial period—and survived British rule for fifteen years, himself ruling Kenya. Today Kenyatta's children and grandchildren are alive and well. Our lack of a nuclear deterrent at the end of the last century denied us the option of nuclear self-destruction as a defence against foreign colonisation.

Supposing the Soviet Union today conquered the whole world. How long will such a vast empire last? "Backward" Afghanistan alone has been keeping thousands of Soviet troops busy and to some extent even scared since 1979. Even if we were all reduced to little Afghanistans—or indeed to Polands—would that really be worse than a nuclear winter? Asia and Africa know only too graphically that empires do not last forever.

Out in the infinite cosmos we live on an island called Earth. A British poet once affirmed: "No man is an island entire unto itself. And therefore never send to know for whom the bell tolls; it tolls for thee."

John Donne has acquired a supreme relevance in the nuclear age. No man is an island—*but every man lives on one*. There is no other island we know in the cosmic sea. Truly, there are no two islands to justify the ethics of dualism. In the face of our cosmic isolation, we must end the dualism—and concentrate on our human singularity. Even a liberal who insists "give me freedom or give me death" must surely realise that he cannot decide for the rest of the human species. For liberals there must surely be one imperative more important than freedom; for socialists one principle more fundamental than economic justice. The two ethical worlds can have no human meaning unless they jointly agree on one thing—that the survival of the human species is a precondition for both freedom and economic justice.

NOTES

1. This chapter is partly based on my "Superpower Ethics: A Third World Perspective," *Ethics and International Affairs* 1(1), 1987, pp. 10–21.

2. Israeli Ambassador Benjamin Netanyahu's *Terrorism: How the West Can Win* (New York: Farrar, Straus, Giroux, 1986), is a defence of state-sponsored terrorism, especially Israeli state terrorism.

14

Role of the Church in Conflict Resolution

Károly Tóth

As my subject is the church and conflict resolution I consider it appropriate to define at the outset the main thrust of my article. Being a churchman I am certainly not expected to speak on the political and sociological aspects of conflict resolution, although some references to this will be inevitable. My contribution is intended rather as theological; that is, I want to dwell on the spiritual, moral, cultural and psychological dimensions of our theme. Of course I will seek to use some of the most recent conclusions of peace and conflict research both within and outside the Christian churches and Christian peace movements. What I have to say seeks to be a specific Christian contribution. But in writing on church and conflict resolution, it is obvious that I cannot pretend to present the view of the whole Christian church on a very complex subject. Secondly, I take it for granted that in speaking of the resolution of conflict we understand it to mean the peaceful resolution of conflict.

The Christian church cannot fit into any political, social or other category, even though the Christian church represents a very peculiar phenomenon from the sociological point of view. This is due to at least four distinctive features of the Christian church.

First, the very foundation of the church is spiritual. The salvation she offers is in its core the reconciliation between God and man, between human beings, and peace with oneself. This reconciliation and peace has been made possible through the love of God manifested in Jesus Christ. "And all things are of God, who hath reconciled us to himself by Jesus Christ, and hath given to us the ministry of reconciliation ... and hath committed unto us the word of reconciliation. Now then we are ambassadors for Christ ...." (II Cor. 5: 18–20). This should create new types of relationships within the human community. Therefore the central message of the church is peace and reconciliation and love. This peace cannot be restricted to the peace of mind and heart of the individual soul, but it must also have relevance for the world, that is for the whole of humankind and creation.

Second, this message of reconciliation has to be proclaimed to human beings in order to become effective, that is to all men and women regardless of their race, sex, social position, nationality, ideology or whatever differences there might be between them. This has implications for the church's direct access to ordinary people if she wants to be a real church.

Third, the church is at the same time a social institution, her activities have social dimensions and therefore there exists a permanent relationship between the churches as institutions and those who have political power. There are indeed various types of church and state relationships, and they may differ from place to place, but the sociological fact remains. This is an extremely important relationship which cannot be ignored, because the church in every age had to work out a delicate balance with the order of political community (Walsh, 1987: 65).

Last, but not least, the church's world–wide nature is important. This means that the church is universal, transcending racial, ideological, national and political frontiers, cutting across all kinds of differences. Because of this, her reconciling potential and responsibility is great. This has been manifested especially through the modern ecumenical movement which understands the search for the unity of the churches as an important contribution to the unity of humankind. "The unity of the church should have a functional character by promoting the unity of humankind" (Huber, 1980: 26.)

The church is metaphysical–spiritual; grass-rooted–popular; national–institutional; and ecumenical–international at the same time. This is why the very nature of the church makes it possible to contribute to conflict resolution on every level of human society.

TRADITIONAL MEANS OF CONFLICT RESOLUTION

It has also to be stressed that the peaceful resolution of international conflicts has become a vital issue for the whole of humanity because of the extreme danger of the destructive capacity of nuclear weapons. No matter what political view people hold, no matter what religion or ideology they profess, there are very few who believe that the "benefits" gained by nuclear conflict could outweigh the cost of a nuclear war. There is also an increased awareness of the danger of escalation from any international conflict so that it becomes a nuclear conflagration. There is a generally accepted view that conflicts should be resolved by means other than war, and that where conflicts emerge they should be managed in such a way that they cannot endanger international peace and security. In the churches there is a strong and growing consensus that war has ceased to be an instrument of politics, that war can no longer be a means of solving international conflicts. The question can of course be raised as to how this vision should be related to the hard facts of everyday life in our world. A well known American publicist puts it this way: "we live in the most cruel period of human history. In the last one hundred years 271 wars were waged, and in the twentieth century alone 207 violent conflicts erupted with more than 80 million dead" (Reston, 1986). This should not however lead us to abandon the vision of a new world order mentioned above in which war will cease to be an instrument of politics. If we did so it would be similar to opposing the training of doctors because there are diseases and illnesses in the world.

That is why instead of wars a new system of institutions for the peaceful solution of conflicts has to be created. There will be no future for humankind if, parallel to the elimination of war, no alternative system of conflict resolution is offered. Of course there will be a long and strenuous road to go but the historic moment has come to start travelling towards this goal. In fact peace on earth and goodwill to all men is being stressed as a value in East and West, in North and South. But there are considerable differences and great difficulties in the means suggested to bring about this state of affairs to create the conditions under which conflicts can be peacefully resolved.

In this context two more remarks have to be made. It is not the increased morality of humankind which has led to thinking about the necessity of abolishing war as an instrument of politics and to seek the peaceful solution of conflicts, but rather a fear of total annihilation in a nuclear catastrophe. We also have to face an extremely great contradiction of human life, namely that the present world situation is so threatening because the ethical development of humanity is lagging behind the lethal mega-instruments with which technological achievements have presented mankind. There is a contradiction between the mega-instruments and the micro-ethics of human life.

There are different views among political leaders concerning the means of bringing about a system for the peaceful solution of conflicts. These means are presented first in the United Nations and the International Court of Justice and the other related bodies of the UN system. But the decisions of these bodies are not accepted and the UN machinery for the peaceful solution of conflicts is hardly used. The Charter of the United Nations

(Article 33) lists the means for the peaceful solution of conflicts—that is for the peaceful settlement of international disputes. Speaking about the UN we can say: "it is an imperfect institution operating in a very difficult environment.... But it is the only multilateral mechanism available for coping with pressing global problems" (Luck, 1985: 143–144). The problem is therefore not to create new instruments, but to improve the present ones and use them; and that would be a challenging task for the universal church as well as the local churches, that they should urge the respective governments to make use of the present institutions to resolve conflicts peacefully.

But there is another school of thought which has come to the conclusion that the existing techniques for conflict solving are no longer adequate and new means and methods have to be found because the old methods have failed. New methods of conflict resolution have to be invented and examined because the international scene rapidly changes while the instruments and methods of solving them do not follow suit. "This mismatch between international reality and the means of dealing with it, particularly the means of managing change, is in itself a contributory cause of the conflicts which exist in the system" (Light, 1984: 147).

There are four special arguments for adjusting the conflict resolution system to the changed international situations. First, the institutions of conflict resolution are operating on the traditional basis, that is on a western, liberal political ground which does not take into account the developing nations and the socialist countries. It reflects too much the traditional international system.

Second, politicians have recently acquired the insight that the settlement of disputes or the resolution of conflicts has to be regarded not only as a legal but above all as a political issue. The resolution of conflicts requires more of a political than a legal approach in our modern and very complex world society, whereas the present means of conflict resolution reflect more the legalistic views than political will. This is obviously the reason why the traditional system of conflict resolution has completely failed.

Third, until now the methods of conflict resolution were designed for the use of governments and governmental bodies. But radical changes have taken place, due to which the emergence as well as the solution of conflicts are no longer caused by governments only. The very nature of modern conflict differs greatly from the old ones, this is why "conflict management institutions can no longer afford to operate only at an inter-governmental level" (Light, 1984: 148).

Fourth, there is another issue which has to be faced in this context. There is a great difference between the views of diplomats and politicians and those of sociologists concerning the function of conflict in human society. "A diplomat probably thinks of conflict as a negative even if inevitable phenomenon, and as being usually dysfunctional. A sociologist, on the other hand, would be more likely to think of conflict as fulfilling a necessary function in human society" (Bailey, 1977: 82). Consequently in all forms of human society there have always been and will always be conflicts. The inevitability of conflict is a fact of life. Problem-solving and conflict resolutions do not imply the elimination of conflicts from society. The rule of probability is that conflicts can exacerbate and take dangerous forms. Within individual societies the management of conflicts is required but in international life conflicts shall be solved in order not to deteriorate and endanger international peace and security.

VALUE TRANSFORMATIONS

There is a further problem to be faced in dealing with the resolution of conflicts. The terms related to the subject matter are not uniform but variably employed. Some speak of "the settlement of disputes," others use the term "conflict resolution"—there are even people speaking of the "management of crisis." Even the United Nations Charter and the majority of related literature speak of "the settlement of international disputes" to be brought about by peaceful means (Articles 1.1, 33.1). These alternatively used terms reflect the difficulties and create the confusions to be clarified.

The Quaker scholar Sydney Bailey makes a serious attempt to define these terms. According to his view dispute is regarded as "a *specific disagreement* which takes the form of claims between parties.... The subject of a dispute is specific in the sense that it must be possible to formulate the question with sufficient clarity" (Bailey, 1977: 81). According to Bailey, settlement means an arrangement adopted by the parties to deal with the matter in dispute. It is the readiness to have negotiations on the matter (Bailey, 1977: 118). In this approach the settlement of a dispute is the imposition of a resolution on conflicting parties by coercion or by other kinds of pressure. The result is that the causes of the conflict are not dealt with adequately, therefore the settlement is likely to leave a lingering sense of grievance in one side with the consequent potential for further conflict at some later stage. Therefore distinctions have to be made between disputes and conflicts on the one hand, settlements and resolutions on the other.

A conflict is defined as "a condition of general *hostility* between States or other authorities ... in which particular differences seem as much a result as a cause of tension" (Bailey, 1977: 81). A conflict situation is normally said to arise between parties who perceive that they possess mutually incompatible objectives. The resolution of conflicts means a new set of relationships emerging from the process and arrived at freely by the parties themselves.

I venture to express my strong conviction that this difference in language reflects a significant shift of thinking. How can this radical change be described? First of all it has to be pointed out that the approach to international relationships from the angle of power politics has lost its attraction. Violence in international relationships is being rejected more and more. Behind this lies "the belief that power is no longer the most important motivating force and organising principle of politics at any level" (Light, 1984: 152). Within individual societies or states seemingly opposing trends become visible: on the one hand decentralisation and democratisation, on the other internationalisation. Internally the politicisation of the wide masses is discernible, more democracy and more participation is required. Even the role of the state has also undergone a change: earlier it was the concern of an elite, now the state has to serve the people and not just those in power. The revolution of growing expectations, and not only of a better material life but also of spiritual, cultural and moral conditions, that is the quality of life, has come. It is against this background that the conflicts between states now arise and therefore the process of conflict resolution has to reckon with all aspects of the modern world.

Conflict resolution is understood to be a process which helps the parties in a dispute to confront the fact that in some sense their definition of the problem may need to be revised and that they may have misunderstood the perception of the understanding of the problem. The idea of winning or losing has to be abandoned and replaced, and the idea of moving away from the present position has to be stressed. It means not to look backward, not to let the past write the future, but to encourage and to speak about the common future. In other words there is a need to start *a process for the transformation of conflict* in the course of which the opposing interests become a problem to be solved jointly. The main task of this process is to define and develop *super-ordinate* goals, the achievement of which is in the interest of all the parties because the cost of continuing the conflict outweighs the benefits to be gained by finding a solution. Thus conflict resolution in the modern (nuclear) age is a learning process of having to adapt to new conditions including the adaptation of new values.

Conflict resolution is therefore to convert conflicts into problems involving a search for alternative futures and accommodations. This type of conflict resolution offers a more viable outcome to conflicts because it converts the conflict into a shared problem by setting up a process of learning and discovering new values and super-ordinate goals.

The difficulty in solving conflicts is to be found in that our world does not have a generally accepted value system. The value system which exists at present is ideologically determined. As long as the resolution of a conflict is far less important than preserving an ideology then there is no hope of solving the problem. If there is no general conviction that the survival of the world should exceed the ideological controversies in importance then the prospet for our survival is not great. Mikhail Gorbachev's recent statement has to be noted in this context. In Leningrad on 14 October 1987 he stressed that class struggle has to be subordinated to the need of the common survival of the human race. At this point one may also see that the most important task of the church is to instil and spread the view of the necessity of having this super-ordinate goal to a greater extent than the churches have done hitherto.

CONFLICT LINKAGES

There are still five further issues related to the resolution of conflicts. The first is the interrelatedness of domestic and international conflicts. "The original, classical assumption that international relations could be studied as a separate discipline, that domestic politics was a matter of domestic jurisdiction, proved to be false. It was agreed that there was a connection between domestic and international relations (Burton, 1986: 143). The fact that international conflicts are usually a spill-over from domestic conflicts proves the truth of this statement. From Afghanistan, to Central America, the Middle East, Sri Lanka, and even South Africa, this is proved. In a domestic conflict it is the natural strategy of the weakest side to seek outside help. In this case the question has to be raised: on what criteria may the help of other powers be legitimately called upon, the help of other centres of power in case of need or so as to prevail in conflict with others? It is extremely difficult to determine where the limits of non-intervention are in the case of oppressed national minorities or the violation of human rights as with the Tanzanian intervention in Uganda. The conflicts arising within countries can endanger international peace and security, therefore solving these conflicts or preventing them is the responsibility of the world community. The purely legal distinction between domestic and international conflicts immediately appears to be artificial as soon as the interdependence of world society expresses itself.

Second, this interdependence is the reality of the world community and is due to the extremely increased technical mobility in the modern age and also to communication technology. It is right to say that "Neither medieval Europe nor Imperial China reflected upheavals at the other end of the continent," and that "the fortunate American Indians knew nothing of the fall of the Roman Empire. But in the modern world any change is far–reaching" (de Reuck, 1984: 104). Indeed, we are living in a world which is not just comprised of states but of transactions of all kinds that cut across state boundaries. That is why conflict resolution must involve all these main transactions.

Another important issue is the problem of justice. Sometimes it may seem as though the requirement of justice is incompatible with the need for the peaceful resolution of conflicts. Has justice to be sacrificed in order to reach the peaceful resolution of conflicts? The great difficulty arises in that there is no generally agreed definition of justice. What is *summa ius* for some, is *summa iniuria* for others. People are freedom fighters to some, heroes to some, but the same people are labelled terrorists by others.

I want only to make three points in relation to justice. Justice is never an absolute notion, it is always socially determined. This also means that justice is a relative concept depending on a point of reference. In relation to what is something just or unjust? Second, in the given world situation the struggle for justice is senseless unless the nuclear catastrophe is averted. Peace without justice cannot be genuine peace, but justice can only be reached in peace, that is in the context of the peaceful resolution of an eventual nuclear conflict. Finally, the church can help to define a generally accepted interpretation of justice because it is a central message of the Gospel of Jesus Christ. One of the greatest tasks of the church is to "make justice understandable for the world which has so widely divergent views on the content of justice" (Kooijmans, 1982).

Fourth, conflict usually arises between nations because of the misuse of the so-called national security and national interest. The traditional understanding of national security has become obsolete. In our interdependent world security is not divisible. Once a country perceives security or independence, this leads to policies that increase its neighbours' sense of security. Conversely, when a country experiences insecurity, its neighbours also feel insecure and thus net insecurity is increased. There will be no effective conflict resolution in our world unless a shared, a common security, prevails. This is simply a requirement of one world and one humanity.

Fifth, in studying conflict resolution in our interdependent world, we have to be aware of the interrelatedness of global and regional solutions. The defusing of nuclear conflict can only be realised gradually; first the nuclear threat has to be got rid of. This should in turn be followed by the removal of conventional weapons and the elimination of war as an institution. The importance of regional arrangements is also stressed by the United Nations Charter which speaks of "pacific settlements through regional arrangements" (Article 52.3). The idea of nuclear-free zones is therefore a special way of preventing situations from becoming conflictual. In this sense the plan for a nuclear-free Pacific, which is the aim of the Treaty of Raratonga, and the role of New Zealand in bringing about this Treaty have to be mentioned specifically. Most of the states of this area of the world have signed the South Pacific Nuclear Free Zone Treaty. The member churches of the World Council of Churches expressed their solidarity with the peoples of the South Pacific who want to keep the testing of nuclear warheads and nuclear armed and powered navies out of this area.

A JUST PEACE DOCTRINE

In conclusion the question has to be answered: what should the church (local and universal) be doing to help conflict resolution?

The churches have made clear in numerous statements and declarations that they categorically oppose and resolutely reject the possibility of nuclear war. The concern for peace, for the prevention of nuclear war and for the promotion of disarmament has been a central focus of the ecumenical movement through this century. The World Council of Churches at all its assemblies, from the first held in Amsterdam in 1948 to the last one held in Vancouver in 1983, has condemned nuclear war as "a sin against God and a crime against humanity." The Second Vatican Council did the same, especially in the Pastoral Constitution on "The Church in the Modern World." In this way it can be said that two Christian bodies, the Vatican and the World Council of Churches representing almost one and a half billion Christians, took a stand on war and peace. The substance of the churches' stand is that there cannot be anything which may justify a nuclear war and the mandate of the church "implies the involvement of the Church in the problem of eliminating wars and their potential sources, as well as in the matter of creating a peaceful future for the world. These tasks are incorporated into the evangelical mission of the Church" (Kondziela, 1987: 415).

The statement of the Sixth Assembly of the World Council of Churches in Vancouver in 1983 named the deeper causes of conflicts, both domestic and international:

> Even without war thousands perish daily in nations, both rich and poor because of hunger and starvation. Human misery and suffering as a result of various forms of injustice have reached levels unprecedented in modern times. There is a resurgence of racism, often in itself a cause of war. Peoples continue to be driven, as a last resort, to take up arms to defend themselves against systematic violence, or to claim their rights to self-determination or independence.

Speaking of the peaceful resolution of conflicts the same Assembly condemned "the growing refusal of many governments to use the opportunites afforded by the United Nations to preserve international peace and security and for the peaceful resolution of conflicts, or to heed its resolutions" as deeply troubling. "We call upon the governments to reaffirm their commitment to the United Nations Charter, to submit interstate conflicts to the Security Council at an early stage when resolution may still be possible short of the use of massive armed force, and to cooperate with it in the pursuit of peaceful solutions" (The Church in International Affairs Report, 1986: 40–41).

Besides making public their views on war and peace, especially on nuclear weapons, the churches have engaged in the practical solution of conflicts. The Vatican helped to resolve the conflict between Argentina and Chile, and the World Council of Churches mediated successfully in the Sudan crisis.

Two statements made by the churches concerning the peaceful resolution of conflicts should be mentioned here. The World Council of Churches published a report on its consultation on the peaceful resolution of conflict in 1982, which declares:

> The church has a special responsibility in initiating and encouraging innovative means for the peaceful resolution of conflicts. The church universal has to create understanding and the significance of the peaceful resolution of conflicts because the churches have an immense responsibility in view of the dangerous situation to encourage the parties in conflict to make use of the existing means of dispute settlements.

The Roman Catholic Church has also stressed the need to support systems capable of settling conflicts by peaceful methods: "It is absolutely necessary that international conflicts should not be settled by war but that other methods better befitting human nature should be found" (Kondziela, 1979).

Among the churches a world–wide network of communication has been established, over the lines of confrontation, which open up channels of information and communication, especially useful for nations in conflict. The church's great opportunity is the movement of her spiritual community across borders and political dividing lines. The church is a spiritual community extending over political, social, national and even ideological divisions. Due to the church's moral authority she can strongly contribute to the creation of an atmosphere favourable for the peaceful solution of conflicts and provide a platform for negotiations and mediation between parties in conflict. In view of the recent evolution of a very complex world community where conflicts can be caused and possibly solved by non-governmental bodies the churches must set up an ecumenical instrument representing the "good offices" of all the churches to help to prevent conflicts, to help to solve them, not only international conflicts but also within nations, especially where ethnic and minority tensions exist.

A major task of the churches must be—due to her peculiar nature—to help demolish the enemy image, to dispel suspicion, to build up confidence and maintain hope. There may be situations where only this hope can free the world from fear. The Christian churches especially in Europe, but not only in Europe, have done a lot in this respect during the last thirty years using the opportunity afforded by regional arrangements which are especially recommended by the United Nations Charter. (In fact, quite a lot of disputes have been managed by regional organisations, given the fact that these know better the cultural peculiarities and background of the region. In this respect the continental ecumenical bodies are playing a noteworthy role.)

But there are specific obligations and challenges for the churches. They have to transform the churches' traditional teaching on war and peace. The just war theory has to be transformed into the theological doctrine of a just peace. There is a further need to pursue the critical analysis of the Christian tradition in regard to war and peace, especially the demolition of the Biblical military tradition. There is now a real opportunity for the churches to elaborate a genuine theology of peace. The Christian churches have now reached the stage where the holding of an Ecumenical Peace Council (originally suggested by Dietrich Bonhoeffer in 1934) is seriously discussed. The churches world–wide are now challenged to demonstrate that Christianity is unequivocally a message of peace. To find one Christian voice on this issue is the missionary task of the church today. What churches have said separately on war and peace up to now, must now be declared by them unitedly. Such a demonstration of unity in relation to the peaceful resolution of the greatest conflict that humanity has ever been confronted with, would be the greatest contribution of the churches to conflict resolution in our age, and it would be the most convincing witness to the Prince of Peace, Jesus Christ.

15

Search for Peace under Conditions of a "Technological Fix"

Rajni Kothari

If peace continues to elude us—as it has now for more than 40 years—it is because we have no theory of peace, no compelling paradigm of peace that will force men and nations to accept its inevitable logic. Its opposite, namely global militarism, does have a theory and is thus able to take nations (and their present institutional embodiment, the states) in its stride. This is the theory of security—for nation-states and alliances thereof, for citizens thereof, for political systems, for ideological alignments. It is a theory that has spurred the state system on to erecting a global military (and political) order.

Not so with peace. Peace continues to be a powerful wish and desire, a passion with millions, a conviction as well, deeply felt and aspired for. It is also leading some (an increasing number though still not large enough) to "action," even if this be in the form of "action against." But nothing that is still as compelling as militarised security systems.

What is more, peace continues to be a negative good, a "good" no doubt but a negative good: an absence of war, absence of militarisation and armament. Its most persistent theme song in our times is di̲s̲armament. By its logic it is a negative demand. And hence also a fragmented one. So that "general and complete" disarmament is fast receding as a compelling force and the defenders and exponents of disarmament are getting engaged in various propositions and formulations that are of a partial and limited kind. Nor is there any assurance that once achieved, disarmament will *be*. There is no such assurance because there is no inevitable logic to peace, no sight of what Kant called "permanent peace." There is no such assurance because the desire for peace, the "movement" for peace is not backed by a cogent and compelling theory. No theory of history, that is to say.

Now there was a powerful theory of history that pushed at least the nation-states of Europe in the nineteenth century in the direction of peace.

There was the theory of progress, of the march of progress based on science and the scientific conquest of nature and societies, of the path of progress being universal (what with the Industrial Revolution, the Imperial unification of the world under its sweep, the "White Man's Burden," the *pax Europeana*)—a key condition of which was peace. Peace was not then seen as an absence of war (for "wars" did occasionally take place and "conquests" were necessary and there was not a little violence in the process of unification of the world) but, rather, as an essential condition of progress and development and science and "modernity." It was all informed by a theory of history.

Now built into this particular theory of history was an inevitable dialectic that was to push the world from a state of warlessness to a state of peacelessness. There were two critical dimensions on which the dynamism of the progressivist world rested—competition for power and technological determinism. The institutional medium of the former was the nation-state, each competing with the other for more power and greater expansion; of the latter it was the whole edifice of science and technology which enabled the pursuit of national power and expansion to move from one threshold of competitive thrust to another. In the course of time, the competitive thrust moved out of the "balance of power" framework and the restraints and "stability" imposed by it and gave in to a logic of technological thrust *per se* which has today achieved an autonomy and momentum of its own, the nation-state framework itself becoming an arena for the struggle for technological supremacy. The interwar period saw the competition for national supremacy in—and beyond—Europe find its nadir in the rise of national fascism; the war itself moved the locus of this competition outside the European framework; the end of the war which coincided with the application of the splitting of the atom to the political arena pushed the world towards a struggle for global supremacy; the decades since then have moved this struggle from its early ideological justification to one of technological momentum and counter-momentum with an inevitable never-ending logic to it. So that today it is not politics that can decide the fate of peoples and nations; if it were politics, there would be scope for "negotiating" our way to some kind of peace. It is technology, military technology above all but technology in its overall comprehensive domination of the world, of societies and cultures, above all of the human mind.

An impressive lot of studies have come out on military technology, military research and development (R&D) and military doctrines, both expert and specialised studies on different aspects of this technology and sociopolitical and ethical studies of the human costs involved in this "mad race." Taken together, they bring out the grand sweep of this new mutation in human evolution based on a wholly new gene that *homo sapiens* have given rise to and which now threatens it like a Frankenstein.

A number of insights have emerged from these studies, as well as from a general overview of the growth of global militarisation, which together project a spectre of gloom verging on total hopelessness. First, technological *progress* has acquired an autonomy of its own and is not subject to either political or ethical restraints, and is not amenable to any "superior" decisions emanating from the state system. Its autonomy extends to becoming autonomous of the very state system that in the first place gave rise to it. Second, recent technological *promise* seeks to shield states and their leaders from public odium or incredulity arising from "ideological wars" that would, *a la* Vietnam, produce long and costly physical involvements in distant lands producing so many dead and maimed which could produce popular reaction. From now on "war" is to be made technologically clean and neat, short and computerised, riding on the high-tech mass fantasy about national security and national ascendancy (witness the mass support for Ronald Reagan and Margaret Thatcher).

Third, the new military technological putsch envelops more than the strictly military field and is based on a close military–civilian nexus, a nexus between military and "science," between the military and the universities, taking in its sweep new "advances" of the modern knowledge system. And, fourth, the new technological *fix* encompasses massive economic—and "scientific"—enterprises and renders large segments of modern economic systems dependent on its onward march and on a new commercial–industrial–bureaucratic complex which makes the technological arena truly global. In its compulsive search for more and more "sophistication," it envelops not just the great industrial powers but also an increasing proportion of world trade and growing penetration of a wide variety of economies around the world. The various "new technologies"—electronics, genetics, biomedical—that are taking hold of enterprises and government-sponsored corporations everywhere are rendering the whole world into an "interdependent" corpus governed by a techno–managerial rationality. To this should be added the phenomenal rise in both profits and salaries of "science-based" industries and personnel engaged in them which have coincided with expansion of space and missile based technologies. Together, these characteristics of modern technology, of which military technology is the key catalyst, have managed to push political elites and mass publics, governments and parliaments, the state itself and the state system, on the periphery of vital decision-making affecting human survival.

In this onward march it is served by a number of other factors—ideological, cultural and intellectual. Ideologically, there is a distinct shift from the doctrine of progress for all to the doctrine of security for a few, from the assumption that the fruits of science and technology will reach all the *peoples* of the world and lay the foundation of a just and peaceful world to the use of the same science and technology to ensure security of *nation states,* and that along a hierarchical scale of nation states. Culturally, the dominant theme is that of "defence of the nation," which is spread through high voltage media blitz as a result of which mass publics are either immunised or mesmerised by the romantic promise of "success," "victory" and decisive "deterrence." This gradually takes hold of the public mind in not just the superpowers but also in other states whose leaders are convinced of force and more and more firepower being the only instrument of their survival. Intellectually, the humanist instincts of democratic consciousness, compassion for the "other" and empathy for the deprived and the oppressed have given place to the compulsions of security, stability and strategic balances so that experts and advisers, "area specialists" and professors of international relations are found to work on trajectories of peace that in effect turn out to be trajectories of strategic balances, assured supplies of essential raw materials and security of high-tech installations. Fragility and vulnerability of every nation in the world have propelled the new "sciences" towards more and more sophisticated games of outdoing the enemy. All but a few of these scientists seem to be engaged in the vast enterprise of somehow forestalling the inevitable—on the clear assumption that we all stand on the brink and will continue to do so. Intellectual fatalism, combined with the new doctrine of security and the new culture of "defence of the nation," has produced the present world order based on rival constellations of nation-states.

It does not seem too likely that the modern state and the state system as they are presently constituted can take us any closer to "peace and security" as these terms are understood by the man in the street. (The same terms mean different things to the experts in science establishments and the universities engaged in contract research.) Nor does it seem likely that these states can provide regimes of equity and justice or of social and ethnic harmony which could remove the sources of tension and violence in a world that is coming apart not just on the strategic but also on the political and cultural dimensions. Disarmament is a non-starter. So are the various proposals for equitable "development," "common security" and "common future" based on environmental conservation as have been advocated by a series of independent commissions whose principal recommendations however are still addressed to states and governments.

Tired and exhausted with the interminable negotiations among superpowers, along the "North–South" dimension and in UN bodies, as well as with national governments and political parties who may be vying with each other with populist slogans of social justice and decentralised democracy but seem to be able to do little to counter dominant global tendencies, the peoples of the world are found to engage in their own acts of intervention through a series of "movements." The most publicised of these is of course the peace movement in Europe, both because of the literally millions of people involved in it and because of the centrality of the issue of nuclear war. But, though less publicised, there are also powerful movements at large led by women, environmentalists, human rights activists and exponents of ethnic diversity and various nationality aspirations, that are taking place in large parts of the world, and which together constitute a mass upsurge of protest and dissent but are also engaged in laying out alternative perspectives on the human condition (though this is still at an early stage).

I have written extensively elsewhere on these social movements and happen to be engaged personally in some of them, as well as in listening to the "voices" that are emerging from the grassroots of various societies and, on that basis, reconceptualising the human agenda (Kothari, 1984a, 1984, 1983b). Many others have been engaged in articulating the aspirations, ideas, alternative strategies and political and technological visions underlying these movements or, more accurately, implied in them. Through the work of *Lokayan* ("Dialogue of the People") in India and through the United Nations University's Programme on Peace and Global Transformation we have tried to articulate the perspectives that are emerging from these movements, the problems they face and their limitations. Increasingly, politically and ethically motivated individuals have been forced to review their earlier faith in the modern nation-state and the world system based on nation-states in producing a just, sustainable and peaceful world and to direct their attention to people's own initiatives, locally for the most part but increasingly regionally and globally too, at redirecting human energy. Furthermore, as the issues get joined and efforts are made to unravel the political and intellectual crisis underlying the more immediate threats to survival, the earlier faith in science and technology as being the harbinger of a "new age" is also being questioned though still only by a few who often do get dismissed as being "abstract" and "theoretical" and even branded as being armchairish and "elitist."

The challenge facing both the intellectual community and the social movements in their effort to reverse major tendencies that threaten human survival is to inter-relate the different dimensions of this threat and the diverse "constituencies" that the different movements represent—the peace movement, the environment and Green movements, the women's movement, the movements for social justice, human rights, cultural survival and non-violence. The peace movement in Europe is one instance where a single focus has emerged for various groups, with both the Greens and the feminists joining forces with peace activists. More recently, the activists of the peace movement in Europe are seeking common cause with the struggles for sustainable development, social justice, economic equity and human dignity launched by various grassroots movements in the Third World and some of the socialist countries. But it is a slow process and so often gets sidetracked because of the felt immediacy of the dangers hovering over Europe, in the end often becoming as Eurocentric as some of the other efforts under way by the more conventional exponents of arms control and limited accords on disarmament, nuclear-free zones and "de-alignment" from power blocs.

One issue that steady research and analysis emerging from both the peace movement and even proponents of "limiting" the nuclear menace has to do with is precisely the problematique posed in this paper, namely the growing menace of a technological race for military supremacy as well as how, through its very logic, this race is going to prove too costly and too hazardous to kep the human enterprise going. First, given the independent momentum of technology and particularly of military technology, it gives rise to an inherently unstable situation. At the turn of the 1960s advances in this technology appeared to affect the interests of both the superpowers adversely, producing what was called "technological deadlock." Hence the willingness on both sides to seriously consider negotiations towards a comprehensive disarmament treaty, starting with arms limitation and control. But in the subsequent decades military technology got developed in an uneven way, giving the edge to one superpower at a time when all the talk on a follow-on system, based on a worst-case analysis, took place. Thus the greater megatonnage of Soviet thermonuclear weapons was soon followed by greater sophistication: multiple independently targetable re-rentry vehicles (MIRVs), tertiary guidance for lower circular error probability (CEP), precision-guided munitions, and many other "innovations" producing a tilt in favour of the US in some respects and a stalemate in other respects, followed yet again by the Soviets catching up and then on to a game of one overtaking the other and then the opposite, in an almost infinite progression.

Second, such a surrender by political decision-makers to technocrats meant an end to diplomacy and the rise of the doctrine of sophistication not just in armaments research but also (as with the Strategic Defence Initiative) in concepts and doctrines of "peace" and "defence," producing an immensely complex system based on unproven technologies simulated in scientific labs. Scientists and university departments are found working on a variety of frontier technologies which are however uninformed by any *policy*. And in the absence of policy, there can be no restraints or reversals, only escalations, including escalations of fantasy.

Third, such a runaway technological race can prove too costly to maintain even strategic superiority. Both the notion of a "weapon system" instead of weapons and the concept of a "follow-on system" under which technological R&D is pursued even before the need for it is felt have together created mind-boggling systems of such complexity that their expense knows no limits. It is by now well known that the argument that the cost of a nuclear weapon is going down is meaningless given the fact that the costs of nuclear *weapon systems* are rising dramatically and that of the "Star Wars" type cannot even be calculated in advance. One has just to project the effect of all this craze for ever more sophistication for the near-nuclear countries in the Third World (and the same is the case with conventional weaponry) to realise that the present technological fix will soon put nations (even the affluent ones but particularly the others) out of business in respect of attending to other needs of societies and peoples.

Add to this the problems of protection and viability of conventional defence systems against counter-measures (like a cheap missile destroying a highly expensive combat aircraft or a barrage of anti-tank missiles immobilising expensive tanks or cheap aluminium "chaff" confusing entire radar systems) as well as the fact of total unreliability of the efficacy of a weapon system demonstrated under non-combat conditions under actual combat conditions, and the extremely expensive and non-sustainable nature of modern weapons systems becomes clear (Deshingkar, 1987).

And yet, all these arguments of "irrationality" of the technological race and its extremely high costs that can only be maintained by progressively eroding and ultimately dismantling the welfare and other components of national budgets only raise uncomfortable questions for policy makers and the lay publics. They do not seem by themselves to reverse dominant tendencies. For, after all, one knows that the same is the case in other fields. Modern medical system, modern education, modern agriculture with its increasing demand for ever more costly "inputs," indeed the whole modern paradigm of development as such, have all been costing themselves out of what people can afford, ending up being available only to a few and rendering millions of people uncared for and shoved off from the concerns and care of national elites. And in all these arenas the reason for national systems costing themselves beyond the reach of people is the growing technologisation of human systems. There is no space to document all this but there are enough studies in each of these areas that have shown this.

Unfortunately, the whole effort at countering world militarisation, including much (though not all) of the effort of the peace movement, is too fragmented and partial to meet the technological nemesis head-on. Peace activists in Europe are still engaged in modes of agitation that remind one of the anti-Vietnam war campaigns; the Greens are found attacking the evils of pollution and acid rain without in fact examining the extent to which their own lives are still dominated by the dynamic thrust of corporate technology and mass media; the women's movement is still (despite some fresh thinking in recent years) too bogged down with mechanistic notions of equality and parity that are rooted in the competitive logic of the modern technologically driven culture; most of the class-based movements in the Third World are similarly too preoccupied with catching up with the upper classes or the western world to realise that they are in fact playing into the very logic of the modern market and of modern technology. Few of them seem to fully realise the sweep of an autonomous and independent momentum of modern technology on various national cultures and the popular psyche everywhere. And inevitably, given the increasing confrontation between the haves and the have-nots (globally and nationally), giving rise to regimes of repression everywhere and the growing power of the doctrine of "security," the technological momentum will inevitably promote militarisation of civil societies.

In the ultimate analysis there is no answer to global militarisation except by shifting focus from merely making the state and the state system less violent and militarist to basic issues of cultural survival, humane governance in which civil society once again comes into its own and promotes decentralisation in which people matter, a conception of economic rationality that is based on subsistence and self-control, restoration of a sense of community and its control over resources and ecologies, and all of this informed by fundamental human stirrings of a spiritual, aesthetic and religious kind. Unless the technological momentum—and its autonomy—are once again brought under human control, unless the *polity* is once again revived and resumes momentum, there is no hope of realising peace on this planet.

Similarly, it is only by focusing on this primary task of de-technologising the civilisational process and resuming its humanist course that we will be able to move towards a new theory of intervention in the historical process. It calls for an effort towards a new enlightenment that transcends the inimical and impersonal momentum generated by the European Enlightenment and the "Theory of Progress."

16

Justice, Peace and the Preservation of Nature

Carl Friedrich von Weizsäcker

CURRENT WORLD PROBLEMS

Mankind is currently in a crisis, the catastrophic climax of which probably still lies ahead.

This statement is the result of a secular analysis.[1] Let us now follow this analysis in three steps which fit in well with the order of the three topics justice, peace, and the preservation of nature.

The problem of poverty, of social justice, is not resolved. The facts indicate that this problem will worsen. Wars continue to be waged as always. The 40–year old armistice between the superpowers in the North still does not secure us from a third world war. Population growth and technological changes in our world disrupt the equilibrium of nature, in which we live.

None of these three catastrophes is necessary, or certain. However, their prevention requires a measure of effective reason, which as yet has overtaxed the imagination of the conservatives as well as the self-critique of the radicals. Later, let us attempt to take a few steps into investigating the necessary course of this secular reason. In so doing, we will not use as guiding concepts the negative expressions of the prophets of doom, such as misery, war, and the destruction of nature, but rather the positive, secular terms social justice, political peace, and the preservation of nature. These terms signify what would have to be done in order to prevent these catastrophes. They also signify the state to which mankind's purified consciousness would have to return after a partial catastrophe. They signify the demands of reason.

Social Justice

No peace without justice; no justice without peace.

This is not only a Christian hope. It is a demand of enlightened reason. Let us explain this term in several steps. First: what does "justice" mean here?

The word has various meanings which are related to each other. In linguistic usage, we differentiate between subjective justice, i.e. the just actions of people, and objective justice, i.e. a just social state, a just form of coexistence between people. The two are related. A person's actions can also be called objectively just if they are in accordance with a written or unwritten standard, a law, or a custom. We can distinguish this as legal or correct action from the motives of the person acting, which can be unjust and selfish even though the action is correct, and in some cases may be just although the action is incorrect. Immanuel Kant differentiates legality, acting according to the law, from morality, acting out of respect for the law. On the other hand, we cannot call a form of society just simply because it has valid, set standards. We judge the standards in themselves just or injust. Finally—and this will be the decisive factor in this section—fundamentally just standards can still be inadequate if the actual social, i.e. economic and power relations, keep the people from enjoying the benefits of justice.

These abstract-sounding differentiations already reflect the major social conflicts of our time. First allow me some preliminary remarks on dealing with these conflicts; let us return to the quest for truth. It is impossible for an author who submits an analysis of these conflicts not to have taken a personal position on them. He should not conceal his own position. He should be willing to listen to an opposing opinion. In this manner, he learned himself. His present position reflects the positions which he attempted to understand. Only someone capable of presenting a coherent defence of those opinions opposed to his own is ready to represent his own opinion convincingly. This would be justice in thought.

In this endeavour, it is essential to understand the viewpoints as well as the motives of both sides. The ways in which motives are reflected in viewpoints are called ideologies. The ambiguity of this reflection can be seen in the ambiguity of the meaning of the word. "Ideology" is above all a word of praise; in Greek it means the expression of forms; in modern language it means a consistent association of thoughts. But as age-old experience shows, the ideals proclaimed by a person or social class are often chosen in such a manner that they provide cover for their particular interests. "Where your treasure is, there will your heart be also," said Jesus; "You say Christ and mean calico," said the socialists of the 19th century. The criticism of ideologies has thus become a popular type of thought of our time, mastered by almost everyone in political debate but applied to one's own ideology by practically no one. This means that the criticism of ideologies is usually applied ideologically. Everyone claims to know his own proclaimed viewpoints as well as the concealed motives of his opponent. The proclaimed viewpoints of one's opponent are therefore not considered worthy of thorough recognition. A person with the strength of character not to lie to himself consciously conceals his own hidden motives. However, whoever cannot bear to recognise his own motives represses them, and whatever he is incapable of repressing fosters the cynicism generally granted to one's own side. Yet, we are taught to "love thy neighbor as thyself." This, too, can be read as a formula of plain reason. You will only learn to understand yourself when you have learned to understand your neighbour. We must learn to take the ideologies of others seriously, as intelligent viewpoints as well as the expression of legitimate motives. Only then will we learn to comprehend how our own legitimate motives are reflected in our own views. Even in this sense of the discussion the motto holds true: no peace without justice.

Let us turn to the real contradictions in the world today. Never before have so many people lived in prosperity as at present, a prosperity which materially surpasses any in the past. Never before have so many people lived in misery and hunger as now; the number of people who have died as a consequence of hunger is greater than the number of dead from all wars of this century. Never before has awareness of the injustice of the distribution of goods been as widespread as today. What must be done?

The banal answer that there are more rich and more poor people living today because the number of people on earth has doubled in the past 60 years and increased tenfold in the past 300 years is true, but not sufficient. Viewed in isolation, this answer expresses acceptance of the age-old difference of rich and poor as fate and thus remains an ideology of the rich. The question is whether modern civilisation should not be in a position to overcome the contradiction of rich and poor, or at least to alleviate it. Only by keeping this question in mind will we be able to discuss the causes and effects of population growth.

Class rule and social injustice are as old as advanced civilisations, at least 6,000 years. The rich masters left behind records of their glory. However, for centuries there have also been written documents of the poor, or of those who spoke out for the poor. There was the lamentation of the poor farmer in ancient Egypt in 2,000 BC, and there was the voice of the

Jewish prophets. God does not want burnt offerings, but rather that you visit the widows and orphans in their poverty, and that you look after the stranger in your land. Jesus went to the poor. It is more likely that a camel laden with treasures will go through the narrow gateway known as the eye of the needle than a rich man will enter the Kingdom of Heaven.

In modern times, on the other hand, we have "real eschatology," the conviction that mankind not only should, but has the power to, change the injustice of our social order. This took place historically in two steps. The first step was the bourgeois revolution of the 18th century which evolved from 1688 in England, broke out as the War of Independence in America in 1776 and in France in 1789, and reappeared in England as the "industrial revolution" of the early 19th century. The second step was the workers' movement of the 19th and 20th centuries, involving militant and revisionist forms of socialism.

With the simplification common to every brief historical statement, we can say that the guiding concept of the first revolution was freedom; the guiding concept of the second revolutionary hope is justice. The word "justice" was introduced to the resolution of the World Council of Churches by the churches of the South. The rich of today believe in the defence of freedom; the poor hope for the attainment of justice. The Latin American theology of liberation is proof of this hope, and, as the bearer of this hope, the church in Latin America has become a social force such as it had long ceased to be.

However, it would be dangerous, even fatal, for freedom as for justice to pit them against each other. Varying the opening sentence of this section, let us dare to state:

No justice without freedom; no freedom without justice.

What is political freedom? It is not, in a modern constitutional state, arbitrariness. Freedom in a viable society is above all not the freedom which I claim for myself and my group, but rather the freedom which I afford to the other person and the other group. This involves two realisations which are not self-evident and are often disregarded: the limitation of our judgment of the actions of our fellow men to a judgment on their legality only (legality principle) and the significance of freedom of expression for the common search for truth (truth orientation).

The legality principle is one of the greatest *moral* accomplishments of modern times. Naturally, a time-honoured, strongly justified conviction exists that mankind should not merely obey moral dictates externally, out of beneficial conformism, but rather out of inner respect for the dictates; that is, to use Kant's manner of speaking quoted above, he should not only act legally, but also morally. This conviction is common to Greek philosophy, particularly late-classical Stoicism, to Christianity, and to the modern enlightenment. However, historically this led much too easily to the political abuse of morality. Societies that morally felt they were right, and governments that morally believed in their legitimacy, demanded of their members or their subjects a moral motive; they took the liberty of morally punishing deviations from the norm, to the extent of using the stake and the executioner's sword. Revolutionaries, on the other hand, who could no longer believe in the moral legitimacy of the government or the social order felt justified in fighting the immoral rulers with all available means, to the extent of political murder and, after their victory, the guillotine. The self-righteousness of morality proved to be unfathomably evil. This is where a distinction between legality and morality is morally required. Human judges can decide whether their fellow men act according to the law; the heart, however, as the old saying goes, is seen by God alone. Therefore, it is the duty of the human court to condemn the unlawfulness of a person's actions, but not the immorality of his motives.

It was this step that made it possible to establish what we now call human rights. They are provided as inalienable, legally inviolable rights of each individual. They are not rights to a spiritual state, but rather to visible behaviour. No government, regardless of how legitimate, and no revolution, regardless of how justified, may violate them without becoming deeply guilty morally, that is, without losing its own legitimacy.

Less generally recognised is the political necessity of truth orientation, of freedom of expression. It represents the institutional form of the common quest for truth. A complex society such as ours in a time of rapid change cannot survive, let alone find the best ways, without insight. However, we do not gain insight in our sleep, at least not without first exerting ourselves greatly in our quest for truth. A social quest for the right insight cannot exist without controversy. Controversy can only exist where there is freedom of expression. Every scientist knows how imperative differences of opinion are for research and how paralysing a prevailing school can become. Dictators and party bureaucrats with a monopoly on opinion tend to fail because their mistakes are not criticised early enough and because they can sweep their scandals under the carpet. A sense of infallibility is suicidal. To close with Kant's words: freedom is the existence of truth. For truth is not dictated, but rather sought and always only partially found.

Thus, the legality principle: no freedom without justice; and truth orientation: no justice without freedom.

However, legally guaranteed political freedom does not solve the problem of rich and poor; at most, it allows it to be made a political topic. Beneath the level of absolute poverty, political freedom is not a utilisable good; at this level, urgently needed food, tools, and a roof over one's head are important. History shows that poor populations do not carry out revolutions. They do not have the necessary strength or time. Relief through nascent prosperity, promotion of education, and political leaders from the ruling classes are part of the liberation movement.

In this regard, however, we are confronted with probably the greatest ideological contradiction of our time, the contradiction between the economic doctrines of the market and those of socialism. At first sight, the statement quoted above now seems appropriate: freedom, that is, freedom of the market, is the guiding concept of the rich; justice, that is, justice in distribution, is the guiding concept of the poor. However, simplified statements do not suffice here either. Classical bourgeois economics as well as genuine Marxism teach us that not merely a moral appeal is needed but also an analysis of the objective causes.

Let us look back about 25 years to the early 1960s. At that time, expectations for further economic and social development were relatively optimistic throughout the world. The world could, and still can, be divided into three regions. Political and military strength was concentrated in the North, with the leading powers the United States of America in the West and the Soviet Union in the East. In the western, "first" world, economic power was also to be found. In the eastern, "second" world, the hope was maintained of catching up, even surpassing, the West economically through technological development. The southern, "third" world, the majority of the earth's population, was poor, but had just been liberated from the political colonial rule of the western North. The third world understood its poverty to be a result of insufficient economic and technological development and now hoped to take swift steps to catch up in their development. In the North, there was a sincere desire to promote the development of the South, which was also expected to open up new markets for the northern economy. At the same time, however, the South was a chessboard on which the capitalistic, northern West with its free market economy and the socialistic, northern East with its planned economy carried out their struggle for power. As long as this struggle was carried out with economic means, the West was and remained superior. From an economic standpoint, there was, and is, one homogenous world market dominated by the "first" world, more precisely by North America and secondly by Western Europe and increasingly by Japan, in which the Soviet Union and socialist China play only a limited role.

The two economic theories, which also provided the framework for this struggle for power, evolved in Western Europe in the 18th and 19th centuries. It should therefore be expected that the conflict between these two theories pertains to a specifically Western European problem. This is important for our statement of the problem from two points of view. On the one hand, we have to understand these theories within their conflict if we are to comprehend the self-interpretation of the economically dominant northern West. On the other hand, there is reason to suspect that their conflict forces inappropriate stereotyping upon the rest of the world, including Russia and Latin America, which both belong to the European cultural complex, and even more so upon the major Asiatic cultures. Which therefore means that, as yet, we will not be able to see the true problem of our modern world in their conceptual terms.

Let us first follow the self-interpretation of the West. According to this interpretation, freedom is not only a great political good, but, as freedom of the market, it is also the cause of economic success, i.e. of wealth. Accordingly, it serves the well-being of those who are still poor today to give them too the origin of prosperity, i.e. the free market. In the period since the origin of the doctrine of liberal economics, approximately 1760 until 1960, the success in the North, especially in industrial production, was indeed striking. The doctrine also provided a very simple, perfectly clear explanation of success. The economy flourishes best when, in a transparent market, each competitor on the market represents his own interests and thus uses his own judgment. For the collective judgment of so many market-competitors brings more good ideas to light than any absolutist or socialist planning authority. It is the same argument as the truth orientation of political freedom. There is also feedback between the free market and political freedom in that free action is learnt in the marketplace.

The socialist criticism is equally simple. The market produces large national products; precisely according to Karl Marx, in historical dialectics it is in fact the role of capitalism to develop productive resources. However, the market does not produce economic equality; according to the socialist view, it does not solve the distribution problem. This also affects the link to politics. Economic dependency turns legally guaranteed political freedom into fiction. Marx carried Friedrich Hegel's enlightening thought further: that freedom, which is impossible without an economic basis, was first accessible to the nobility, then, after the bourgeois revolution, to the middle-classes and capitalists, and that—according to Marx—after a last proletarian revolution, it will be accessible to all people in society.

However, the progressive impoverishment of the industrial proletariats awaited by Marx failed to materialise in any of the major capitalistic countries. Under the protection of the constitutional state, it was headed off by the workers' movement, the establishment of purchasing power for the masses, and social legislation. In the form of social democracy, socialism put through a significant number of its ideals by conforming to the market system, and not by political revolution. Revolutionary socialism only came to power in those regions which, according to its own doctrine, were not yet historically ready for it, in the pre-bourgeois, old, absolute monarchies in Russia and China. What could have been more plausible in the West around 1960 than to sincerely hope for the transfer of this favourable development of the market to the South?

In the quarter century since, there have been partial successes in all three regions of the world, but there have been even greater disappointments. The big socialist powers have quite simply not been able to lessen their economic backwardness as compared to the West; China, and more slowly, the Soviet Union, were forced to give priority to the reform needs of their own systems. In the northern West, the problem of rich and poor has been diminished, but not solved, and is now growing again. The industrial working class as a whole is integrated in society with petty-bourgeois status; the majority of the population of the western countries, as compared to the rest of the world, belongs to the rich. In contrast, however, a poor minority of the population is being increasingly excluded from society: the permanently unemployed, the growing ethnic minorities. Yet, the most serious, potentially most catastrophic problem is found in the South.

In the South alone, as well, more people live today in prosperity and more people in misery and hunger than ever before. Industries were founded which not only brought wealth to the upper class but, to a certain degree, also established an educated middle-class, which is indispensable to society, and a working class with growing purchasing power. At the same time, the number of poor in the slums of the cities with several million inhabitants is increasing continuously. Industrialisation was made possible through heavy indebtedness, which is now upsetting the international financial market. An understandable, yet self-defeating policy of the creditors is aimed at maintaining the debtor countries' ability to pay interest and repay capital by forcing them to orient their economies almost entirely to exports; by doing so, the sole economic basis of social and political stability, a flourishing domestic market, is hindered in its development, or even destroyed. As a result of these economic conditions, the form of government vacillates between democracy and military, ideological, or religious dictatorships. Human rights violations by governments and revolutionary terrorism, which outrage and terrify the complacent citizens of the North, are indications of this political instability.

Prognosis and therapy are difficult without a reliable causal diagnosis of the disease. Where does the misery come from? However, it is precisely this diagnosis which is controversial in the conflict between the ideologies. Three causes have been named; yet, depending on the ideology, they have been accorded greater or lesser importance.

Today, the view that misery is in itself a result of the dependency of the South on the capitalistic world market, known as the dependency theory in Latin America, enjoys a wide following, particularly among the intellectuals of the South. It is one of the reasons for the South's demand to place justice before peace as the topic of a Christian world assembly. In fact, socialists already pointed out in the early 1900s that the advancement of the working class in the industrial countries of the North not only succeeded (as stated above) due to domestic developments such as trade unions, the domestic market, and social legislation, but also due to the shift of material exploitation to the "periphery," i.e. the world of the South and East, which was made dependent through colonialism and imperialism. A consistent socialist theorist will not look for the cause in the ill-will of certain groups, such as the "multinationals," but rather in the compulsory profit maximisation incorporated in the competitive system. A consistent market theorist, however, will ask why the solution, which succeeded on the domestic market of the industrial countries, should not ultimately succeed on the world market as well. Who is right?

There is evidence indicating why this solution would presumably be much more difficult on the world market today than it once was on the national domestic market. The national solution required the support of a comprehensive constitutional state which guaranteed the right to strike, labour legislation, an infrastructure, and external peace. An analagous world-state encompassing the world market does not exist, and the nation-states themselves, especially the economically dependent states of the South, are in the role of competitors on the world market. Current international economic policy is determined by the powerful competitors. The danger exists that through their economic and financial policies they will unwittingly keep the democracy in the South, which they theoretically believe in, from the success which a democracy needs in order to be viable.

There are two further causes of need and misery, regardless of how we judge the role of the world market.

Population growth must be mentioned in this connection. It threatens to devour all economic progress. India and China are aware of the problem.

A vicious circle has become apparent in these countries. It is precisely the poorer populations that grow most rapidly. This is economically understandable. It is a burning interest of every family living in poor, especially rural conditions to have many children; the children alone are available as unpaid labour, and the children alone will some day provide for their parents. How are we to create the prosperity that could bring this growth to a standstill?

Finally, the development optimists underestimated the problem of cultural adaptation. Technological modernisation, which has been developing for centuries in the North, has been given to the peoples of the South in a matter of decades. It is destroying ways of life which were stable for centuries. And this brings us back to the question of whether our own culture can actually tolerate so much technology.

Political Peace

The time has come when the political institution of war must be, and can be, overcome.

What does "peace" mean? We will first ask this question in a limited sense; we will speak of political peace. Initially, we will even limit this to international peace, which is generally considered to be the absence of war.

However, comparing hope to realisation, must we not fear that our hope of overcoming the political institution of war has relapsed into the realm of fantasy? The facts point to continuing bloodshed in the South in approximately 130 wars since 1945 and the continuing threat of a nuclear world war in the North. And it is horrible to have to admit that the present wars in the South are closer to the normal course of world history than the four decades of armistice in the North.

War itself is at least as old as civilisation. The oldest accounts of peoples are epic poems on heroes and documents of victory. The old myths describe battles between the gods. The afflictions of war are age-old. The proclamation of the prophet in the Old Testament sounds like an Utopian hope, expressed in the language of a poetic parable: the lion shall lie down with the lamb, and the swords shall be beaten into ploughshares.

Nevertheless, the present situation is fundamentally different than all others in the past. A change of awareness about war and peace has set in, hitherto unprecedented.

People are beginning to perceive overcoming the institution of war not as a hope belonging to another world, but as a relevant, solvable problem belonging to this world. And they must view it this way if they are to hope for the survival of mankind. The reason for this change of awareness is also relevant and belongs to this world. It lies in the destructive power of modern weapons technology. In the past, mankind, but not always every race, survived the major, then technologically feasible wars. War was a horrible, yet feasible institution. It is still feasible today, though not permanently survivable. It is necessary to overcome war as an institution.

We are practically as far from achieving this as ever. The wars of the South and particularly the general staff planning of the North involve the limited use of weapons. The purpose of this deliberate limitation is to allow for the continued use of the instrument of war. We do not know how to settle the conflicts surrounding justice, political systems, and the numerous national and regional interests without recourse to weapons; we do not know how to pursue major foreign policy without the threat of war.

Specifically ascribing the guilt to one's respective adversary is always a standard political tool. For overcoming war as an institution this is inappropriate, even in cases where the guilt is rightly placed. In war, both sides usually feel justified and on the defensive; the military principle "attack is the best defence" then justifies aggression. In fact, our entire, age-old political system is based on the possibility of an armed settlement as the *ultima ratio regum,* the final argument of the rulers.

In the North as in the South there is a certain blindness for the respective other region and, therefore, for the interdependence of the two. In the North, each of the two superpowers views the other as a great danger, and the smaller nations of the North fear nothing more than the consequences of this conflict. Openness for discussion requires of me the clear personal statement that I do not view the conflict between the ideologies of the two superpowers symmetrically. The previous observation that justice is not possible without freedom represents an unequivocal belief in the western interpretation of freedom. This domestic partisanship, however, does not spare me from the international analysis, which teaches me that, in this regard, two international candidates for hegemony are locked in a long-term struggle. From the perspective of this struggle for power, both generally view the South, as previously mentioned, merely as part of a chessboard which they are using to play their game; in the South, each views the influence of its adversary above all with utmost suspicion. This is dangerous blindness to the real problems of the South.

In the South, as a direct reflection of this, the simultaneous aversion to both northern powers is growing today: "Don't bother us with your conflict." One even hears extreme sentiments in the South expressed in such forms as: "Why don't these two northern barbarians finally wage their war against each other? Then we would be rid of both of them!" Even among lenient, discriminating discussion partners in the South no response can be found for the northern idea of a council on peace alone: "That's your problem, not ours." This reaction of turning away from the concerns of the North is highly understandable, but it is dangerous blindness in the light of an international danger.

The fates of both halves of the world are, in fact, almost inseparably bound up with each other. The economy of the northern West, as we have seen, dominates the southern world market and is dependent upon it. The weapons used in war and terrorism in the southern conflicts are produced in the North. Arms build-up in all countries devours funds which should be used for other ends. The hot spots which could cause a northern war to break out are located in the South. However, a major northern war would not spare the South; even without radioactivity and nuclear winter, a war of this nature would bring about an unrivalled hunger catastrophe in the South through the temporary destruction of the world economy alone.

It is therefore in the vital interest of all mankind, as well as of every effort towards justice and the integrity of nature, that the war between the superpowers of the North be avoided. This prevention of war, however, is not guaranteed. New measures are necessary. Time is running out.

We must go into greater detail regarding this problem.

Atomic weapons are not the cause of the danger of war. On the contrary, in the past 40 years war has only been waged on this earth in those regions where it appeared certain that it would not become nuclear. However, nuclear deterrence through mutually assured second-strike capability, a clever invention of American scientists, is not appropriate and was never intended to solve the problem of the prevention of war conclusively. It was only intended to provide a reprieve in which it would have been possible to provide for the political guarantee of peace.

In the final analysis, necessary world peace can by no means be guaranteed technologically, but only politically. Technology, which, in addition, is caught in the constant stream of development, cannot provide a permanent guarantee against technical failure, the escalation of regional conflicts, and human madness. And *one* failure a century is enough for the catastrophe. Precisely the success in the prevention of war during the 1960s and 1970s has temporarily lulled world opinion into sleep. The new wakening of fear in the early 1980s was a chance. Will it be used?

Since the early 1960s I have expected an international political cycle and then watched it take its course. The cold war, a system of antagonistic bipolarity, led to the mutual paralysis of the foreign policy of both superpowers in the light of an increasingly pluralistic world structure [Mao

Zedong, Charles de Gaulle, and later the Organisation of Petroleum Exporting Countries (OPEC)]. Consequently, the superpowers discovered their interest in a more cooperative bipolarity, which was then called *détente*. However, it was foreseeable that the superpowers would rediscover their struggle for hegemony, should they have ever forgotten it. The Soviet Union obviously never did; in the 1970s, the Soviet Union incessantly continued its arms build-up.

While at present the Soviet side, under the pressure of the recognised urgent necessity of economic reform and therefore of the primacy of domestic policy, is beginning to push for disarmament, American policy has again reverted to complete distrust of its hegemonial adversary. This is a common occurrence even in private conflicts: alternately only one of the two adversaries is willing to compromise; distrust is the decisive element.

One of the greatest barriers to an—inherently possible—peaceful *modus vivendi* between the superpowers is their mutual perception, the way in which they view each other. The contradiction between their ideologies is certainly not the most profound reason for their elementary and banal power conflict. The ideological contradiction is much more the way in which each of the two sides makes it psychologically tolerable to continue with this struggle for power. Power conflicts between countries are a legacy of advanced civilisation. The most profound reason for this conflict would seem to be mutual fear, a fear which is nurtured by any arms build-up, itself born out of fear, or aggression by the respective adversary.

Naturally, the contextual contradiction between the two ideologies is important and, for the present, cannot be settled in principle. An understanding of its origin, however, could contribute to the superpowers' ability to negotiate. Both ideologies come from the same "real eschatological" modern-European model, the model of political revolution. However, the American ideology originates from the first, liberal-bourgeois phase, and the Soviet ideology originates from the second, radical socialistic phase. In addition, the eminently important difference in the formative historical experience of both nations plays a role.

Both nations are characterised by expansion, by the historical settlement of, in European terms, a practically endless region. North America was conquered and settled by Europeans seeking freedom. The original wish of the United States was to have no part in the reprehensible struggles for power between the European princes, which was made possible by the fortunate isolation between two oceans. Freedom of the market and the size of the country then allowed the United States to become the greatest economic power of the world. The self-inflicted slaughter of Europe during this century forced the United States into the role of international political hegemony. No other power in the history of the world took on a politically imperialistic role with as much reluctance as the United States. Yet, precisely its inexperience in an imperialistic role, as well as the primacy of domestic policy in a system of constantly recurring elections, combined with the only constant, namely the unavoidably expansive economic interests, has recurringly blinded several of the American governments to the true interests of both their partners and their adversaries. This blindness is threatening to nullify the glad tidings of political freedom which America sincerely intends to bring to the peoples of this earth.

Geographically and historically, Russia is in the opposite situation. The peasantry, living on a naturally borderless plain bound by more advanced civilisation to the West and nomads on swift horses to the East, was historically only able to exist for 1,000 years due to the military strength of the country. Excessive military build-up and expansion to the point of confrontation with insurpassable borders is the natural, subjectively viewed as defensive reaction in this situation. Action and reaction to power is then basic political practice. Domestically, this spiritually rich, emotionally strong, passionately pious people had been under a system of absolute supremacy since coming to nationhood. The intellectual opening to the West led to self-awareness in the grandiose Russian literature of the 19th century, and, in this century, to revolution based on the Marxist, i.e. western, doctrine. This doctrine also promises the peoples of the earth freedom through economic justice. The weakness of their specifically Soviet version derives from the fact that throughout Russian history there was never an opportunity to experience bourgeois democratic freedom. Consequently, on the Soviet side as well there is a specific blindness for the true interests of both their partners and their adversaries. The consequences can be seen in China, Eastern Europe, and now practically everywhere in the South.

An author who, without himself being an American or Soviet citizen, diagnoses blindness in both superpowers, must ask himself whether this diagnosis is not in itself the result of his own blindness, specifically of his own frustrated, Western European, political arrogance. Especially for a German, who experienced Hitler's criminally blind great-power policy as a grown man and did not resist it sufficiently, this would be unforgiveable. Perhaps it can be said that experiencing the involvement of one's own country and of oneself in this power mentality leaves behind a sensitivity for its inherent dangers. History shows that great power always creates certain delusions, and perhaps even presupposes them. To the outsider, this appears as the "arrogance of power." The true reason, however, is fear. Fear numbs the sensitivity that could lead to rescue through self-criticism and instead projects this criticism onto the external adversary.

The danger of the present situation, therefore, is that the two international powers perceive each other almost exclusively as adversaries, since each has elevated the in-and-of-themselves limited power interests of the other to the point of being intolerable by taking the ideology of its respective adversary literally.

The 40 years of armistice during the arms race are no consolation. Allow me to use a simile. In the arid zones of Australia and America, for example, there have often been devastating forest fires, after which the forests nevertheless recovered. We have now learned to prevent forest fires better and better. Consequently, however, more and more combustible material has accumulated. If a fire then nevertheless breaks out, it grows to an inextinguishable intensity, leaving behind an area in which the flora and fauna of the forest can no longer regain a footing. The northern peace of the past 40 years could have been the period of the prevented forest fire of mankind.

After depicting the dangers, we must now come back to describe the hope of political peace. Hope alone creates strength to face danger. Let us repeat three older theses:

1. World peace is a prerequisite for the survival of mankind in a technological civilisation.
2. Politically guaranteed world peace would not be the Golden Age. It would be the overcoming of a specific, no longer tolerable form of settling conflicts.
3. The establishment of world peace requires exceptional moral effort.

A few comments on these theses.

1. The reasons why a major world war must be prevented are obvious. Regional wars involve the danger of escalation if they move into the conflict zones of the superpowers. In particular, however, they are almost insurmountable barriers to the creation of an international legal system, without which the transition of the world market into a phase of social justice would be impossible. Naturally, in a world of social and national oppression, revolutionaries, as belligerents, and later as the victors of a revolution, understand their struggle as a war of liberation, as a moral duty. In spite of Mahatma Gandhi's eminent example, the customary reaction is to take up arms. In a world full of superior strength, injustice, and arms, this reaction can only be expected. It is not the protected citizen of a well-to-do democracy who is entitled to criticise this, but only the non-

violent fighter. However, it can be seen in many cases that the taking up of arms creates a vicious circle. It increases the resistance which it intends to break. In the revolutionary, it often produces a frame of mind which entices him, after the victory, to establish a new tyranny: "Revolution devours its children." Viewed objectively, arms build-up consumes the funds needed for economic growth, and war prevents the creation of a functioning international legal system. If we want international social justice, then we have to want international political peace. No justice without peace.

2. The second thesis is the answer to the argument that conflicts are simply a part of human nature. The answer is yes; however, not conflicts in the form of politically organised, reciprocal collective murder as a means of settling a conflict. War between fortresses and between cities has long since disappeared in well-organised nation states. Under a legal system, people can live together without organised war even if they envy or hate their neighbours. Election campaigns can be morally as revolting as war propaganda. However, the legality principle, wherever it functions, prevents a violent settlement.

The question, however, is how a legal system of this nature is to be established internationally. The *de facto* renunciation of the exercise of the sovereign right to wage war, today still granted under international law to all nations, would be imperative. In certain regions of the earth, this has become reality, as for example between the Scandinavian countries long since, between the USA and Canada, and for a few decades now between the countries of Western Europe. However, special domestic and international conditions exist in each of these cases. In the European examples, in particular, democracy and the loss of their former positions as great powers combine with the threat of having more powerful neighbours. The question is how the most powerful nation can be compelled to renounce its right to sovereignty. As the mice asked: "Who is going to bell the cat?"

All historical examples of the establishment of long-term peace in a large region are based on the military victory of a prospective candidate for hegemony and, usually, on the creation of a huge centralised state after the victory, as in China and Rome. Now, the most conservative solution according to these parallels would be the creation of a world-state by the victor of a final world war. The general public at present verbally agrees that this is no longer possible today. In view of the constant instability of technological arms development, however, it is not certain whether this will always be the case. It is also not certain whether all responsible parties even believe in this impossibility today, or for the near future. It is only certain that we must not *want* this solution.

A seemingly easier but actually more radical solution would be the voluntary establishment of an international federation which would expressly, in a legally binding form, renounce the sovereign right to wage war and would reduce the national armies to the size of mere police forces. To freely renounce, on grounds of reason, a right from which not even force has been able to separate us, would presuppose a change of consciousness in mankind, which has indeed begun, but still remains far from its goal. At present this thought remains Utopian. However, this change of consciousness is imperative. What we are incapable of wanting, we will not receive.

What is indeed happening today is completely pallid in comparison. Nations reserve the right to wage war, yet renounce the exercise of this right according to their own evaluation of the danger. The United Nations is important because it creates publicity. However, it is only a first step towards the hope for peace. *De facto,* the United Nations is largely a body for the voice of the powerless majority. Its measures guarantee peace at best in those regions where the powerful nations are also interested in peace. There are formal conventions on the banning of war; however, they conceal the reality of warfare so little that their existence is hardly known among the general public. As if in a dream, the majority of the people delude themselves in the hope that the great war will never come, or that it will not reach their own region; however, the smaller wars have to be, and can be, lived with, especially if they are far away. And every small war is far away from the majority of the people. This day-dreaming is the actual barrier to a change of consciousness.

3. The exceptional moral effort is the effort of a change of consciousness. This is the third thesis, following the two theses which call for *political* world peace. Later we will need to address the profound change of awareness needed to attain genuine peaceableness. I am convinced that this change is possible within the realms of human nature and human society. The path to this change is at best paved by political systems and moral behaviour; this path in fact leads through suffering and mercy. The present thesis, however, calls for something less pretentious. It calls for a change of awareness based on reason, allowing for the creation of political systems which will prevent a spiritually unredeemed mankind from destroying itself. Such reason cannot come about without moral effort and without the strong impetus of love. One of its most important accomplishments, however, is the intellectual effort to understand the current political realities.

The Preservation of Nature

No peace between people without peace with nature.

People do not fight over things that are available in abundance. The economy produces and manages goods which are naturally scarce. Political supremacy means control over scarce goods. Social injustice is the unjust distribution of scarce goods. War is waged over living space and supremacy, i.e. over scarce goods. Modern technology appears to be a path to liberation from the scarcity of goods. Supremacy over people, it is hoped, will no longer be necessary and will disappear when we have gained technological supremacy over nature.

Have we, with this hope, backed the wrong horse? The ecological movement of the past two decades has rediscovered this danger. The West has become wealthy and intermittently dominates the world through technology. There have been critics of this course in every decade. Never has their criticism been forgotten more than since 1945. Now, in the rich northern West, the reaction, fear, has come, in the form of water pollution, erosion, dying forests and reactor disasters. Several of the greatest ecological dangers already recognised today can be found in the South, for example the felling of the rain forests. However, in the South, it is easier to see the present poverty than the suspected future danger. What solutions for this poverty are being proposed by the ecological admonishers in the North?

The scientific and technological environmental problems are detailed in nature and therefore highly complex. It is not possible for us to treat these problems here. Let us keep to two basic questions. First, on a more superficial level: can the protection of nature be realised in political and economic terms? This in turn gives rise to the more fundamental historical, anthropological question of whether nature and civilisation are even compatible.

In the northern countries, we still have reason to hope that the environmental problems will be kept within reasonable limits, of course only if we are determined to act politically. Everything stated previously under the topic of justice and freedom with the catchwords "legality principle" and "truth orientation" is valid here. For the private competitor on the market, environmental damage, or the avoidance thereof, represents above all external costs, which do not appear in his direct costs of production and sales revenue. He therefore often cannot afford to produce or consume in an environmentally safe manner if this leads to competitive disadvantages for him. Environmental protection, as with the creation of an infrastructure (lighthouses were the example in the 18th century), is the duty of the government, even according to the classical theory of liberal economics. The government is now obligated to create equitable conditions for environmentally safe behaviour for all market competitors through binding regulations. This will never be carried through without public debate and without political uproar. For this reason, the political uproar over environmental damage is a blessing. When the environmental awareness of the people is sufficiently developed, then pressure will even arise on the market in favour of environmentally safe products. In a transparent market and a democracy capable of making decisions, national ecological problems should consequently be solvable. For example, if I may now speak as a Central European, the air in the industrial centre of West Germany, the Ruhr Valley, is cleaner now than fifty years ago and the lakes of Switzerland and Bavaria are cleaner than twenty years ago.

Yet, at the present speed of technological development, the timely recognition of environmental damage remains an unresolved problem in many cases. Systematic research is indispensable in this regard and is indeed not hopeless.

What do in fact seem unsolvable so far are the environmental problems that cross national borders. Even a regional organisation created exclusively for joint decision-making, such as the European Community, faces the difficulties of cooperation between sovereign states in this regard. In addition, world-wide environmental protection, just as presumably the overcoming of poverty, has so far been unsuccessful due to the lack of a binding, acceptable, and enforceable legal system. These two problems are related. There can be no lasting peace among men without a degree of social justice. There can be no social justice if mankind saps the resources of nature. Therefore, as stated at the beginning of this chapter, there can be no peace among men without peace with nature. Likewise, however, there can be no peace with nature without peace among men. We cannot allow our planet, through the world market, to become an economic and functional unit without authorities for joint political decision-making. The result can only be catastrophic.

One example of the unresolved problems which in themsleves would not have to end in disaster is long-term energy policy. Modern technology is largely dependent on an adequate supply of energy. The decisive step took place during the past centuries when coal surpassed and replaced the potentially regenerative sources of energy such as wind, water, and firewood. The major burden of our energy supply today lies on fossil fuels. They have two inherent weaknesses. First, at the present or a growing rate of consumption they will be depleted within a period of at most a few centuries and in some cases in a few decades. Thus, they provide growth at the cost of longer term stability. Furthermore, they are high-grade chemical substances which could be used much more practically than for combustion. Second, they produce pollutants in the atmosphere. Waste-gas purification is possible, but expensive, and very difficult to enforce beyond national borders. In addition, the threatening problem remains unresolved of a progressive change in climate on our earth due to the fact that carbon dioxide, inevitably released during combustion, is heating the atmosphere in the 'greenhouse effect'.

Physicists, including the author, have therefore set their hopes now for almost five decades on nuclear energy as an environmentally safe alternative. Using breeder technology or fusion, nuclear energy would indeed be inexhaustible for centuries. And, in principle, the more concentrated a source of energy is, the more technologically profitably, i.e. sparingly, it can be used on a large scale. One danger, the extent of which we have realised too slowly (although it was the experts and not the opponents who first noticed the problem), is the resulting radioactive waste. Subsequently, we should not be surprised that a reaction which normally does not occur on the earth's natural surface can have consequences to which life on earth is not adapted. In principle, this also applies to the massive combustion of coal and petroleum.

Personally, even after Three Mile Island and Chernobyl, I venture to presume that, with continuously improved safety technology, reactors in normal operation should cause less damage to the environment in the long run than fossil fuels; of course, I am not a technical expert in this regard. However, acts of violence cannot be ruled out, and their consequences could be devastating. The American reactor specialist Alvin Weinberg said long ago: "Guarantee me a thousand years of political peace, and I will guarantee you a thousand-year supply of energy." It is a misleading argument then to use the nightmare of a total nuclear war as an excuse for reactors not being secured against violence, along the lines: "If the war doesn't come then nothing will happen. If it comes, then everything is over anyway." Neither biological evolution nor the evolution of civilisation are compatible with such all-or-nothing alternatives. "Error tolerance" is a prerequisite for viable progress. Certainly, the political institution of war must be overcome. However, at present, it has not been overcome, and it is a sign of foolish wishful-thinking if we act as if it had been overcome. The limited use of arms, in war or terrorism, is a part of daily life on earth today. For ten years, presumably without a sufficient assessment of the technological and financial conditions, in any case without any appreciable success, I called for safety for reactors (and reprocessing facilities!) against the possible use of arms. Today, for the period for which we can plan, I can no longer advise the use of nuclear energy as the chief source of energy.

However, negative conclusions such as this do not solve the energy problem. Today, photovoltaically derived solar energy stored in hydrogen has given rise to long-term hopes. Of course, solar energy is primarily diffuse; it does not fulfil the large-scale technological criterion of high concentration and will therefore require an expanse of facilities, which, it is estimated today, will take seven decades to establish it adequately as the leading source of energy. In the meantime, we would largely be dependent on the insufficiently utilised possibilities of energy conservation. The concern does not appear unfounded that energy conservation could slow economic progress, especially in the South, and consequently further stimulate population growth, thus making poverty inevitable.

These are considerations within the conceptual field of the present technocracy. Will we be forced to assume a completely different manner of acting and thinking? Are we heading towards an ascetic universal civilisation?

Hard-line critics, in fact, do not see the conflict between economics and ecology in the political decision-making system, but rather in two incompatible principles: growth in the interest of the economy, and stability as a condition for the survival of nature. Allow me to underscore this conflict using a historical hypothesis.

The Old Stone Age civilisations of hunters and gatherers, embedded in the bosom of nature, were stable for hundreds of thousands of years. They were, so to speak, nature themselves. Through the invention of farming and the domestication of animals, man began to master nature. Now the earth's population is growing. Can it remain embedded in nature?

From our superficial, historical point of view, ancient civilisations also appear stable. They often preserved the fundamentals of their political system and its artistic means of expression, i.e. its conception of itself, over several millenniums. Ancient Egypt for three thousand years, China for four thousand years, and three thousand years of Hindu civilisation with the most stable of all social systems of advanced civilisations, the caste system, are examples. And, if we did not sense conflicts intensely from within, then we would also add Europe and its three thousand years. However, people always see the transition from stable planes to deep crises more clearly from within. The phases of political stability in Egypt and China also seldom lasted longer than two or three centuries. A dynasty, according to the chroniclers, begins with strong, good rulers and ends with evil, weak rulers, in China often with an evil woman. Does the moralism of the chroniclers and contemporaries suffice to explain this phenomenon?

Now to the hypothesis. Political stability in advanced civilisations always presupposed economic growth, albeit moderate, to be somewhat faster than population growth. For a stable government carried by the consent of the governed means governing with humanitarian compromises: "Right now there is no job for you, but in five years one will be available." However, every civilisation has run up against the limits of its growth, contingent on geography and the state of technology. When the limits to growth have been reached, the rulers must govern uncompromisingly. Those who are capable of this are considered evil rulers by the chroniclers, and those who are incapable are considered weak rulers. The result is political catastrophe, and after centuries of disorder, the country has shed enough blood to begin the next two hundred years of growth.

The respective limits to growth are a result of the respective state of technology. Modern technology is developing so rapidly that we do not know the objective limits of our own growth. It is certain that the consequences of technology have begun to equal the order of magnitude of the natural geoclimatic changes, that the variety of organic species has been rapidly decreasing during the past decades; in short, that mankind has unknowingly assumed responsibility for the continuance of organic life on earth.

Under what conditions can we bear the responsibility for earth?

THE ORIGIN OF THE PROBLEMS

War as an institution, social injustice, and environmental destruction are consequences of the previous history of advanced civilisation. They are not the result of an unalterable human nature. The combined application of political, economic, and moral reason could overcome them.

However, common sense does not come about simply because we call for it. It has in itself political, moral, affective, and—the use of the word permitting—transcendent prerequisites.

Politically: *communication* is necessary, open discussion, the arousal of political will, and the creation of authorities with legally binding competence.

Morally: *will* is what matters. Willingness to listen, to help, to make our own inevitable sacrifices.

Affectively: common sense requires an affect to support and enliven it. In our traditional language this is called *charity*.

Transcendentally: neither affect, reason, nor success are controlled by our will. Our will is necessary, but does not suffice. *Mercy* is with us.

The History of Civilisation

Let us presume that the origin of the present world problems lies in the development of civilisation.

By doing so, we are dissociating ourselves from two other current, popular interpretations of these problems: from seeking a villain and from resigning ourselves to the unalterable nature of man. We do not seek the origin of our problems in a current misfortune nor in eternity, but rather in the long, yet comprehensible history of six thousand or ten thousand years, in historically understandable structures.

Naturally, we have to be willing to ask ourselves what lies on the other side of these structures and makes them possible, just as this question is asked in the field of natural science and also in theology. We begin with the scientific question.

The theory of evolution teaches us that man is a child of nature. Nature itself is historical. The origin of the struggle among men was sought in the struggle for existence, which hastened evolution. *Homo homini lupus,* man is a wolf to man—this is a thesis which claims to understand man as a creature of nature. It is not far from this pessimistic view to the optimistic, cynical "social Darwinism." In the struggle for existence, the superior species or race, it is said, will survive or should survive. Viewed in light of the history of civilisation, however, it becomes apparent that this doctrine of late 19th century Europe projects an image of nature which reflects its own social prerequisites: a competitive society, militarism, and racial conflict. It is an image of temporary victors. In particular, it is bad natural science. It is a bad theory of evolution. It is not on the same level as the Darwinian theory.

Reality is much more discriminating. "The struggle for survival" means not primarily combat, but a hard effort. A contemporary of Darwin's beginnings was the pessimistic economics of Robert Malthus: the population will continue to grow until foodstuffs become scarce. Darwin reverses this idea evolutionally and optimistically: the species that best masters the problem of hunger will survive. It remains true that in the process of evolution thousands of creatures perish whilst one species flourishes. Death itself is an "invention of life": evolution presupposes that individuals will die in order to make room for new, perhaps better adapted beings. The Buddhist doctrine, that life is thirst and sorrow, is closer to the actual history of nature than many western harmonisms. However, there is nothing in these realisations which justifies the glorification of murder as heroism.

How does evolution come about? Selection, survival of the fittest, is merely the final stage. If something is to survive, it must first come into being. New forms come into being by mutation; and an abundance of forms, a decisive prerequisite for evolution, requires spacial isolation (literally: "island formation"), i.e. protection from the most difficult struggle with competitors. The term "error tolerance" covers these conditions for evolution. Only those who endure, and even promote, the interplay of variants are viable in the long run.

Behavioural science teaches us that "the wolf is not a man to the wolf." The struggle for rank among animals fit to fight, such as the wolf, is not ended by death, but rather by the gesture of submissiveness by the loser. A species can only survive if the inhibition to kill members of the same species and blood-relatives is effective to a reasonable degree. Man, who is by nature unarmed, does not have enough of this instinctive inhibition. He has to acquire it as a conscious achievement during the development of civilisation.

For hundreds of thousands of years, early man lived in small groups adapted to these laws of all life before him; he could not do otherwise. It has only been for approximately the past ten thousand years that agriculture, the founding of cities, river-valley civilisations, and large empires have created a new advanced and unstable civilisation, the stabilisation crises of which we still live in today. The performance and instability of this civilisation are largely dependent on the fact that it is a civilisation of "large" societies.

Let us define a small society as a group in which the reciprocal relations between its members can be governed solely by personal acquaintance and a large society as a group in which this is no longer possible. Herds of higher mammals correspond to small societies. Their coexistence is governed largely by the hierarchy of their members. Nomadic or rural large families of people are also small societies. However, since those early millenniums, cities and empires have formed large societies. In them, cooperation and rank were objectified by the division of labour, barter and monetary economies; law, which made the economy possible; supremacy, which guaranteed the law; power, which stabilised supremacy; knowledge, which made power possible; and finally war, which was the result of the mutually threatening accumulation of power.

This is not to say that there had not been any bloodshed between men prior to advanced civilisation. The 'primitive' civilisations known today are themselves products of several millenniums of history, and it is not certain to what extent we may draw a link from them to earlier forms of civilisation. In any case, they demonstrate a wide spectrum of generally highly stylised forms of social intercourse within and between the small groups, from great peaceableness to ritualised warfare. The stylisation, however, changes in advanced civilisations. This was already suggested by the use of the term "objectify." This objectification may be seen as a stage in the development of human possibilities.

Let us concentrate on three central concepts: money, power, and knowledge. **Money** is the means to quantify, to make measurable, reciprocal services. In the personal relations of a small society, for example in a family, there is an almost implicit ban on the quantification of reciprocal services. Personal intercourse within a stable human relationship is error tolerant; it requires ample room for action and the irreplaceableness of a spontaneous give-and-take. It is the quantification through the exchange of goods and then through the neutral standard of value of money which then isolates the objective service from the person who renders the service and from the person who receives it. In personal intercourse, services are always accompanied by an affect, whether affectionate or sullen. This cannot be the basis for an economy in advanced civilisation. Earlier, we discussed the legality principle, the conscious renunciation of the affective or moral valuation of actions as the basis of a legally structured society. The optimistic hope of market theory is that the transparent market will likewise not depend on the emotions of people, which can never be understood objectively, but rather will be an "objectively altruistic structure." The socialist criticism is that the real market did not fulfil precisely that, but rather that it was an instrument of supremacy, i.e. of power. The counter-criticism is that a planned economy fulfils this even less.

What is **power**? The word "power" is used here in a specific sense, referring to human civilisation. We define power as the accumulation of means for reserved purposes. In this sense, power is a humanum, something that differentiates human from animal societies. Man is capable of accumulating means for purposes: foodstuffs, tools, hunting weapons, money, arms for use against men, political followers.

Power makes it possible to transform a basic phenomenon of animal groups, hierarchy, into the widely established, objectified, social supremacy. At this point, an observation on the current feminist debate is perhaps appropriate. Is thinking in power categories not a symptom of male society, of a patriarchate? And is this not contrary to nature? This question is of utmost importance. As usual, however, the correlations are even more complicated. As far as we can tell, the social groups of our closer animal ancestors, i.e. mammals, and particularly apes, are organised in primarily patriarchal fashion. Thus, for man, the patriarchate could be considered a continued social development as defined by his natural origin. The equal status of women and the domestic matriarchate are all the more so a humanum, a trait of earlier stages of civilisation, in which men ruled the forest and women ruled the home. Then, however, advanced civilisation created the large society outside of the home, i.e. in the male domain, and thus organised human society in secondary patriarchal fashion as well.

Even in animal groups, rank is usually associated with constantly vibrant competition. Even the means of winning this competition are objectified in a large society. Castes or classes stabilise the inherited hierarchy of large groups. Families and regional societies separate themselves from each other with property, for example the possession of land, the prototype of which can be seen in the territorialism of animals, and ultimately with weapons.

This vibrant competition leads to the luxuriation of power, an unavoidable surplus of power. "Luxuriate" is a term used in the theory of evolution. If a physical trait or pattern of behaviour affords the species an advantage, and if there is selection pressure, as it is called, in favour of this trait or pattern of behaviour, then it is possible that in the course of many generations this trait or pattern of behaviour will develop more and more, beyond the limits of practicality: for example, the physical size of the dinosaurs, the mammoths' tusks, and the mating rituals of many birds. Patterns of behaviour directed towards members of the same species, in particular, can luxuriate because the reactions of members of the same species can luxuriate in turn. This applies to slow genetic changes, and, above all, to the historical development of human learning processes.

This is also how the luxuriation of power works. Whoever avails himself of the means of power in competition has a chance of emerging victorious. Such is the case with the accumulation of capital in market competition. Thus, for millenniums, there have also been military arms races in which each party has sought security through superiority in arms. *Si vis pacem, para bellum:* if you want to live in peace, be armed for war. It is not military balance that has historically been the preserver of peace. Military balance provokes the comparison of strength. A party can only feel secure if it is militarily superior to its adversary. A vicious circle can be seen in these arms races. Security through superiority can only be had by one of two adversaries. The balance of arms will then stabilise at the limits of the economic feasibility of the arms race. In general: during the race, it is advantageous for every party to be ahead in the competition. In the final analysis, however, regardless of how much the competition increases its means, it can bring destruction to the whole.

The key concept is "**knowledge.**" Power is the accumulation of means for purposes; this presupposes knowledge of purposes and means. Money is a form of abstract power in an already objectively structured society. What is knowledge?

This chapter is not a philosophical discourse. We must limit ourselves to intimations. Present-day Westerners generally picture knowledge in the form of judgments, that is, affirmative propositions, which can be true or false. We thus depict knowledge in the form of language. Speech is a symbolic act, an act which means something. The intended meaning, in the form of a request or command, can itself be an act, or in the form of a statement, a fact. However, there is also knowledge which is largely non-language oriented: perception, practical ability. Symbolic action creates perception by creating form; all art is like this. All elementary perception is at the same time affective. The advantageous and disadvantageous are perceived as such, and are desired or fled. The inexhaustible nuances between affects bear the meaning of the perceptions.

One of the main forms of perceiving reality by creating a form which symbolically represents reality is mythology. That which is essential to life bears in itself the major affect. The grand reality which bears our life is presented to us in a mythical image. This is the divine essence. Today, we call the mythological gods anthropomorphic. We know how they vary from civilisation to civilisation. Yet, they have a background of archetypes. Our images are anthropomorphic, but not the realities which the images depict.

From the outset, civilisation explained its own foundations in mythological terms. This is reflected in the traditional founders' myths. The basis of the vital, social supremacy system is reflected in the divine consecration of royalty. Power is symbolised in the figures of gods. Money in the form of gold is a symbolic metal, which guarantees the exchange value.

The luxuriation of wealth, however, leads, among other things, to the misery of the poor. The luxuriation of the struggle for power leads to the never-ending misery of wars. The luxuriation of man's access to resources leads to the destruction of their natural basis. This is the source of the problems which we described earlier. In the increasingly difficult competition, everyone views the competitor as the evil one, and none of them notice how together they have created the competition in which everyone then makes everyone else the evil one.

Naturally, there have always been people who have understood the origin of misery. In the mythological self-perception of early civilisations, the battles of the gods reflect the battles of the powers. The battles of gods also reflect cultural revolutions—devotion to a new god who promises to bring salvation, i.e. peace.

Probably the greatest change in man's conception of himself, prior to our modern era, occurred in the first half of the first millennium before Christ. We owe to this age the new religious experience of the Jewish prophets and Greek philosophy, Zoroaster, Upanishads and Buddha, Taoism, and the political ethics of Confucius. No two of these figures are the same. We are not concerned here with their highly complex diversity, only wishing to observe one common trait. An ethic against luxuriating power can be observed in each and every one of them. We can speak of the counter-luxuriation of ethics against the luxury of power.

We can differentiate between two forms of counter-movement of ethics against the struggle for power, a cool form and a passionate form. The cool form may be called reason and the passionate form love. Reason can be defined as a conceptually explainable perception of the whole. Politics is the compromise between power and reason which must continually be re-coordinated. Charity, as taught by the major religions, is the concern for one's fellow man. It is a surplus, that is, a counter-luxuriation against luxuriating power. Only as a surplus is charity love. And in its wake we find an excess of human effort to the point of martyrdom.

Reason and love are not identical, but are dependent on one another. Political reason must avail itself of the objectifying means of large societies. It must also objectify the patterns of behaviour which preserve society. It requires law, creates standards of justice, and calls for political morality. Charity, however, is connected to the pattern of behaviour in a small society and enhances it. The care of one's fellow man takes place through the affect, not through calculation. Therefore, charity does not evoke measured morality, but rather excess; in Christian terms: not law, but gospel.

The radical ethic was before its time in two senses: religiously and politically.

In regard to religious experience: in most Asiatic doctrines, an ethic is not a commandment, but rather insight in the context, which is known as *karma* in India: behold, and recognise the consequences of your actions! In Greek philosophy, which is also a major religion, the purged soul has insight into that which is good: it is true. In Israel, the distinction between good and evil is a divine commandment. However, the god who commands the good is a different god from the mythical god whose son is the king of an empire. The god who revealed himself in the commandments on Mount Sinai is then also understood as the creator of the world. The commandment pronounces conditions for survival in God's creation. All of this is insight, new knowledge, concern for the whole, reason before logic.

In regard to political experience: several of the Asiatic doctrines address, above all, the individual. Buddha founded an order of monks, that is, a radically different society from the large societies of ancient advanced civilisations. Whoever addresses political society in a positive manner, such as Confucius, Zoroaster, the Greek philosophers, Moses, and the prophets, must demand a radical transformation of the political structures. The Old Testament is incomprehensible without this demand. This is the Sinai covenant: an entire people shall live as no people has lived before, under the commandment which makes real life possible. This is the demand of the prophets, from Elijah to Micah. The promise for the world is what is meant in the coded language of the strange parables, such as the Apocalypse in the Book of Daniel. We do not understand the Apocalypse at all if we do not understand it as the hope for a changed world.

NOTES

1. This paper is excerpted from chapters 4–7 of Carl Friedrich von Weizsäcker, *Die Zeit Drängt* (Munich: Carl Hanser Verlag, 1987), translated from German into English by Elaine Griffiths; reprinted by permission. The book was originally written for a Church Assembly. "Secular" here means non-theological.

17

The Quest for Security
Viewed as a Whole–System Problem

Willis W. Harman

The world faces a dilemma that is all too clear. All nations, and all peoples, seek security; that is, they seek to insure the integrity of their territory and possessions, and their freedom to pursue their own destiny in their own chosen way. In their attempts to achieve security nations have armed, have threatened war, and have conducted wars. As technology has advanced, the capability of mass destruction has increased until, with modern nuclear and biological weapons, civilisation itself is at stake. Thus the time-honoured ways in which nations have sought to assure their security are now obsolete; instead of security, they bring global insecurity.

Regarding this dilemma we can draw two conclusions: (1) an alternative to nuclear deterrence for achieving national and global security is absolutely essential if there is to be a viable future at all; and (2) such an alternative, involving some kind of global management of the peace, requires a degree of mutual trust and cooperation among nations that has not been present in the past and does not seem likely to be easily achieved in the future.

And yet our sobering dilemma is that such an alternative *has* to be found and made to work. It has to work with one hundred percent reliability: the world cannot afford *one* nuclear war. Nowhere else in human affairs do we demand such reliability.

Clearly some very substantial shifts in perspective and changes in values will be required for the world's peoples and leaders to accept and participate in the degree of global management necessary to keep the peace, provide general security, and permit the complete or nearly complete dismantling of the present nuclear arsenal.

Thus we find ourselves concerned with something like the following three questions:

1. What are possible alternative approaches to achieving national and global security?
2. What shifts in perspective and changes in values will be necessary for successful operation of such an alternative system?
3. What is the likelihood that such changes could take place? What might be done that would contribute in a positive way to these necessary changes?

We will investigate these questions in the following discussion. But first we need to explore some preliminary issues.

SECURITY ALTERNATIVES

It is apparent that the world is not yet ready for the kind of transnational authority that is an inherent part of an effective global security system. Nevertheless, there are a number of policy directions that could be implemented without delay which would reduce the likelihood of major war, especially nuclear war. These include progressively reducing reliance on nuclear deterrence (i.e. dependence on *offensive* capability), while increasing reliance on defensive structures; implementing effective arms limitation and overall arms reduction; providing for effective peacekeeping through cooperative action; strengthening peacemaking procedures and institutions; building trust between nations; etc. All of these measures together do not provide security; they do not solve the nuclear weapons dilemma. But they make nuclear war more improbable, and they buy time. They amount to a sort of *transitional security*.

Meanwhile we can be moving towards the day when the powerful nations agree to pool sovereignty sufficiently to allow for effective peacekeeping structures, and to remove legitimacy from preparation for armed conflict as an element of national policy; to arrive at last at the goal of *mutual security structures, jointly designed and supported*. National security, and global security, achieved through means other than nuclear deterrence, are not goals to be reached in one move, but through a longer evolutionary process. Furthermore, the problem of national security and the arms race to which it has led cannot be separated from the problems of chronic global poverty and the many facets of the global ecological crisis;

they are all too intertwined for there to be a solution to one without dealing with the rest.

Thus the security alternative we seek is not a single policy action, but getting and staying on a constructive path that eventually leads to peace and common security, satisfactory equity and justice around the world, and a stewardship relation to the Earth and its other inhabitants of the plant and animal kingdoms.

Obstacles

Why have alternative security approaches seemed implausible to most people? If there are paths to security other than the nuclear arms race, why has it seemed too difficult for us to view them objectively, to see what has to be done, and to set out to do it? This is not a trivial question. All of us experience resistance when challenged to break out of old ways of thinking and explore the new and untried; that resistance may be the greatest source of peril in the world today

It is necessary, first of all, to fully grasp the implications of the fact that the problem of alternative security is not an isolated problem. The approach to national security to which the powerful nations are presently committed has tremendous momentum. It is deeply rooted in the same thought system that created modern industrial society, and it is intimately linked to the economic, technological, social, and ecological aspects of modern society. The achievement of alternative security can come about only through a change in that whole system. It is not a matter of a technological or management add-on, or of minor adjustments and modifications of that system.

Three temptations. Thus there are three temptations to be avoided if we wish to escape the kinds of frustrations that have characterised our past.

One is the temptation to believe in solution by technology: Third World poverty will be solved by the Green Revolution in agriculture; environmental degradation will be solved by anti-pollution technologies; the nuclear missile threat will be solved by Star Wars anti-missile systems; etc. The world's current problems result in large measure from the technological successes of the past; for that reason they are unlikely to be solvable through application of further technology. It seems far more likely that the solution lies, at least in part, in a fundamental change of mind. If so, the technological approaches are a costly diversion—not only in terms of money, but in lost opportunity.

A second temptation is to believe that the problems can be solved by negotiations and agreements: disarmament will be achieved by strategic arms limitation agreements; North–South tensions will be resolved by non-violent conflict resolution approaches; environmental problems will be solved by getting industry to agree to take better care of the environment. If the sources of the problems are to be found deeply embedded in the structure of sociopolitical systems, it is not realistic to expect agreements to furnish the answers.

A third temptation is to believe in the effectiveness of organisations: we can deal with environmental problems by setting up an Environmental Programme, with poverty through a Development Programme, and with the threat of nuclear holocaust by a Security Council. If the origins of the problems include a need for system change, generating programmes within the unchanged system can be expected to be ineffective, and in fact to impede the necessary system change.

Need for a change in perspective. Suppose one can imagine a future state of the world in which the goal of global and common security is achieved. If such a state could be described, then we would be in a position to ask what conditions would have to be met before that state would seem to be a feasible goal. And then we could see about getting to work on those conditions.

We may take for granted that if this task can be done at all, it will require a shift in perspective. Even to think about it requires a shift in perspective. Most current analysis, and all of the history of peace and disarmament efforts, convincingly demonstrate that we cannot get there from the present perspective. The corollary to this proposition is that the road to conviction is not through impartial examination of evidence and rational argument. It is through a change of *Gestalt,* a paradigm shift, a discontinuous shift in perception.

The discussion below invites such a shift. It does not compel it, and no argument can. It does attempt to make plausible the following conclusions:

1. To achieve the goal of common security will require a fundamental shift in perspective. The nature of that shift can, to some extent at least, be identified;
2. That shift in perspective, or something closely resembling it, appears to have spontaneously taken place in a fraction (a small minority) of persons over the past two decades;

3. There is considerable reason to expect the shift to continue to spread fairly rapidly. On the one hand, it has positive appeal, because it promises much more than a mere cessation of the arms race. On the other hand, we are increasingly forced into some kind of shift because the old perspective is so obviously failing;

4. The shift in perspective can be fostered. (It probably could not have been generated if we were not at a point in history when it is beginning to appear spontaneously);

5. Thus we conclude on an optimistic note: there are things that can be done to urge the shift along. Equally importantly, through widespread understanding of the signs of profound change, it is possible to reduce anxiety and feelings of threat that naturally accompany such a shift, and hence to avoid generating the sorts of human misery that have often in the past accompanied fundamental societal change.

SECURITY OBJECTIVES

We need to distinguish between three different security objectives as held by nations and peoples: (1) One of these is the specific and immediate goal of **national security.** This requires particular attention *vis-a-vis* the confrontation between the United States and the Soviet Union, with its attendant potentiality of a nuclear holocaust. (2) The second is a longer-term goal of **global international security,** taking into account the growing and fundamental tensions between the rich and poor countries. (3) The third is the goal of **general security,** in the sense of assurance of satisfaction of fundamental human needs. Much of the emphasis in contemporary debates has been on the first objective. However, it may be the case that this objective cannot be achieved (except in the limited sense of transitional security defined above) without paying more attention to the other two.

Each of these three security objectives has an associated fundamental puzzle. Let us try to identify these.

National Security

We often speak of the goal of national security as though it were something objective and obvious, easily agreed upon. It will be helpful to remind ourselves of the particular conception of national security that gripped the United States two decades ago. Communist China was perceived by the US government as an evil menace, in league with the Soviet Union, poised to take over Southeast Asia, and thence to proceed to other parts of the world. Once Vietnam became controlled by the Communists, according to the "domino theory," the other nations in Southeast Asia would fall one by one. National security lay in preventing the first "domino" from toppling, almost regardless of the military, economic, and moral costs. It was the moral costs that eventually split the nation asunder and determined the outcome of the war. In the service of a particular misguided concept of national security, the United States paid a terrible price in terms of ethics and ideals set aside, high values compromised, and innocence lost.

Security and the measures taken to insure it are matters of perception. Present US concepts of national security depend fundamentally upon perceptions of the Soviet Union, its characteristics and motivations. Many visitors to the Soviet Union who have sought out intimate communication with the Soviet people conclude that US stereotypes of the Soviets are as dangerously delusive as were previous perceptions of the Chinese—or, for that matter, earlier perceptions of the Japanese and the Germans. It seems clear that Soviet perceptions of the United States are likely to be equally in error.

Presently, the people of the world probably feel less secure than at most times in history; this is partly because of the measures that have been taken by the powerful countries in the name of "national security." It is not the fear of an invader that haunts the populace, but the fear that some accident or misjudgment may loose the hell that is contained within those tens of thousands of missiles that each of the superpowers has aimed at the other. Agreement is fairly widespread that living under the cloud of nuclear doom is not "security" by any stretch of the imagination—yet there is also widespread despair that anything can be done about it. Now that the scabbard has been discarded, the nuclear sword of Damocles hangs over all of our heads for evermore.

Many have pointed out recently the disturbing parallel between the present world situation and Europe in 1914. No one "decided" to start World War I. "We all muddled into war" said Lloyd George. But the preparations had been made (to insure "national security"), and a minor catalytic event triggered off what for its time, and in a limited area of the globe, amounted to a holocaust of shocking proportions. The analogy fits in a frightening way.

Much of the discussion of the nuclear peril proceeds as if the danger posed by modern war systems were fully in the hands of rational national leaders, and we might safely depend on their prudence so long as it remains clear to reasonable men that a big war would be a big mistake. If one assumes that war is a rational endeavour—a deliberate attempt to seize something by military force—then one might reasonably conclude that no sane leader would initiate a nuclear war. But if one thinks of war as something that is fundamentally irrational—an unpredictable and explosive release of primitive social emotions—then the mere inadvisability of unrestrained war may strike one as rather scant protection.

Thus it is hard to see that there is a realistic goal of national safety for the US and the USSR short of the denuclearisation of security and the delegitimation of war. If we assume that for the present the world is divided into two hostile blocs, there has to be a re-perception of security that takes that into account. But that leaves the key question: are there satisfactory alternatives to the nuclear threat system for the assurance of national security?

This is the question that has occupied the world for four decades The answer would seem to be that something like the security system envisioned in the Charter and other early documents of the United Nations will be required. But for that to work necessitates different attitudes on the part of the superpowers, and a new spirit of North–South cooperation. So the first puzzle is how to engender those attitudes.

Common Security

Practically all the nations of the world have been moving towards the Rule of Law as the only legitimate form of government. The Rule of Law (as contrasted with other more arbitrary and authoritarian forms of government) is expressly assumed as an essential precondition in the 1950 European Convention for the Protection of Human Rights and Fundamental Freedoms. The 1948 UN Universal Declaration of Human Rights declares that "it is essential if man is not compelled to have recourse, as a last resort, to rebellion against tyranny and oppression, that human rights should be protected by the Rule of Law." Jawaharlal Nehru, the first Prime Minister of India, saw the Rule of Law as "synonymous with the maintenance of civilised existence."

The doctrine of the Rule of Law, a cornerstone of the Anglo–American common law system, has been characteristic of all modern nations. It is fair to say that the Soviet Union has lagged somewhat behind because of the peculiarities of its history; nevertheless the direction is clear. But one thing has been clear throughout the history of the United Nations: however much the larger countries may be committed to the Rule of Law and to democratic institutions *within their boundaries*, not even the United States believes strongly in the Rule of Law for the world.

The Palme Commission report made the basic point forcefully. In a nuclear age, in which catastrophic destruction can be accomplished by even a small number of nuclear weapons, there will not be security for anyone unless there is common security. And there will not be common security until there is replacement of the Rule of Force by the Rule of Law—until the stronger nations are willing to pool sufficient sovereignty to allow some such supranational organisations as the World Court and the United Nations peacekeeping provisions to function effectively.

Why has security seemed achievable through national defence? Throughout most of the history of the nation-state, security seemed to be primarily a matter of keeping any enemy from encroaching on national territory. To equate security with having the military capability to prevent invasion was reasonable enough.

World War I was a confidence-shattering experience for the western world, in many ways. First and foremost, of course, was that it happened at all, when no nation desired it and no nation can be said to have started it. By the end of the war, or within a few years after, it was becoming clear that development of the aeroplane (and later on, of course, the guided missile) changed the nature of the game. Now an enemy could inflict unlimited damage on a country without ever invading it with a single soldier. Related to this was one of the most shocking developments of all. Wars had been largely matters of armies contesting in the field. Even though civilian lives had been uprooted and terminated by the activities of war, still it was appalling that in World War I a full twenty percent of the casualties were civilians.

In World War II, fifty percent of the casualties were civilians; and in the Vietnam war ninety percent! War has become the mass slaughter of civilians. That fact alone renders obsolete all concepts of security through a strong national defence that can insulate civilians from the hostilities. There is no real security for the superpowers through deterrence. There is no real security for Europe as long as it is at the mercy of the decisions of the superpowers, or of accidental initiations of hostilities.

But also, there is no real security for the peoples of the Third World nations. In a world which permits outlawry there is no security for the weak. And in the present world system some of the weak seem to be rather permanently relegated to that position.

Responsibility for protection of the weak *within* national boundaries has been increasingly assumed by the civilised nations of the world. In some of these countries, including the United States, enactment of social security programmes was preceded by many years of debate. Many people questioned the appropriateness of this assumed right and its actualisation through transfer payments or provision of services. (In the United States, Franklin Roosevelt encountered keen opposition to his proposed social security programmes.) Nevertheless, national-level programmes aimed at implementing the concept of a right to satisfaction of basic needs have been adopted by over 120 countries (although in the majority of cases this has happened only within the past few decades).

However, the idea of extending this right to the global level, to insure that all people everywhere can have their basic needs satisfied, is far from being recognised as a valid concept. Furthermore, just as poverty within a nation is not satisfactorily dealt with by benevolent welfare programmes (keeping people as pets), so there is little reason to think that the matter will be satisfactorily dealt with by putting poor nations on welfare—that is, by conventional development aid programmes. This problem is recognised in the current debates over the need for a New International Economic Order.

In brief, it is not clear that common security can be obtained around the globe by means short of a major system change. But we have no idea how to bring about a major system change, and doubt that such a deliberately managed fundamental change is possible. Puzzle number two.

General Security

It is not casually that the Charter of the United Nations, which has as its first purpose to maintain international peace and security, links so intimately the issues of peace, development, and human rights. The concept of universally felt needs is woven throughout the fabric of the United Nations documents. These needs include something like the following:

- Need for "enough" food, shelter, health care, and security of the person;
- Need for connectedness and a self-affirming social role—which in modern and modernising societies involves education and employment;
- Need for a sense of the dignity of being human, a sense of becoming (a chance to achieve a better life through one's own efforts), a sense of achievement;
- Need for a sense of justice or equity;

- Need for a sense of solidarity—of belonging to a worthy group and of participation in decisions that affect the group's, and one's own, destiny.

In its most fundamental sense, security involves a feeling of adequate satisfaction of some such set of fundamental needs. It is true that needs are to some extent in the eye of the beholder. Peoples (e.g. under conditions of feudalism or slavery) may go for generations assuming that a lack of such satisfaction is a "misfortune." When through increasing awareness and education, perception of this lack shifts from "misfortune" to "injustice," then a sociopolitical force for change results. (The American sociologist Ralph Turner has interpreted in this way such major transformations as the Reformation, and the liberal, democratic, and socialist revolutions.) The last half century has seen minority groups within countries, and subnational and national political groups around the planet, evidence in a multitude of ways such a shift in percetion.

The felt lack of security has a firm reality base. Elements of this, manifesting in various parts of the world, include the following:

- The ever-present threat of a nuclear exchange being triggered, with massive loss of life and mass creation of human desolation;
- Persistent "local" wars with "conventional" weapons leaving a steady wake of human misery;
- A global arms race involving expenditures of over a billion dollars a day, with some of the poorer countries spending more on military preparation than on health care, education, and human welfare all together;
- Widespread poverty, with accompanying disease, malnutrition, and starvation, and with strains on the natural environment that include overgrazing, deforestation, soil erosion, and surface water pollution;
- Environmental degradation and resource exploitation stemming from the economic activities of the industrialised societies;
- Increasing tensions between the industrialised, mass-consuming North and the poverty-stricken South.

Reaction to these factors is manifested in the activities of peace movements, environmental protection groups, Third World liberation movements, women's movements, and assorted private voluntary organisations. In one way and another, these various movements are registering the public shift in perception that all of the elements listed above, comprising the contemporary lack of security, are no longer to be considered as unavoidable misfortunes, but rather as correctable ills and fundamental injustices. That is the fundamental observation that makes whole–system change imperative and also identifies the driving force that could bring it about. But it also poses a third puzzle: if such a powerful transformational force is loose in the world, how can it be managed in such a way as to achieve nondisruptive change—change unaccompanied by wrenching social disruption and widespread human misery?

In summary, serious consideration of the nature of the security challenge makes it apparent that alternate means to assure common security will require (a) fundamental changes in attitudes, around the world but particularly in the most powerful countries; (b) changes in perceptions, especially in those perceptions which build up mutual distrust; and (c) changes in basic assumptions, to an extent which will be tantamount to basic system change. One factor in the plausibility of such fundamental change is the changing perceptions of vast numbers of people that the elements of contemporary insecurity are pervasive throughout modern society and do not have to be accepted.

SYSTEM CHANGE

We asked earlier why people question the feasibility of an alternative to the nuclear deterrence security policy. Part of the answer, at least, is to be found in the preceding remarks. Without a major system change—in attitudes and perceptions, and basic assumptions—security alternatives are not very convincing. And the idea of a major change is dismissed as being too complicated, and requiring too much in the way of resources, to be even worth thinking about. However, the stakes are high enough to make it worth an effort to see if that dismissal may be premature.

Let us address the issue of complexity through an analogy. Consider an individual who falls prey to a series of illness, each serious and difficult to diagnose and treat. If the suggestion is put forth that the illnesses may be better looked at in terms of some basic underlying cause rather than individually, then at first thought that may seem to make the analysis more complex. But to the contrary, that recognition—that the person's attitudes towards job, marriage, and other life circumstances are inducing stress; and that stress is interfering with the proper functioning of the body's immune system; and that failure is leading to susceptibility to illness—that recognition leads to a simpler diagnosis and prescription: namely, to change attitudes and eliminate stress.

Of course it may not be as simple as the above statement makes it sound. The individual is likely to have considerable internal, unconscious resistance to discovering the basis for, and releasing, the attitudes that underlie the problem. Perception of one's employer, for instance, may be influenced by unconsciously held beliefs about authority; to change these may require confronting inner contents of the unconscious in a way that generates resistance.

With this analogy we are suggesting that focusing on the limited goal of national security narrowly defined may be less fruitful than focusing on the broader goal of general security. In so doing we cannot dismiss the possibility that our own present perceptions of the Soviet Union, or of the rebel forces in Central America, or of the impact of American business on the Third World, are influenced by unconscious beliefs which we are loathe to reexamine. In other words, in assessing current reality the role of unconscious forces shaping perceptions must be taken into account.

Perhaps the point is clearer with a slightly different analogy. The success of Alcoholics Anonymous in dealing with the notably recalcitrant problem of alcoholism depends on a regime summarised in the well-known "Twelve Steps." The first of these is recognised to be the most difficult. It is: we admitted that we were powerless over alcohol—that our lives had become unmanageable. The second step is: we came to believe that a Power greater than ourselves could restore us to sanity. Strong resistance is invariably encountered in recognising that life has become unmanageable, to admitting that sanity is the issue, and to giving up control by the rational ego-mind.

Let us suggest a direct parallel. Strong resistance is encountered to the idea that in some fundamental way, western industrial society (including both capitalist and communist forms) has become unmanageable; and also to the possibility that sanity might be the issue. But is it sane to insist that "national security" can be achieved by increasing the armaments technology that has contributed so much to our feelings of _insecurity_? Is it sane to insist that our economic health requires ever-increasing growth when that growth has a direct correlation with consumption of scarce resources and deleterious impact on the environment? Is it sane to assume that the planet could stand the Third World populations becoming mass-consumption society like America; or, contrariwise, that they will be content not to? The rationalisation of agriculture and industry over the past two or three centuries has systematically created rapidly increasing numbers of marginal people—the unemployed, underemployed, and unemployable; if that continues, then can we imagine a viable global future?

Probably one reason why we have not paid more attention to the powerful unconscious forces involved in the global security issues is that it was not clear what might be done about them. Once again, let us make use of an organic metaphor. In the process of dealing with a crisis in the human body, the individual's immune system may take some actions that are perceived by the individual as inconveniences or even problems. For instance, in dealing with an infection the body may create a painful boil. The person may think of this as a nuisance and an affliction—yet with more understanding it appears as a healthy sign of the body's creative response to the infection. Similarly, some of the contemporary social movements, bizarre lifestyles, and even revolutionary tendencies may in retrospect seem as benign and creative as do now the heresies and noncompliances at the times of the Reformation and the scientific revolution. In other words, these may be the unrecognised indications that the required change of mind to make security alternatives practicable is already taking place.

At the risk of overdoing the use of analogies, let us make one more. Many, many people have undergone a fundamental reorganisation of their "inner maps of reality." Typically, this change was brought about by life's crises. Sometimes it was characterised by trauma and breakdown; sometimes the passage was aided by formal psychotherapy or a spontaneous spiritual awakening. However diverse their individual experiences, person after person has learned the same lesson: no matter how insoluble and overwhelming may seem the problems faced—emotional, financial, in relationships, at work, or in the family—perceived another way, they are all solvable and, furthermore, all the resources necessary for their solution were available all along! No one could have persuaded the person before his or her transformation that such a conclusion was possible. We are implying, of course, that a parallel discovery may be made regarding the complex of seemingly unsolvable global problems that perplex us at this point in history.

In all of the above we are suggesting two points. On the one hand, the security problem and its attendant global problems comprise a crisis unprecedented in human history. There is no solution that does not involve fundamental change in the way that we perceive ourselves, our deepest motivations, our relationship to one another and to the planet, our perceptions of reality, and our most basic assumptions. On the other hand, there may be a solution nearer at hand than we imagine, which does indeed involve at its core such a total system change as happens extremely rarely in history—but which may well be happening spontaneously, already.

Mind Change

It is not difficult to see signs of change and reassessment—they surround us. What is more difficult is to discern the pattern and significance of the changes. In industrialised countries, there are those who perceive the system in difficulty and sense that the need is to "get back on the track" of steady technological advance and economic growth, low unemployment, and virile military strength. There are others who want to return to the days when things worked, values and morals were unconfused, families and communities held together, and society's destiny was clear. There are yet a third group of persons who see fundamental change happening (be it to the "Age of Aquarius," the vision of Green politics, respiritualisation of society, "Third Wave," or whatever), and are participative in it and exhilarated by it.

For our purposes here it will be useful to put the question: in all these indications of reassessment and change, do we see something analogous to the first two of the "Twelve Steps" of Alcoholics Anonymous? Do an increasing number of people seem to conclude that within our present paradigm the world has become unmanageable? And do an increasing number of people seem to conclude that by tapping into the deep intuition, inner wisdom, or spiritual centre we can "restore ourselves to sanity"?

Approaching these two questions, we could for example look at the changing attitudes, value emphases, and beliefs of the sector of society that is most visibly involved with change of lifestyle, "New Age" values, social movements (peace, ecology, women's, holistic health, etc.), and so forth. Instead, let us explore what appears to be the leading edge of one of the most pragmatic sectors of society—the world of business. In business, the important question is: does it work? There is relatively little concern about whether it is in accordance with what used to be believed, or with what "science says."

As to the perceived unmanageability of the world, the more senior and the more international the executive, the more frankly (s)he will admit that—perhaps starting with the oil shocks of the seventies—it has become clear that nobody really knows what to do about the world debt structure, deteriorating environment, ceaseless armed conflict, increasing terrorism, international industrial competition, persisting unemployment, and a score of other world-level problems. Neither economic nor social science theories seem to fit the real world, and there is little confidence that things will not get a lot worse before they get better (despite the optimism that would seem to be reflected in the stock market).

On changing attitudes and values, it is instructive to look into the kinds of management training workshops and executive development seminars that companies are sending their managers to in order to prepare them for the future. These courses are far more responsive to the changing business culture than are the graduate schools of business, and better indicators of the foreseen future needs. They have been changing significantly over the past couple of decades, and the few that seem to be most in tune with the changing times emphasise aspects of leadership that would not have been featured even a half dozen years ago.

From such indicators we can summarise an overall change of mind, which is in the direction of:

- A rejection of extreme positivism and reductionism in science, and a reassertion of the value of the inner search (see appendix for amplification);
- An affirmation of the existence of consciousness in the universe, and of the essential spirituality of the individual;
- An affirmation of the brotherhood of man/woman and of a non-exploitative stewardship relationship to the planet;
- A stand that social institutions (the economy, the military) are legitimate only when they are guided by the highest values and principles;
- An insistence that the legitimacy of war and preparation for war as instruments of national policy are obsolete in a nuclear age;
- A growing global awareness, and willingness to have rights that have long been guaranteed in the nation (e.g. Rule of Law, freedom of association, minimal satisfaction of basic needs) apply globally.

As noted earlier, these trends are by no means unambiguous; tendencies in the opposite direction can also be noticed. This kind of ambiguity is characteristic of periods of fundamental societal change, and relates to the simultaneous existence of backward-looking and forward-looking segments of the public. In other words, while fundamental system change may be a plausible scenario, it is by no means assured.

The Potentiality of Common Security

World Without War Council has identified seven requirements for a world in which security is achieved by means other than armed force. They comprise a concise summary of the requirements as discussed in the main body of this report:

- **Disarmament** —universal, general, inspected, and enforceable;
- **World Law**—to protect the peace and resolve international conflict;
- **World Community** —to sustain law;
- **Change and Development** —to promote justice, human dignity, and political freedom;
- **Agreement Among Nations**—the key to achieving the four requirements above;
- **Forcing Change Without Violence**—getting agreement while defending core political and moral values;
- **Root Values**—to provide the moral ground from which all the rest can occur.

Past experience, including especially that associated with the creation and nurturing of the United Nations, suggests that the likelihood of meeting these seven conditions in the absence of some fairly fundamental change is low. On the other hand, the kind of system change that could make the conditions relatively easy to meet may not be so improbable as is typically assumed. Therein lies the real hope of assuring our common security in a nonmilitarised way.

Appendix 17.1: The Metaphysical Crisis in Science—Its Relevance to the Security Dilemma

Science is the official knowledge-validating system in our society. Thus if there is a crisis in science, with regard to whether it is presenting us with an accurate picture of reality, then that crisis has an impact on every institution in the entire society.

The remarkable advances of modern science have been achieved on a foundation set of metaphysical assumptions which included:

a. **objectivism** —the assumption that there is an objective universe which can be explored by external observation and scientific inquiry, and approximated, progressively more precisely, by quantitative models;

b. **positivism** —the assumption that what is (scientifically) real is what is physically measurable;

c. **reductionism** —the assumption that scientific understanding is to be found in the reducing of phenomena to more elemental events (such as the motion of elementary particles, or the configuration of electromagnetic field).

One of the great surprises of the past decade is that the adequacy of these assumptions is being vigorously challenged, and the possibility is being considered of re-erecting science on the basis of metaphysical assumptions that more directly include consciousness (not physically measurable), connectedness (in empathic, nonphysical ways), and purpose (a non-reductionistic explanatory principle).

Several contending kinds of replacement assumptions are under consideration. One is some sort of "new dualism" (science having been more dualistic in its very early, formative years). Another is "pan–psychism"—that is, the assumption that matter has as an inside aspect, not physical in the usual sense, a mind-like dimension. Yet another contender is the sort of assumptions that are found at the esoteric core of the world's spiritual traditions, sometimes referred to as the "perennial wisdom." The latter candidate fits well with the rather surprising spread of "metaphysical" interests in recent years, especially apparent in northern Europe, North America, and Australia.

The way in which this issue is finally resolved will affect not only science, but every major institution in global society. The exact form of the emerging authority system (whether or not it is called science) is by no means clear at this point. On one item there is clarity, however. Whereas the older science had nothing to say about values, and in fact tended to imply an extreme relativism in that regard, the contending authority system (probably an expanded form of science) will place particular emphasis on values and intuitive sense of purpose.

Consciousness as Causal Reality

The heart of the issue is perhaps best expressed in a recent paper by Roger Sperry of the California Institute of Technology. Sperry shared the 1981 Nobel Prize in Physiology and Medicine for his work in human split-brain studies. As an accompaniment to this honour, he was invited to write the lead article for the 1981 *Annual Review of Neuroscience.* This was entitled "Changing Priorities," and spoke to the importance of a neglected area of science, namely the study of human subjective experience, and the kind of "downward causation" implied when our mental activities influence the physical and physiological world. The paper signalled a profound development, which Sperry described as follows (emphasis added):

> Social values depend ... on whether consciousness is believed to be mortal, immortal, reincarnate, or cosmic ... localised and brain-bound or essentially universal .... Current concepts of the mind-brain relation involve a direct break with the long-established materialist and behaviorist doctrine that has dominated neuroscience for many decades. Instead of renouncing or ignoring consciousness, the new interpretation gives full recognition to *the primacy of inner conscious awareness as a causal reality.*

How does science accommodate to "the primacy of inner conscious awareness as a causal reality"? Or must it? These are the questions at the heart of the present crisis in science.

When the modern world view began to take shape in Western Europe around the 17th century, it involved a revolt of common sense against the authoritarian excesses of Scholasticism. It was a declaration of faith in the senses as opposed to the speculative mind, and in the visible world as opposed to the unseen. For good reason it emphasised the empirical and the reductionist, as yielding a more fruitful kind of explanation than the medieval concepts of ruling spiritual forces.

There were also ample grounds for science separating the objective, which can be viewed by all, from the subjective, which the individual experiences in the privacy of his own mind—and good reasons to concentrate on the former. Not only did concentration on the objective accelerate scientific progress, but it also avoided a territorial clash with the Church, which viewed the soul and spirit as its special domain.

As Western Europe and North America put increasing emphasis on industrialising economic production, they naturally supported research into knowledge that would improve the abilities to predict and control and generate new technologies. This strengthened still further the deterministic and behaviouristic tendencies in science. It was not until the last decade or so that the counteraction to these tendencies gained any appreciable strength.

Thus the issue raised with regard to consciousness is not to criticise the past, but rather to ask whether science has outgrown its positivistic, reductionistic bias—while recognising the past productiveness of this bias.

Challenges to Positivism and Reductionism

As strong as the positivistic and behaviouristic biases had become by the mid-twentieth century, there was nonetheless a feeling on the part of many scientists (and non-scientists) that something important was being left out. After all, the only experience of reality that we have directly is our own conscious awareness. There was something very unnatural about a science which seemed to deny consciousness as a causal reality when everyday experience seemed to confirm again and again that it is the *decision* to act that causes action.

In order to be in accord with the sophisticated scientific view of the day, one tried to accept that it is the brain which is real, and consciousness is an "epiphenomenon"; that the question "Does mind exist?" had been finally answered in the negative. The complex products of creative imagination were supposed to have come about through some sort of random recycling of a brain-computer, together with some kind of selection of "best fit." We were supposed to believe that the complex instinctual behaviours of animals, and complex physiological systems such as the two eyes giving binocular vision, had developed through our evolutionary past solely as a result of random mutations plus natural selection.

Disturbing as these demands were, there were also the anomalies to remind us that all was not well with the orthodox scientific world view. Down through the centuries a variety of anomalous, "psychic" phenomena have been reported, all having in some way to do with *mind* having some effect in the physical world—directly, as in the reported instances of dramatic healing, or indirectly, as in the clairvoyant "remote viewing" that has recently attracted the attention of personnel in military intelligence. A half-century ago it seemed that (in spite of the claims of a few parapsychologists researching these phenomena) the better educated and more sophisticated public felt confident that scientific advance was making the genuineness of such phenomena decreasingly plausible; now the reverse is the case.

But if one looked closely, everyday and commonplace phenomena were equally mysterious, in the same way. The phenomena of attention and volition are good examples. What stimuli I perceive and react to depends upon what I "pay attention" to. I decide to act on the environment in a particular way—but how can this be explained "scientifically"? Attitudes towards one's work bring about tension and stress, and an ulcer results. Patients told that a plain sugar pill has curative powers experience remission of the symptoms of their illness (placebo effect). In our everyday experience it would seem strained and artificial to deny that what goes on in our minds affects our actions. Yet *as scientists,* more than one generation of students was trained to engage in that denial.

It is in the light of these decades of denial of consciousness as causal reality that Sperry's pronouncement comes with such impact. It is similar to the impact of Copernicus' observations after centuries of denying that the earth could possibly move.

The jury may yet be out, as far as the question of a second Copernican revolution is concerned. Our point here is that if such a conceptual revolution turns out to be taking place, the system change postulated earlier is seen as part of an even more profound ongoing transformation, and becomes far more plausible.

References

ABRAMS, H. L. (1982) Survivors of Nuclear War: Infection and the Spread of Disease. In *Last Aid: The Medical Dimensions of Nuclear War*, edited by E. Chivian *et al.* San Francisco: W. H. Freeman.

ADOMEIT, H. (1982) *Soviet Risk-Taking and Crisis Behaviour: A Theoretical and Empirical Analysis.* London: Allen & Unwin.

ALBINSKI, H. S. (1987) *ANZUS, the United States and Pacific Security.* Washington, DC: University Press of America for the Asia Society.

ALTERNATIVES (1986) Movements. Special issue, 11(1).

ARONSON, J. D. (ed.) (1979) *Debt and the Less Developed Countries.* Boulder, Colo.: Westview.

BAILEY, S. S. (1977) Peaceful Settlement of International Disputes. In *Dispute Settlement through the United Nations*, edited by K. V. Raman. New York: Oceana Publications.

BANKS, M. (ed.) (1984) *Conflict in World Society: A New Perspective on International Relations.* Brighton: Wheatsheaf.

BERCOVITCH, J. (1984) *Social Conflict and Third Parties: Strategies of Conflict Resolution.* Boulder, Colo.: Westview.

BETTS, R. (1977) *Soldiers, Statesmen, and Cold War Crises.* Cambridge, Mass.: Harvard University Press.

BLACKBURN, P. (1986) Nigeria: The Year of the IMF. *Africa Report* 31(6): 18–20.

BLECHMAN, B. M. and S. S. KAPLAN (1978) *Force Without War: U.S. Armed Forces as a Political Instrument.* Washington, DC: The Brookings Institution.

BOUTHOUL, G. and R. CARRERE (1976) *Le defi de la guerre, 1740–1974.* Paris: Presses Universitaires de France.

BRANDT, W. *et al.* (1980) *North–South: A Programme for Survival.* Report of the Independent Commission on International Development Issues (Brandt Commission). Cambridge, Mass.: MIT Press.

281

282

BROWN, A. (1986) Change in the Soviet Union. *Foreign Affairs* 64(5): 1048–1065.

BRUNDTLAND, G. H. (1987) *Our Common Future: World Commission on Environment and Development* (Brundtland Commission). Oxford: Oxford University Press.

BUENO DE MESQUITA, B. (1981) *The War Trap*. New Haven, Conn.: Yale University Press.

BULL, H. (1980) The Great Irresponsibles? The United States, the Soviet Union, and World Order. *International Journal* 25(3): 437–447.

_____. (1977) *The Anarchical Society: A Study of Order in World Society*. London: Macmillan.

_____. (1971) The Objectives of Arms Control. In *The Use of Force*, edited by R. J. Art and K. N. Waltz. Boston: Little, Brown.

BULL, H. and A. WATSON (eds.) (1984) *The Expansion of International Society*. Oxford: Clarendon Press.

BURTON, J. W(1987) *Resolving Deep-Rooted Conflict: A Handbook*. Washington, DC: University Press of America.

_____. (1986) *Global Conflicts*. College Park, Maryland: University of Maryland Press.

_____. (1984) *The Domestic Sources of International Crisis*. College Park: Center for International Development.

BUTTERWORTH, R. L. (1978) *Moderation from Management*. Pittsburgh: University of Pittsburgh Press.

BYROM, T. (1976) *The Dhammapada: The Sayings of the Buddha*. New York: Vintage.

CABLE, J. (1981) *Gunboat Diplomacy 1919–1979: Political Applications of Limited Naval Force*. New York: St Martin's Press.

CALOGERO, F. (1982) Dynamics of Nuclear Arms Race. In *Scientists, the Arms Race and Disarmament*, edited by J. Rotblat. London: Taylor & Francis.

CAMPBELL, K. M. (1986) *Soviet Policy towards South Africa*. New York: St Martin's Press.

CARR, E. H. (1977) *International Relations between the Two World Wars, 1919–1939*. London: Macmillan.

CASSESE, A. (1978) Recent Trends in the Attitude of the Superpowers towards Peace-keeping. In *United Nations Peace-keeping: Legal Essays*, edited by A. Cassese. Alphen aan den Rijn: Sijthoff & Noordhoff.

CHAUHAN, S. K. (1983) *Who Puts Water in the Taps? Community Participation in Third World Drinking Water, Sanitation and Health*. London: Earthscan.

CHOMSKY, N. (1983) *The Fateful Triangle: The United States, Israel and the Palestinians*. Boston: South End Press.

CHUTA, E., and S. V. SETHERAMAN (eds.) (1984) *Rural Small-Scale Industries and Employment in Africa and Asia: A Review of Programmes and Policies.* Geneva: International Labour Office.

COMAY, M. (1983) UN Peacekeeping: The Israeli Experience. In *Peacekeeping: Appraisals and Proposals,* edited by H. Wiseman. New York: Pergamon.

COSER, L. A. (1961) The Termination of Conflict. *Journal of Conflict Resolution* 5: 347–353.

CRUTZEN, P. J. (1985) The Global Environment after Nuclear War. *Environment* 27: 6–11, 34–37.

CRUTZEN, P. J. and J. W. BIRKS (1982) The Atmosphere after a Nuclear War: Twilight at Noon. *Ambio* 11: 114–125.

DE REUCK, A. (1984) The Logic of Conflict: Its Origin, Development and Resolution. In *Conflict in World Society: A New Perspective on International Relations.* edited by M. Banks. Brighton: Wheatsheaf.

DESHINGKAR, G. (1987) Arms, Technology, Violence and the Global Military Order. In *The Quest for Peace,* edited by R. Vayrynen. London: Sage.

DOBRYNIN, A. F. (1987) Nuclear-Free World: Towards the 21st Century. In *Peace and Disarmament: Academic Studies.* Moscow: Politizdat.

DORAN, C. (1971) *The Politics of Assimilation: Hegemony and its Aftermath.* Baltimore: Johns Hopkins University Press.

ELARABY, N. A. (1983) UN Peacekeeping: The Egyptian Experience. In *Peacekeeping: Appraisals and Proposals,* edited by H. Wiseman. New York: Pergamon.

FANON, F. (1963) *The Wretched of the Earth.* New York: Grove Press.

FRANK, J. D. (1967) *Sanity and Survival: Psychological Aspects of War and Peace.* New York: Random House.

FREEDMAN, L. (1984) The "Star Wars" Debate: The Western Alliance and Strategic Defence. *Adelphi Paper* 199. London: IISS.

FREI, D. (ed.) (1982) *Managing International Crises.* Beverly Hills, Calif.: Sage Publications.

———. (ed.) (1978) *International Crises and Crisis Management.* Farnborough, Hampshire: Saxon House.

GORBACHEV, M. S. (1987a) *Perestroika and New Thinking for Our Country and the Whole World.* Moscow: Progress Publishers.

———. (1987b) *October and Perestroika: The Revolution Continues.* Moscow: Progress Publishers.

———. (1987) Reality and Guarantees for a Secure World. *Pravda,* September 17; English translation in *Moscow News,* supplement to issue no. 39 (3287).

———. (1986) *Selected Speeches and Articles.* Moscow: Progress Publishers.

GRAY, C. S. (1971) The Arms Race Phenomenon. *World Politics* 24(1): 39–79.

GREEN, W., T. CAIRNS and J. WRIGHT (1987) *New Zealand after Nuclear War.* Wellington: New Zealand Planning Council.

GURR, R. (ed.) (1981) *Handbook of Political Conflict: Theory and Research.* New York: Free Press.

HAMMARSKJÖLD, D. (1960) Introduction to the *Annual Report of the Secretary-General on the Work of the Organization 1960.* New York: United Nations Organisation.

HARDIN, G. (1974) Living on a Lifeboat. *Bioscience* 24(October): 561–568.

_____. (1968) The Tragedy of the Commons. *Science* 162(December 18): 1243–1248.

HARVARD NUCLEAR STUDY GROUP (1983) *Living with Nuclear Weapons.* Cambridge, Mass.: Harvard University Press.

HARWELL, M. A. and H. D. GROVER (1985) Biological Effects of Nuclear War. 1: Impact on Humans. *Bioscience* 35: 570–575.

HARWELL, M. A. and T. C. HUTCHINSON (1985) *Environmental Consequences of Nuclear War. Volume II: Ecological and Agricultural Effects.* SCOPE 28. Chichester: John Wiley & Sons.

HAWKES, N. (1987) Russia takes an interest. *Otago Daily Times,* October 14.

HITLER, A. (1939) *Mein Kampf.* New York: Reynal and Hitchcock.

HOFFMANN, S. (1962) In Search of a Thread: The U.N. in the Congo Labyrinth. *International Organization* 16(2): 331–361.

HOLSTI, K. J. (1988 and 1977) *International Politics: A Framework for Analysis.* Englewood Cliffs, NJ: Prentice–Hall.

_____. (1986) The Horsemen of the Apocalypse: At the Gate, Detoured, or Retreating. *International Studies Quarterly* 30(4): 335–372.

HOLSTI, O. R. (1972) *Crisis, Escalation, War.* Montreal: McGill–Queen's University Press.

HOUGH, J. F. (1985) Gorbachev's Strategy. *Foreign Affairs* 64(1): 33–55.

HUBER, W. (1980) *Der Streit um die Wahrheit und die Faehigkeit zum Frieden.* München: Kaiser.

HUNTINGTON, S. P. (1971) Arms Races: Prerequisites and Results. In *The Use of Force,* edited by R. J. Art and K. N. Waltz. Boston: Little, Brown.

INTERNATIONAL JOURNAL (1985) The Management of International Conflicts. Special issue, 40(4).

JACOBSEN, H. K. (1979) *Networks of Interdependence.* New York: Knopf.

JAMES, A. (1969) *The Politics of Peace-Keeping.* New York: Praeger.

JONSSON, C. (1984) *Superpower: Comparing American and Soviet Foreign Policy.* London: Frances Pinter.

KAPLAN, S. S. (1981) *Diplomacy and Power: Soviet Armed Forces as Political Instruments.* Washington, DC: The Brookings Institution.

KENNAN, G. F. (1987) Foreword. In *The Pathology of Power* by N. Cousins. London and New York: W. W. Norton.

KENNAN, G. F (1981) The Only Way Out of a Nuclear Nightmare. *The Guardian Weekly,* May 31.

KHAN, K. M. (1986) *Multinationals of the South.* New York: St Martin's Press.

KHAN, S. A. (1986) *Nuclear War: Nuclear Proliferation and Their Consequences.* Oxford: Clarendon Press.

KONDZIELA, J. (1987) Catholic Perspectives on Life in Peace. *Bulletin of Peace Proposals* **18**(3): 415–432.

_____. (1979) Justice in the World. *IDOC Bulletin:* 184–190.

KOOIJMANS, P. H. (1982) Peaceful Settlement of Conflicts. In *The Security Trap.* Rome: IDOC.

KOTHARI, R. (1987) Peace, Development and Life. *Bulletin of Peace Proposals* **18**(3): 261–267.

_____. (1984a) Party and State in Our Times: The Rise of Non-Party Political Formations. *Alternatives* **9**(4): 541–564.

_____. (1984) The Non-Party Political Process. *Economic and Political Weekly* **19**(5): 216–224.

_____. (1983a) Concept of Common Security and the Reality of Common Insecurity. *Bulletin of Peace Proposals* **14**(4): 371–377.

_____. (1983b) *Survival in an Age of Transformation.* New Delhi and Tokyo: United Nations University.

_____. (1983) Peace in an Age of Transformation. *Alternatives* **9**(2): 177–217.

LALL, A. (ed.) (1985) *Multilateral Negotiation and Mediation.* New York: Pergamon.

LIGHT, M. (1984) Problem-solving Workshops: The Role of Scholarship in Conflict Resolution. In *Conflict in World Society: A New Perspective on International Relations.* edited by M. Banks. Brighton: Wheatsheaf.

LUCAS, G. R. and T. R. OGLETREE (eds.) (1976) *Lifeboat Ethics: The Moral Dilemmas of Hunger.* New York: Harper & Row.

LUCK, E. C. (1985) The U. N. at 40: A Supporter's Lament. *Foreign Policy* **57**(Winter): 143–159.

MCMILLAN, S. (1987) *Neither Confirm Nor Deny.* Sydney and Wellington: Allen & Unwin/Port Nicholson Press.

MAOZ, Z. (1982) *Paths to Conflict: International Dispute Initiation, 1816–1976.* Boulder, Colo.: Westview.

MAZRUI, A. A. (1986) *The Africans: A Triple Heritage.* New York: Little, Brown.

_____. (1980) *The African Condition: A Political Diagnosis.* New York: Cambridge University Press.

MITCHELL, C. R. (1981) *The Structure of International Conflict.* London: Macmillan.

286

MITCHELL, C. R. (1976) Peace-keeping: The Police Function. *Year Book of World Affairs* **30**: 150–173.

NELSON, R. (1984–1985) Multinational Peacekeeping in the Middle East and the United Nations Model. *International Affairs* **61**(1): 67–89.

NETANYAHU, B. (1986) *Terrorism: How the West Can Win.* New York: Farrar, Straus, Giroux.

NEW ZEALAND GOVERNMENT (1987) *Defence of New Zealand: Review of Defence Policy.* Wellington: Government Printer.

NYE, J. S. (1986) *Nuclear Ethics.* New York: The Free Press.

OGARKOV, N. (1985) *History Teaches Vigilance.* Moscow.

ONWUKA, R. I., and O. ALUKO (1986) *The Future of Africa and The New International Economic Order.* New York: St Martin's Press.

OPHULS, W. (1977) *Ecology and the Politics of Scarcity.* San Francisco: W. H. Freeman.

ORGANSKI, A. F. K. and J. KUGLER (1980) *The War Ledger.* Chicago: University of Chicago Press.

OTT, M. C. (1972) Mediation as a Method of Conflict Resolution: Two Cases. *International Organization* **26**(4): 595–618.

PALME, O. (1982) *Common Security: A Blueprint for Survival.* Report of the Independent Commission on Disarmament and Security (Palme Commission). New York: Simon and Schuster.

PAYER, C. (1974) *The Debt Trap: The International Monetary Fund and the Third World.* New York: Monthly Review.

PEARSON, L. B. (1957) Force for U. N. *Foreign Affairs* **35**(3): 395–404.

PELCOVITS, N. A. (1984) *Peacekeeping on Arab–Israeli Fronts: Lessons from the Sinai and Lebanon.* Boulder, Colo.: Westview.

PITTOCK, A. B. *et al.* (1986) *Environmental Consequences of Nuclear War. Volume I: Physical and Atmospheric Effects.* SCOPE 28. Chichester: John Wiley & Sons.

PREDDEY, G. F. (1985) *Nuclear Disaster: A Way of Thinking Down Under.* Wellington: Asia Pacific Books.

PREDDEY, G. F. *et al.* (1982) *Future Contingencies. 4: Nuclear Disaster.* Wellington: Commission for the Future.

REDMAN, C. (1986) *Come as You Are: The Peace Corps Story.* New York: Harcourt Brace Jovanovich.

REPORT OF THE DEFENCE COMMITTEE OF ENQUIRY (1986) *Defence and Security: What New Zealanders Want.* Wellington: Government Printer.

RESTON, J. (1986) A World of Wars Past, Wars in Process and Wars to Come. *International Herald Tribune*, May 26.

RIKHYE, I. J. (1984) *The Theory & Practice of Peacekeeping.* London: C. Hurst.

RIKHYE, I. J., M. HARBOTTLE and B. EGGE (1974) *The Thin Blue Line: International Peacekeeping and its Future.* New Haven: Yale University Press.

ROSENAU, J. N. (1987) Patterned Chaos in Global Life: Structure and Process in the Two Works of World Politics. (Mimeo) Institute of Transnational Studies, University of Southern California.

SCALAPINO, R. A. (1987) *Major Power Relations in Northeast Asia.* Washington, DC: University Press of America for the Asia Society.

SCHELLING, T. C. (1976) *Arms and Influence.* Westport, Conn.: Greenwood.

_____. (1960) *The Strategy of Conflict.* Cambridge, Mass.: Harvard University Press.

SCHLOMING, G. C. (1987) *American Foreign Policy and the Nuclear Dilemma.* Englewood Cliffs, NJ: Prentice–Hall.

SCIENTISTS (1986) Statement on Violence. *Sciences et Devenir de L'Homme* 5: 50–58.

SEITZ, R. (1986) In from the Cold: "Nuclear Winter" Melts Down. *The National Interest:* 3–17.

SHARP, G. (1985) *Making Europe Unconquerable: The Potential of Civilian-Based Deterrence and Defense.* Cambridge, Mass.: Ballinger.

SHETH, D. L. (1983) Grassroots Stirrings and the Future of Politics. *Alternatives* 9(1): 1–24.

SHEVARDNADZE, E. A. (1987) For New Thinking in World Politics. In *Peace and Disarmament: Academic Studies.* Moscow: Politizdat.

SINCLAIR, K. (1986) *A Destiny Apart.* Sydney and Wellington: Allen & Unwin/Port Nicholson Press.

SINGER, J. D. and M. SMALL (1972) *The Wages of War, 1816–1965.* New York: John Wiley.

SIVARD, R. L. (1985) *World Military and Social Expenditures 1985.* Washington, DC: World Priorities.

SMALL, M., and J. D. SINGER (1982) *Resort to Arms.* Beverly Hills, Calif.: Sage Publications.

SMOKE, R. with W. HARMAN (1987) *Paths to Peace: Exploring the Feasibility of Sustainable Peace.* Boulder, Colo.: Westview.

SNYDER, G. H. and P. DIESING (1977) *Conflict Among Nations.* Princeton: Princeton University Press.

SOROOS, M. S. (1984) Coping with Resource Scarcity: A Critique of Lifeboat Ethics. In *The Global Agenda: Issues and Perspectives,* edited by C. W. Kegley and E. R. Wittkopf. New York: Random House.

SPECTOR, L. S. (1984) *Nuclear Proliferation Today.* New York: Vintage.

SPERRY, R. (1981) Changing Priorities. *Annual Review of Neuroscience* 4: 1–15.

STEGENGA, J. A. (1983) The Immorality of Nuclear Deterrence. *International Studies Notes* 10(1): 18–21.

STEPHENSON, C. M. (1982) *Alternative Methods for International Security.* Washington, DC: University Press of America.

STEPHENSON, M. and R. HEARN (eds.) (1983) *The Nuclear Case Book.* London: Frederick Muller.

STOKES, W. M. (1983) Technology and the Future of Peacekeeping. In *Peacekeeping: Appraisals and Proposals,* edited by H. Wiseman. New York: Pergamon.

STRANGE, S. (1987) Review of K. J. Holsti *The Dividing Discipline: Hegemony and Diversity in International Theory,* in *International Journal* 42(2): 398–400.

Survey: A Journal of East and West Studies.

SWIFT, R. N. (1974) United Nations Military Training for Peace. *International Organization* 28(2): 267–280.

TEMPLETON, M. (1987) Independence in Foreign Policy: How Valid a Concept? Unpublished paper.

THAKUR, R. (1987) *International Peacekeeping in Lebanon: United Nations Authority and Multinational Force.* Boulder, Colo.: Westview.

_____. (1986a) A Dispute of Many Colours: France, New Zealand and the 'Rainbow Warrior' Affair. *The World Today* 42(12): 209–214.

_____. (1986) *In Defence of New Zealand: Foreign Policy Choices in the Nuclear Age.* Boulder, Colo.: Westview.

THANT, U (1963) Address at Harvard University, 13 June 1963. *United Nations Review.*

THOMPSON, S. L. and S. H. SCHNEIDER (1986) Nuclear Winter Reappraised. *Foreign Affairs* 64: 981–1005.

THORSSON, I. (1984) *In Pursuit of Disarmament: Conversion from Military to Civil Production in Sweden.* Stockholm: Liber.

TIMOFEEV, T. (1987) On Democratisation of International Relations. In *Peace and Disarmament: Academic Studies.* Moscow: Politizdat.

TURCO, R. P. *et al.* (1983) Nuclear Winter: Global Consequences of Multiple Nuclear Explosions. *Science* 222: 1283–1292.

UNGAR, S. J. (1985) *Estrangement: America and the World.* New York: Oxford University Press.

UNO (1986) *Disarmament and Development: Declaration by the Panel of Eminent Personalities.* New York: United Nations Organisation.

_____. (1985) *The Blue Helmets: A Review of United Nations Peace-keeping.* New York: United Nations Organisation.

URQUHART, B. E. (1983) Peacekeeping: A View from the Operational Center. In *Peacekeeping: Appraisals and Proposals,* edited by H. Wiseman. New York: Pergamon.

US GOVERNMENT (1980) *The Global 2000 Report to the President, Vol. I: Entering the Twenty-first Century.* Washington, DC: US Government Printing Office.

VAYRYNEN, R. (ed.) (1987) *The Quest for Peace.* London: Sage.

WALKER, R. B. J. (1987) *One World, Many Worlds: Struggles for a Just World Peace.* Boulder, Colo.: Lynne Rienner.

WALSH, D. (1987) The Role of the Church in the Modern World. *Journal of Church and State* (Winter).

WALTZ, K. N. (1959) *Man, the State and War.* New York: Columbia University Press.

WARMBAUGH, S. (1933) *Plebiscites Since the World War.* Washington, DC: Carnegie Endowment.

WARNER, F. (1987) Severe Global-Scale Effects of Nuclear War Reaffirmed. *Environment* 29(4): 4–5, 45.

WEHR, P. (1979) *Conflict Regulation.* Boulder, Colo.: Westview.

WEISS, T. G., and A. JENNINGS (1983) *More for the Least: Prospects for Poorest Countries in the Eighties.* Lexington, Mass.: Lexington Books.

WHO (1983) *Effects of Nuclear War on Health and Health Services.* World Health Organisation: Report of International Committee of Experts in Medical Sciences and Public Health; Document A36/12.

WIONCZEK, M. S. (1982) *Some Key Issues for the World Periphery: Selected Essays.* Oxford: Pergamon.

WISEMAN, H. (ed.) (1983) *Peacekeeping: Appraisals and Proposals.* New York: Pergamon.

WOHLSTETTER, A. (1976) Racing Forward? Or Ambling Back? *Survey* 22(3 & 4): 163–217.

WOLFERS, A. (1962) *Discord and Collaboration.* Baltimore: Johns Hopkins University Press.

WOOD, R. E. (1984) The Debt Crisis in North South Relations. *Third World Quarterly* 6(3): 703–716.

WRIGHT, Q. (1942) *A Study of War.* 2 vols. Chicago: University of Chicago Press.

YOUNG, O. (1967) *The Intermediaries: Third Parties in International Crises.* Princeton: Princeton University Press.

ZAGLADIN, V., I. PANTIN and T. TIMOFEEV (eds.) (1985) *Struggle for Peace and the Future Destinies of Mankind.* Moscow: Politizdat.

ZIEGLER, D. W. (1987) *War, Peace, and International Politics.* Boston: Little, Brown.

Contributors

GEOFFREY BLAINEY has taught at the University of Melbourne since 1962, being Professor of Economic History from 1968 to 1977 and the Ernest Scott Professor of History since 1977. He has written 17 books, some of which are widely known, including *The Rush that Never Ended* (Melbourne University Press, 1963), *The Tyranny of Distance* (Macmillan, 1968), and *Triumph of the Nomads* (Macmillan, 1975). His book *The Causes of War*, first published in London in 1973, has aroused much controversy because of its argument that the causes of peace and war are closely related. He is Dean of the Arts Faculty at the University of Melbourne, and has also served on many federal government bodies, including being chairman of the Australia Council (1977–1981) and chairman of the Australia–China Council (1979–1984).

ALAIN BROUILLET is Assistant Professor of Law at the University of Paris (Panthéon–Sorbonne). He has published widely in the fields of public international law and constitutional law, edited the debates and proceedings of the 1985 and 1987 sessions of the Institute of International Law in Helsinki and Cairo, and been parliamentary and legal correspondent for the press group "L'EXPANSION."

WREN GREEN is a member of the New Zealand Royal Society's Scientific Committee on Problems of the Environment (SCOPE), and was the New Zealand delegate to the 1985 SCOPE General Assembly in Washington DC where the findings of the international study of nuclear winter effects were presented. Dr Green is a past President of the New Zealand Association of Scientists. As a Council member of the New Zealand Ecological Society he coordinated the 1984 Statement on the Environmental Impacts of Nuclear War on New Zealand. He is editor of *Focus on Social Responsibility in Science* (Wellington, 1979), and is a principal author of *New Zealand after Nuclear War* (New Zealand Planning Council, 1987).

WILLIS HARMAN is Professor of Engineering–Economic Systems at Stanford University. A Senior Social Scientist at the Stanford Research Institute and President of the Institute of Noetic Sciences, Professor Harman received his Ph. D. in electrical engineering from Stanford in 1948. He taught for several years at the University of Florida before joining the Stanford faculty in 1952. He is the author of numerous texts and papers in various aspects of electrical and systems engineering, futures research, social policy and analysis, and the current societal transition. He was listed as an "Exemplary Futurist" in the World Future Society's reference work *The Study of the Future* (1977). He wrote *An Incomplete Guide to the Future* (W. W. Norton, 1979), and is the co-author of *Changing Images of Man* (Pergamon, 1982), *Higher Creativity* (Jeremy Tarcher, 1984) and *Paths to Peace* (Westview, 1987).

KAL HOLSTI joined the Department of Political Science at the University of British Columbia in 1961, where he has been Professor since 1971. He is the author of several notable books and articles in international relations, including one of the most widely used textbooks, *International Politics: A Framework for Analysis* (Prentice–Hall, 1967; 5th ed. 1988). His latest book is *The Dividing Discipline: Hegemony and Diversity in International Theory* (Allen & Unwin, 1985). Professor Holsti has won many international awards and distinctions, was President of the Canadian Political Science Association (1984–1985), President of the International Studies Association (1986–1987), and has also been involved in an editorial role in several scholarly journals.

JIN JUNHUI is head of the Department for American and Latin American Studies of the Institute of International Studies in Beijing, where he has been since 1979. Having studied at Beijing University and Charles University in Prague, he worked for the Ministry of Foreign Affairs of the People's Republic of China. His articles on US–Soviet relations have been published in several Chinese journals, and he also held a visiting appointment at the International Institute for Strategic Studies in London during 1985.

RAJNI KOTHARI, a gifted intellectual from India, is a household name among social scientists interested in peace and a just world order for humanity. He has held many notable visiting appointments around the world, been involved in some of the leading research institutes and endeavours of recent decades, authored many distinguished books, monographs and journal articles, and was a founding editor of the journal *Alternatives*. He is presently Director of the United Nations University's Program on Peace and Global Transformation in Delhi, and active in civil rights issues in India.

VICTOR KREMENYUK is Head of the Department of the Institute of USA and Canada Studies of the USSR Academy of Sciences. He is a Soviet expert on the problems of developing countries and of regional conflicts. Dr Kremenyuk is the author of several works on these subjects, including *International Conflicts in the Present Period* (Moscow, 1983). He has written extensively for Soviet and other journals on the prevention, control and settlement of international conflicts and crises.

SIR GEORGE LAKING KCMG, now retired, has had a long and distinguished career in New Zealand public service. He joined the Prime Minister's and External Affairs Department in 1940, was Acting High Commissioner to the United Kingdom (1958–1961), Ambassador to the European Community (1960–1961), Ambassador to the United States of America (1961–1967), Secretary of Foreign Affairs and Permanent Head of the Prime Minister's Department (1967–1972), Ombudsman (1975–1977), and Chief Ombudsman (1977–1978). Amongst other activities, Sir George was also Privacy Commissioner (1977–1978), a Member of the Human Rights Commission (1978–1984), and President of the New Zealand Institute of International Affairs (1980–1984).

HON. RUSSELL MARSHALL, a former Methodist Minister, joined the Labour Party in 1968 and was elected to Parliament in 1972. Before entering politics he was involved in CORSO (the New Zealand Council of Organisations for Relief Service Overseas) and the United Nations Association, and was also active in campaigns against New Zealand participation in the Vietnam war and sporting contacts with South Africa. He was the Minister of Education (1984–1987) before being made Minister of Foreign Affairs and the first New Zealand Minister for Disarmament and Arms Control (1987–).

ALI MAZRUI is one of Africa's leading social scientists. Born in Kenya, he was educated at the universities of Manchester, Columbia and Oxford, and taught at Makerere University as Professor of Political Science (1965–1973). He is presently Professor of Afroamerican and African Studies as well as Professor of Political Science at the University of Michigan, Research Professor of Political Science at the University of Jos in Nigeria, and Andrew D. White Professor-at-Large at Cornell University. He has authored and co-authored some 20 books in the past two decades, and published more than 50 articles in the last dozen years. He has also been editor since 1986 of Volume 8 of UNESCO's *General History of Africa;* author, narrator and presenter for the British Broadcasting Corporation (BBC) and the Public Broadcasting Corporation (PBC, Washington DC) since 1981; BBC Reith lecturer (1979); President of the African Studies Association of the USA (1978–1979); Vice President of the International Political Science Association (1970–1973); Director of the African Section of the World Order Models Project (1969–1983); and a member of the editorial boards of about a dozen journals in Africa, the UK and the USA. His television series *The Africans: A Triple Heritage* (BBC and PBC, 1986) aroused enormous interest, generating controversy and tributes in Africa, America, Britain and elsewhere.

RAMESH THAKUR received his educational training in India and Canada and taught at the University of the South Pacific in Fiji before joining Otago in 1980, where he is Senior Lecturer in Political Studies. A past President of the Dunedin branch of the New Zealand Institute of International Affairs, he is the author of *Peacekeeping in Vietnam: Canada, India, Poland and the International Commission* (University of Alberta Press, 1984), *In Defence of New Zealand: Foreign Policy Choices in the Nuclear Age* (Westview, 1986), *International Peacekeeping in Lebanon: United Nations Authority and Multinational Force* (Westview, 1987); and co-editor of *The Soviet Union as an Asian Pacific Power* (Westview and Macmillan, 1987). He has written more than 40 articles for journals around the world, is the New Zealand correspondent of the *Asian Defence Journal,* and also writes occasionally for newspapers in New Zealand.

INGA THORSSON, a former Under-Secretary of State in Sweden's Ministry of Foreign Affairs, was Chairman of the United Nations Governmental Expert Group on the Relationship between Disarmament and Development (1978–1981), and President of the First Non Proliferation Treaty (NPT) Review Conference in Geneva in 1975. Having spent her earlier public life in the city politics of Stockholm and in the diplomatic service of Sweden, she has devoted most of her professional life for the past 15 years to the cause of disarmament and peace. In 1983, Mrs Thorsson was commissioned by the Swedish government to examine the relationship between disarmament and development for Sweden; her two-volume report *In Pursuit of Disarmament* was published in 1984. She is President of the Great Peace Journey which began in Sweden in·1984, was awarded the UN Peace Messenger Award in September 1987, and is due to onclude with a Popular Global Summit in 1988.

TIMOUR TIMOFEEV is a Corresponding Member of the USSR Academy of Sciences and Director of the Institute of the International Labour and Social Studies. He is also Vice President of the Soviet Scientific Council for Peace and Disarmament Research. Professor Timofeev is the author and editor of many monographs dealing with international affairs, world economics and socio–political problems, as well as several articles published in leading Soviet periodicals.

K´AROLY T´OTH, President of the Christian Peace Conference, Vice President of the World Alliance of Reformed Churches, General Secretary of the Hungarian Bible Council, has been Bishop of the Danubian District of the Reformed Church in Hungary since 1977. Educated in Hungary and France, Bishop Tóth received his doctorate from the Theological Faculty of Debrecen.

At the World Council of Churches Assembly in Vancouver in 1983, Bishop Tóth became a member of the WCC's Central Committee and Executive Committee; in March 1987, he was elected President of the Synod of the Reformed Church in Hungary. Bishop Tóth has received many church and state distinctions in Hungary, Poland, the USSR and Czechoslovakia, and has authored and edited several books and articles, including *Seven Years Christian Peace Conference* (Prague, 1978), *Living as a Christian in Today's World* (Prague, 1981), *A Reorientation to Peace* (Delhi, 1985). He is widely acknowledged as having made important contributions to ecumenical dialogue, to revealing the Biblical message of peace and justice, and to finding forms of international and ecumenical cooperation.

CARL FRIEDRICH FREIHERR VON WEIZSÄCKER received his Ph.D. in 1933 and was Professor of Physics at the universities of Strassburg and Göttingen. He has also been Professor of Philosophy at the University of Hamburg (1957–1969), and Director of the Max Planck Institute in Starnberg (1970–1980). One of Germany's foremost thinkers, having received the most prestigious German scientific and literary awards, Dr. Weizsäcker is a physicist and philosopher of worldwide reputation. He has published widely on the economic and political realities of the nuclear age, including *Wahrnehmung Der Neuzeit* ("Perception of Modern Times," 1983), *Wege in Der Gefahr* ("The Politics of Peril," 1979), and *Einheit Der Natur* ("The Unity of Nature," 1971).

Index

308